BALLOONS AND AIRSHIPS

Balloons and Airships

(originally published as 'Airships Past and Present')

by

A. Hildebrandt

Captain and Instructor in the
Prussian Balloon Corps

Translated by W. H. Story

EP Publishing Limited
1973

PREFACE.

THE modern application of ballooning to scientific purposes has caused a widespread interest to be taken in the sport, and this has been intensified by the successes which have attended the efforts of Santos Dumont and the brothers Lébaudy in another direction. The present moment, therefore, seems to be suitable for a survey of the development of the art, and, in making this attempt, the author has drawn on a large number of sources that have not hitherto been accessible to the general reader, and has also supplemented the historical outline with the result of many years of practical experience. The following pages contain a rough sketch of the past and present state of the art, and its applications to scientific ends, and further it is hoped that the looker-on may find in them something to help him towards understanding the various problems which are now calling for solution and afford such a fruitful subject for discussion in the daily press. Certain matters have been described in some detail, such, for instance, as balloon photography and the use of the carrier pigeon ; and this has seemed to be desirable, seeing that hitherto no trustworthy information on these subjects has been forthcoming.

Balloon photography has been very carefully studied of late years. The author can lay claim to considerable experience in this department, and has made about eighty ascents, mainly for photographic purposes. He has also had the advantage of Professor Miethe's assistance on many of these occasions, and Lieutenant-Colonel Klussman, who was formerly in command of the Prussian Balloon Corps, has also kindly contributed much valuable information as to the various optical phenomena that arise in balloon photography.

Herr Bernhard Flöring, of Barmen, has also been good enough to give the author the benefit of his long experience in the matter of the carrier pigeon. The chapter which deals with this subject contains a good deal of general information, and is not merely confined to the use of carrier pigeons in connection with balloons. The author has for many years devoted himself to the breeding and training of these birds, and feels that the sport deserves every encouragement. It is hoped that something may be done towards increasing its usefulness, seeing that it might be of untold value in time of war ; but it must be admitted that up to the present little has been done on a systematic basis, and it is entirely neglected by most balloonists.

The importance of the scientific application of ballooning entitles it to careful consideration, and such work is here fully discussed. The author had the honour of being elected a member of the international commission which was appointed to consider matters connected with the application of ballooning to scientific ends, and has had the pleasure of working with Professor Assmann and Professor Hergesell, whose work in exploring the upper layers of the atmosphere places them in the front rank of meteorologists.

The flying machine, which includes all devices which aim at the imitation of the flight of birds, is on the other hand rather briefly discussed, inasmuch as from the practical point of view little of real importance has been accomplished in this department. But it is more than probable the future will have surprises in store for us, and that the hopeful views, lately expressed by the Académie des Sciences, will prove to be justified in so far as the results which may be expected from work on these lines is concerned.

Generally speaking, it may be said that in the following pages all questions are fully discussed which lend themselves to popular treatment and appear to be of general interest. Many years of experience in connection with balloon clubs, specially those of Strassburg and Berlin, coupled with the outcome of lectures delivered in connection with the Prussian Balloon Corps, lead the author to think that information on many of the points which are here discussed will be of service to those who take interest in these matters.

A certain amount of theoretical investigation was unavoidable, but it has been reduced to the smallest possible limits. There is not enough of it to frighten anybody, and it may further be said in self-defence, if any should be found to complain that there is too little of it, that the author had no intention of writing a technical textbook. It has been his wish that the reader may find amusement and instruction to be pleasantly combined in these pages, and may derive both pleasure and profit from the review of past and present.

BERLIN, *October*, 1906.

CONTENTS.

LIST OF ILLUSTRATIONS.

LIST OF ILLUSTRATIONS. xiii

LIST OF ILLUSTRATIONS.

AIRSHIPS PAST AND PRESENT

CHAPTER I.

THE EARLY HISTORY OF THE ART.

THE folklore of almost every race contains some myth, embodying the aspiration of man to add the conquest of the air to that of the sea. Phrixos and Helle flew over the sea, mounted on the ram with the golden fleece. Dædalus and Icarus attempted flight, but Icarus ventured so near the sun that the wax which fastened the wings to his body was melted, and he fell headlong into the sea.

Passing from myth to semi-legendary history, we are told that Xerxes received, as a gift from his courtiers, a winged throne, to which were harnessed four tame eagles. Food was held before the hungry birds, and their struggles had the effect of raising the throne from the ground. Somehow or another, Xerxes seems to have survived the start, and our picture shows him sailing quite pleasantly through the air. The philosopher Archytas of Tarentum devised a pigeon, which could raise itself if air were pumped into it, but it soon fell to the ground ; and here we may have an early attempt to construct a " Montgolfière." The Chinese, to whom the invention of gunpowder has always been credited, possibly made still earlier efforts to imitate flight, but of these little is known, though a French missionary in 1694 states that a balloon was sent up on the day of the coronation of the Emperor Fo-Kien at Pekin in the year 1306.

Mention ought also to be made of the celebrated name of Leonardo da Vinci, who devoted much attention to the study of the problem. Sketches made by him are still in existence, and

A. B

from these it appears that he proposed to mount the rider on a
kind of framework, to which devices of the nature of wings were
to be attached.   The technical details bear witness to the extraordinary aptitude which the artist possessed for dealing with
mechanical problems.   The arrangement of the bat-like wings
is particularly interesting.   On their downward movement they
were to strike the air over the whole of their surface, but they
were so arranged as to
oppose very slight resistance to upward motion, in
consequence of the folding
together of the various
sections. Fauste Veranzio
was the first human being
who is ever known to have
risked his life over the
work.   In 1617 he let himself down from a tower in
Venice by means of a very
primitive parachute, which
consisted of a square framework covered with canvas.
But for many years there
were no further imitators
of his methods. Proposals
of more or less historical
interest   were,   however,

FIG. 1.—The throne of Xerxes drawn
through the air by four tame eagles.

made about that time.   John Wilkins, Bishop of Chester, constructed a flying machine in 1648, and first drew attention to
the enormous force which could be developed by the application
of steam.   Cyrano de Bergerac developed the original idea of
fastening air-bags to his body, and then allowing them to heat
in the sun.   He supposed that the heated air would have the
effect of making him fly, and his muddle-headed notions are
very similar to those which bore fruit in the practical hands of
Montgolfier.

Francisco de Lana showed great ingenuity in his contrivance

of the flying ship, and in spite of his mistakes it is impossible not to admire the acuteness of his reasoning. He clearly understood that the air has a definite weight, just like any solid or liquid body, and supposed that at a great height the density of the atmosphere would be less, owing to decrease of barometric pressure. He also clearly understood that all bodies which are lighter than air would rise in the same way that a piece of wood rises from the bottom of a basin of water. Consequently he

proposed to make four great metal spheres, which were to be connected together by pieces of wood, and attached by ropes to a boat, fitted with oars and sails in the usual way. He proposed to exhaust the air from the metal spheres by filling them with water through an opening at the top, and then allowing the water to flow away through a tap at the bottom. He assumed that a vacuum would be created if the tap at the bottom were closed at the right moment. In order to prevent the boat from starting with a sudden jerk it was to be suitably

FIG. 2.—Fauste Veranzio in his parachute.

loaded with weights ; the height to which it would rise would then be conveniently regulated either by the admission of air to the spheres, or by throwing overboard some portion of the ballast. His ideas on the theory of the problem were undoubtedly correct, and he carried on a vigorous controversy with those who advanced objections to his proposals. But he came finally to the pious conclusion that he could scarcely hope for the accomplishment of his scheme, seeing that God would prevent such a revolution in human affairs. In the year 1680 Borelli makes some interesting observations with regard to the construction of an artificial

bird in his book " De Motu Animalium," and tried to show that
it was impossible for a man to fly by his own unaided efforts.
A man was, indeed, much too heavy, at any rate in comparison
with birds, neither had he sufficient muscular energy in the parts
about the chest; and further, the weight of any appurtenances
to take the place of wings would place him at a still more
serious disadvantage.   This reminds us of the results published
by Helmholtz in 1872, when he was a member of the committee

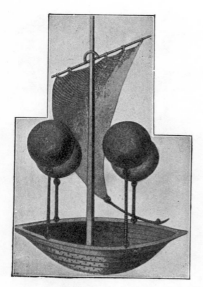

appointed to examine into
aeronautical problems.   He
there states in the most definite
manner that it is extremely
improbable that, with the aid
of the most perfect mechanism,
a man will be able by his own
muscular exertion to raise his
body into the air and to maintain it in that position.

But Borelli gave a very clear
exposition of the law of Archimedes, and considered in consequence that an imitation of the
flight of birds was impracticable.
On the other hand he thought
that the bladder of a fish was a
more hopeful suggestion, but
he strongly opposed all schemes

FIG. 3.—The flying ship, designed by
Francisco de Lana.

which necessitated the creation of a vacuum.   In view of the
external pressure of the atmosphere, any vacuum apparatus
would have to be constructed of metal and must be of great
size.   Its consequent weight made the whole thing impossible,
and arguments of this nature might well be considered by some
of the inventors who are still at work on the problem.   His
conclusions, which were at once thoughtful and clearly expressed,
came into the hands of many scientific men and interested them
in the possibility of a solution.

The science of aeronautics may be divided into two parts, of which the one may be called aerostatics, and the other aerodynamics. Aerostatical devices include those in which the load is lifted by filling certain spaces with a gas which is lighter than air, whereas in aerodynamical machines the effect is produced by means of propellers or other arrangements of a similar kind, tending to cause motion through the air. Bartholomaus

FIG. 4.—Photograph of Augsburg, showing the cathedral. Taken from a balloon by A. Riedinger.

Laurenzo de Gusmann constructed an airship in Lisbon in the year 1685 out of a wooden basket covered with paper, and if the facts were true, he would seem to have been the first to work on aerostatical principles. His basket is said to have been filled with hot air, and the apparatus rose from the ground in the presence of the royal Court at Lisbon. But the investigations of Lecornu clearly show that two totally separate experiments have been put together and ascribed to one man. It seems to be a fact that the monk Bartholomaus Laurenzo invented a machine and carried out certain experiments with it, about which nothing is known; and twenty-five years later, a scientific man, named de Gusmann, announced the construction of a flying machine, with which he proposed to descend from a certain tower in Lisbon. His scheme merely called on his head the derision of the mob, and the French are justified in refusing to allow any special merit to his experiments, and in claiming for Montgolfier the invention of the aerostatic airship.

The monk Galien ought also to be noticed, inasmuch as he may be regarded as the forerunner of the brothers Montgolfier. His book, entitled "L'art de naviguer dans l'air," was published in 1757. He points out that careful investigation should be made into the constitution and properties of the atmosphere, and by experiment it might be found whether the principle of Archimedes was likely to be able to be usefully applied towards the solution of the problem. He concludes that in order to rise from the ground, a ship might be filled with the air found at a considerable height, which would be a thousand times lighter than water, and if one went still higher, would be two thousand times as light. If the force tending to raise the ship were greater than that tending to sink it, it would be possible to lift a weight corresponding to the difference of these forces. Galien made the most careful calculations, according to which his airship was to be as large as the town of Avignon, and to be able to carry 4,000,000 persons and several million packages. It seems marvellous to think that a fantastic scheme of this kind should commend itself to a mind that was fully capable of dealing with theoretical subtleties.

In the meantime, the rival school of thought, which believed in the construction of an airship that should be heavier than the air, had not been without their successes. In 1742 the Marquis de Bacqueville built a flying machine, with which he descended from the window of his mansion, succeeded in crossing the gardens of the Tuileries, and finally landed on the top of a washerwoman's bench in the middle of the Seine. The apparatus acting as a parachute, the descent was very gradual and without accident. However, the axioms laid down by Borelli and Helmholtz still

hold true, and progress in the matter of a mere flying machine
seems very unlikely.　New types of a more promising kind were
however invented.　The mathematician Paucton suggested the
principle of the propeller, which he called a " Pterophore."　One
propeller was to be on a vertical axis for raising the dead weight,
and another on a horizontal axis for any forward or backward
movement, a parachute being provided for the descent.　The
propellers were to be driven by hand, and though nothing came
of these proposals, it must be allowed that a definite step had
been made on the path, which was to lead to future success on
these lines.　The Abbé Desforges invented a flying machine,
called the " Orthoptère," which was in no way remarkable.　On

the other hand, men-
tion should be made
of the flying car of the
aeronaut Blanchard,
which in some respects
seems to have been on
the lines of the modern
motor car. As a matter
of fact, it was fitted
with sails and wings,
and moved at a great

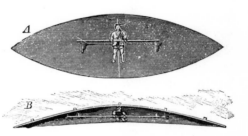

FIG. 5.—Meerwein's flying machine.　From
Moedebeck's " Pocket Book for Balloonists."

rate on the Place Louis XV. and the Champs Elysées.　Still
Blanchard never succeeded in raising himself from the ground
with his marvellous mechanism, and so fell a ready victim to the
wits of the day.

　Karl Friedrich Meerwein was architect to the Grand Duke of
Baden, and managed to construct a flying machine, which gave
proof of a very accurate knowledge of the laws of air-resistance.
In order to sustain the weight of a man, he calculated that an
exposed surface of 130 square feet would be sufficient, and this
is indeed a wonderfully good approximation to the truth.　He
suggested that serious accidents would probably be avoided if
experiments were made at sea and not on land, and if this idea
had been adopted by Lilienthal, Pilcher and others, they would
doubtless have escaped their untimely ends.　But of late years

something has been done in this way.   Zeppelin on the Bodensee
and Langley on the Potomac have helped to lessen the danger
attaching to experimental work of this kind.

It may be of interest to examine the construction of a flying
machine, worked by a propeller, which was shown by the Frenchmen Launoy and Bienvenu to a committee of the Académie des
Sciences in 1784.   A wooden bow was pierced at its centre, and
through the hole thus made there was passed a spindle which
carried at either end some birds' feathers, so arranged as to serve
the purpose of a propeller.   The string of the bow was wound
several times round the spindle, and the apparatus was intended
to start in a vertical position.   The pull of the bow on the
cord tended to rotate the spindle and put the two propellers
in motion.   The feathers, which were arranged at an angle, drove
the air downwards, and the little model, weighing about 3 oz.,
flew up to the ceiling.   This ingenious device had many imitators,
but no great success was achieved owing to lack of suitable
motive power.   In 1870 Pénaud replaced the bow by strong
rubber bands, but without effecting any marked improvement.
None the less, these things deserve mention, and smoothed the
way for Santos Dumont.

CHAPTER II.

WE now reach the history of a second attempt which has been made to deprive the French of the laurels attaching to the invention of the air balloon. In 1776 Cavendish discovered hydrogen, and showed that it was much lighter than air. Dr. Black later asserted that in 1777 or 1778 he discussed with his friends the possibility of filling certain spaces with hydrogen, and, by a proper design of the dimensions, he hoped to raise a body in the air. He consequently considered himself to be the inventor of the air balloon. But it is only fair to point out that he made no attempt of any sort on a practical scale. Leo Cavallo did indeed blow soap bubbles filled with hydrogen, and also experimented with rubber solution, varnishes and oils ; he noticed that such soap bubbles moved much faster than usual. He then tried to fill bladders and small bags made of special paper with the gas ; but it immediately escaped through the pores. He was on the point of trying goldbeaters' skin, when he was anticipated by the brothers Montgolfier.

Stephen and Joseph Montgolfier were sons of a rich paper-maker in Annonay, and are undoubtedly the inventors of the aerostatic airship. Naturally enough, tradition reports that the whole thing was due to an accident. One of the brothers is said to have dried his silk coat over the oven and to have noticed that the heated air tended to lift it. But such tales lose much of their force when it is stated that both brothers had long and carefully studied both mathematics and physics, and that numerous improvements introduced by them into the working of the paper factory were ample evidence of practical capacity. Joseph Montgolfier was the first to interest himself in aeronautics, and he is stated to have descended from the roof of his house by means of a parachute in 1771. He occupied his mind with the possibility of mechanical devices as applied to flying machines, and discussed frequently with his brother the various treatises which existed on the subject, and the feasibility of suggestions which had been made. Galien's idea of filling receivers with air drawn from higher levels specially interested them, and the movement of the clouds seemed to justify hopes. Accordingly they passed steam into a receiver, and noticed that the vessel had a tendency to rise in the air. However, the steam soon condensed; they

FIG. 6.—Clouds photographed from a balloon.

therefore repeated their experiment with smoke, which produced the same effect. The smoke escaped through the pores of the paper bag which acted as receiver; the results were therefore no better than before, and the experiments were temporarily suspended. Priestley's work on the different kinds of " air " was translated into French in 1776, and suggested to them the use of hydrogen. They filled paper bags with hydrogen, which escaped at once through the pores. Their next idea was that the clouds were supported by electrical means. They lighted a fire below their balloon and fed it with wet straw and wool. The first balloon was soon burnt; but they constructed another

which held 700 cubic feet and rose to a height of 1,000 ft.
Gradually they carried out their experiments on a larger scale,
and the first public exhibition was made on June 5th, 1783.
They constructed a paper balloon, 112 ft. in circumference, and
filled it with hot air by means of a fire placed below it. The

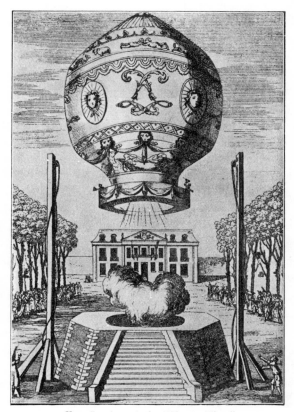

FIG. 7.—Ascent of a " Montgolfière."

balloon rose in the presence of the astonished spectators to a
height of 1,000 ft., but fell to the ground in ten minutes owing to
the gradual escape of the hot air.

The Académie des Sciences, which has always turned its
searching glance on any mechanical improvement, forthwith
invited the brothers Montgolfier to repeat their experiment in
Paris. But before they were able to undertake the journey

Paris had become familiar with the sight of a balloon in mid-air. Professor Faujas de Saint-Fond started a subscription list for the purpose of raising funds, and the physicist Charles was entrusted with the practical work. Charles was familiar with the properties of hydrogen from his laboratory work, and saw at once that the lightness of the heated air had caused Montgolfier's balloon to rise. He therefore concluded that the use of hydrogen would constitute a still further improvement, and would have the obvious advantage of decreasing the size of the receiver owing to its greater buoyancy. He also knew that hydrogen escaped much more easily than air through the pores of the envelope, and consequently well understood the necessity of making the silk covering thoroughly airtight. The brothers Robert, who had succeeded in dissolving rubber, were able to provide him with an excellent medium for coating his balloon, and it is interesting to note that even at the present day no better covering is known for the purpose. Hydrogen was prepared from sulphuric acid and iron turnings. But notwithstanding the apparent simplicity of the arrangements, it took four days to fill a balloon, 13 ft. in diameter, and required half a ton of iron and a quarter of a ton of sulphuric acid. The booming of cannon on August 29th, 1783, announced to the Parisians the impending flight of the balloon. In spite of heavy rain, 300,000 spectators collected in the Champs de Mars, and so great was the enthusiasm that silks and satins were completely forgotten till the balloon had made a start. It weighed rather less than 20 lbs., and speedily rose in the air, disappearing in the clouds. After a short time it was seen again at a great height, but appeared to be ruptured, presumably owing to its having been too strongly inflated. The treatment it received on reaching the ground in the neighbourhood of Paris was amusing. The peasants saw it falling from the clouds, and ascribed its presence to the agency of the devil. They therefore attacked it with rakes and hoes and anything else that was handy. It was finally fastened to the tail of a horse, and dragged about, trailing on the ground, till nothing was left. The Government therefore thought it necessary to acquaint the rustic mind with the nature of the new invention, and to request better treatment for it in future.

In the meantime, Montgolfier had reached Paris, and under the auspices of the Académie des Sciences, constructed a linen balloon of curious shape. The middle portion was cylindrical, being 42 ft. in diameter, and 26 ft. in height; above this there was a conical portion, 30 ft. high, and at the bottom the cylinder was closed by a similar conical piece, 20 ft. in length. The framework was covered with paper, both on the inside and outside. The balloon presented a magnificent appearance, and was decorated with gold on a background of blue. But the Fates were against the inventor. A heavy rainstorm loosened the paper from the linen; the linen in its turn was torn at the seams; and finally, a strong wind completed in twenty-four hours the entire destruction of the work of many months. Montgolfier at once constructed a new spherical balloon, having a capacity of 52,000 cubic feet, out of waterproof linen, and made an ascent in the courtyard of the palace at Versailles on September 19th. The car attached to the balloon took up three passengers in the form of a sheep, a cock, and a duck. The apparatus came to earth eight minutes after the start, the descent being caused by a rent at the top, which was probably made during inflation. The duck and sheep were just as lively as they were before the start; but the cock appeared to have suffered some injury, which was ascribed by the learned to the effects of the rarefied atmosphere, whereas it was later clearly shown to have been due to the fact that it had been trodden on by the sheep.

The brothers Montgolfier were everywhere received with the greatest enthusiasm. The King conferred the Order of St. Michael on Stephen, and a pension of £40 on Joseph, while their father received a patent of nobility with the motto, " Sic itur ad astra." The Académie des Sciences also conferred honours on them, in addition to a prize of money, which had been set apart for distinction in the arts and sciences. Both were made members of the Legion of Honour, and a deputation of scientific men, headed by Faujas de Saint-Fond, presented Stephen with a gold medal, which had been struck in honour of his achievements.

CHAPTER III.

THE enthusiasm in Paris was great, and people amused themselves with the manufacture of small balloons on the Montgolfier pattern. Baron de Beaumanoir was the first to construct them of goldbeater's skin, a method which has since found favour in the English army. The diameter of his balloon was 18 in., and it was filled with hydrogen. The small skins, which measure about 30 in. by 10 in., are very suitable for the purpose, being light and airtight. Still, it must be admitted that it is a costly form of construction. Naturally enough many doubted whether anything likely to be really profitable to humanity would result. Benjamin Franklin, who was present at one of these ascents, was asked by a man what was the use of it all, and replied by asking "What's the use of a baby?" Similar questions are often asked about dirigible balloons, but the enthusiasm of the inventor is not easily damped.

Stephen Montgolfier proceeded to build a new balloon, intended to carry passengers. It was therefore much bigger than its predecessor; its height was 85 ft., and its diameter 50 ft., the capacity being 100,000 cubic feet. The exterior was highly decorated, and the car, intended to hold the passengers, was suspended below. The balloon was filled through a short cylindrical opening, constructed of linen; beneath this a pan was suspended on which the fire was lighted. Pilátre de Rozier was the first to ascend in a captive balloon; this he accomplished on October 15th, 1783, when he rose to a height of 80 ft. His presence of mind was shown on an occasion when the balloon was blown against a tree at a considerable height; by diligent stoking of the fire he caused it to rise above the tree and so free itself from the entanglement. In the same year Rozier undertook the first expedition in a free balloon with the Marquis d'Arlandes as a companion. It was only with great difficulty that the King was persuaded to give his permission, as it had been intended to experiment on two criminals who were condemned to death, and their lives were to have been spared if they succeeded in reaching the ground in safety. The King, however, finally gave his consent, and on November 21st, 1783, Pilâtre de Rozier and the Marquis d'Arlandes made a journey lasting twenty-five minutes. They came safely to the ground, but the balloon immediately collapsed, and Rozier was almost

FIG. 8.—Portjengrat, an Alpine peak.   Photograph by Spelterini.

buried beneath the ruins. He was, however, rescued by his companion, and able to crawl out into the open. Similar accidents happen nowadays in calm weather if the landing causes any rupture in the body of the balloon. The gas then escapes very suddenly, and the balloon collapses without any warning. Some years ago, an Austrian officer would have been suffocated in this way if he had not received timely help from his friends.

Increased interest continued to be taken in the sport, and venturesome ladies occasionally mounted the car. On June 4th, 1784, at Lyons, Madame Thible ascended in a free balloon in the presence of King Gustavus III. of Sweden. The journey lasted three-quarters of an hour, and a height of 9,000 ft. was reached. Still it soon became apparent that great disadvantages attached to balloons of the hot-air type, and the danger of fire was great, both before and after the start. Fire-extinguishing contrivances were always at hand during the filling operations, and notwithstanding this, more than one balloon was completely destroyed by the flames. On landing there was always trouble owing to the fact that the body of the balloon fell on the pan, which was often still glowing hot. The danger both to person and property which arose from the use of hot air made any extended use of

Fig. 9.—A successful landing.

this type of balloon out of the question. It was further impossible to carry any large amount of combustible on the journey, and this limited the distance that could be travelled. The method originally used by Montgolfier of burning a mixture of straw and wool was found to be the best, as it produced a bright and lively flame without much smoke. Saussure, the well-known physicist, had proposed to use alder wood in place of straw. In order to study the question carefully and to note the necessary conditions he had remained on the car of one of Montgolfier's balloons for eighteen minutes during the preliminary inflation, in spite of the great heat. He proved thereby that the hottest air at the top is free from oxygen, but contains great quantities of the gases of combustion and water vapour. He also showed by means of laboratory experiments that the ascent of the balloon is caused not by the heat directly, but by the rarefaction of the air thereby produced. The weights and lifting powers of the air at different temperatures are somewhat as follows, assuming a barometric pressure of 30 in. of mercury : —

Temperature in degrees Fahrenheit.	Weight per cubic foot of air in lbs.	Lifting power per cubic foot in lbs., compared with 40° F.
40	0·08	0
80	0·074	0·006
120	0·069	0·011
160	0·064	0·016
200	0·06	0·02
212	0·059	0·021

At a height of 8,330 ft., a cubic foot of air at a temperature of 32° Fahr. weighs only 0·059 lb., and therefore a " Montgolfière " cannot reach a greater height than this, seeing that the " lift " then disappears, unless the temperatures, given in the above table, can be exceeded.

All these considerations tended to show that the type associated with the name of Professor Charles was better. He had indeed specially built a new balloon 30 ft. in diameter, for the purpose of atmospheric observations. The construction of Charles' balloon was very similar to that in use at present, and it may therefore be of interest to describe it more minutely. The silk covering was coated with rubber solution, as has been already stated. An outer net was also employed, which was intended partly to support the silk covering, and partly to distribute the pressure more uniformly over the whole surface. The net, as used by Charles, covered only the upper half of his balloon, and ended in a wooden ring, which was connected to the car by ropes. The length of these ropes is a matter of importance. From the point of view of diminishing the load, it is well to keep them as short as possible; but on the other hand, the danger which may attend the escape of gases from the balloon makes it impossible to place the car too close to the body. In

c

Germany it is usually suspended about 8 ft. below the body; in France the two are placed much nearer to one another.   Many accidents have taken place in France with balloons filled with hydrogen prepared from sulphuric acid and iron.   Sulphuric acid is very liable to contain arsenic, which easily passes with the hydrogen into the balloon, and is fatal in very small doses, several aeronauts having met their deaths in France owing to this cause.   The method which Charles used for the construction of his net is still in vogue, but it is now so arranged as to cover the entire balloon.   He made a marked improvement by placing a valve at the top, and by this means he was able to allow the gas to escape at will.   The most ordinary kind of valve is some form of the plate or butterfly type.   The original construction consisted of a wooden ring with a transverse strip, to which two flap valves were fastened by means of hinges.   These valves were operated from the car by means of ropes, and were normally kept closed by springs, which pressed them against their seatings. In another form of valve a flat plate is pulled away from its wooden seating, allowing the gas to pass out sideways.   In order to ensure the tightness of the valve, the plates or flaps have sharp edges, which are pressed against a rubber packing.   It was formerly the practice to use a special kind of luting to ensure a good fit, but after the valve has been opened and shut a few times, such a joint becomes almost useless.   Generally speaking, the valve is only used for the purpose of effecting a descent; any other use only results in loss of buoyancy with a consequent shortening of the time during which the journey can be continued. It is of course also used in order to fall to a lower level, in the hope of finding more favourable breezes.

At the bottom of Charles's balloon he had a tube about 7 in. in diameter, through which the gases were passed into the body of the balloon, and through which they could also escape in case of any rise of internal pressure.   This neck is nowadays generally left open.   The diminished pressure on rising causes the gases to expand, a result which may also be caused by an increase of temperature.   If, therefore, this opening were closed, and the gases were unable to escape, the whole balloon might be shattered.

The length and diameter of the opening must be somewhat in proportion to the contents of the balloon, and suitable sizes can be calculated by anyone with sufficient general experience.

The gas was prepared by Charles by the reaction of sulphuric acid on iron turnings, which were therefore mixed with water in barrels, and on the addition of sulphuric acid the reaction immediately took place. The gas must be washed by passing through water, and is then cooled and dried. The various processes are not, however, quite so simple as would appear at first sight. Sulphuric acid is a corrosive fluid, and lead is one of the few substances which it does not attack; consequently it is extremely difficult to get the gas in a state of purity. As a matter of historical interest, it may be pointed out that the first gas explosion took place over the filling of one of these balloons, and was caused by a lamp which was brought near a leaky barrel. This is caused by a mixture of two volumes of hydrogen with five of air; the heat of combination expands the water vapour, which is formed by the reaction, to such an extent as to cause a very violent explosion. It took three days and three nights, with the aid of twenty barrels, to generate 14,000 cubic feet of hydrogen, but at last, on December 1st, Charles had completed all his arrangements for the ascent.

The fittings carried on the car of the balloon included many novelties. For the purpose of facilitating the descent during a heavy wind, he carried a kind of anchor, which was fastened at the end of a long rope. His idea was that the grapnel would hold the balloon at a safe distance from the ground until it was possible to allow a sufficient amount of gas to escape through the open valve and so complete the descent. He also carried a barometer, which he had himself constructed for the purpose of determining the height to which the balloon had risen, and herein may be seen the result of the ideas which originated with Lana and Galien. In order to determine the direction of the wind before starting, Charles had provided a small pilot balloon, 6 ft. in diameter, which he handed to Montgolfier with the words, " C'est à vous qu'il appartient de nous ouvrir la route des cieux." The good feeling thus shown to Montgolfier showed that

c 2

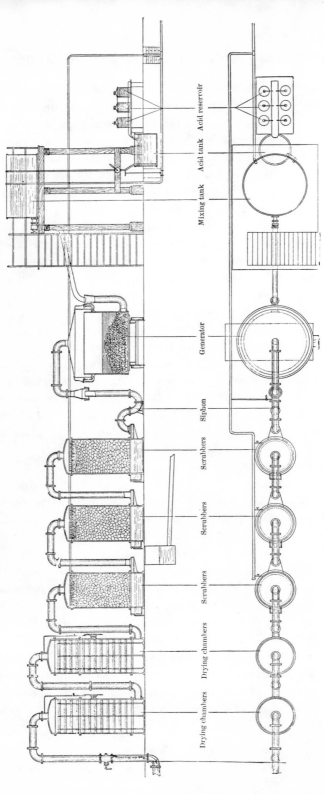

FIG. 10.—Apparatus for generating hydrogen, from the design of Dr. Nass.

no bitterness existed between the two inventors, although it is undoubtedly true that there was a very lively controversy as to

FIG. 11.—Paris, showing the Eiffel Tower.   Photograph by Count de la Vaulx.

the merits of the rival schemes.   It is impossible to deny that Charles showed great originality in all his work.   The shape of his balloon was indeed the same as that of his rival's design, but it is obvious that no other shape was reasonably possible,

seeing that he must have well known that a sphere combines
the greatest volume with the smallest surface. In the pilot
balloon he invented an auxiliary which is of great use in meteorology as well as in aeronautics, and it is obviously of importance
to know beforehand the direction of the overhead breezes. The
Abbés Miollan and Janinet had a special method for using them
during a voyage. They proposed to keep one small balloon,
filled with hydrogen, at a height of 150 ft. above the main track,
and a second, filled with air, at the same distance below. In this
way they would be able to determine the direction of the breezes
over a vertical space of 300 ft. Suggestions of this kind are,
however, of no great value. The direction of the wind at a level
below that of the car can easily be found by throwing out small
pieces of paper; and an overhead pilot would be completely
hidden by the body of the main balloon, unless the rope by
which it was attached was inordinately long. Moreover, there
are other and obvious difficulties attaching to their use.

These pilot balloons have played a great part at popular
festivities, on which occasions their weird shapes and many
colours have added to the gaiety of the scene. From the
professional point of view, displays of this kind are of no importance, but one occasion may be noticed on account of its
historical interest. A man named Garnerin was well known on
account of his many descents by means of a parachute. He
was therefore commissioned to send up a pilot balloon on the
occasion of Napoleon's coronation in 1806. This was done, and
the balloon found its way to Rome, where it descended on the
tomb of Nero. Napoleon regarded this as an evil omen, and
is supposed to have conceived a violent antipathy to ballooning
in any form, even in its application to military purposes.

Charles made his ascent with one of the brothers Robert
on December 1st, 1783, in fine weather before a large concourse of people. He afterwards wrote in glowing terms of the
delight which he experienced on journeys of this kind. On this
particular occasion they covered about 40 miles in $3\frac{3}{4}$ hours and
arrived at Nesles, where Robert landed, while Charles continued
his journey alone. He then rose to a great height, and was

exposed to the unpleasant effects of the rarefied atmosphere. In consequence of the very rapid ascent he experienced great pain in the ears, besides suffering acutely from the cold; he therefore opened the valve, and came to earth in 35 minutes from the start, at a distance of a few miles from the spot where he had left his friend. The balloon had been satisfactorily tested in every way. In particular, the benefit of the open tube at the

FIG. 12.—A balloon in the act of landing. To the right of the basket is seen the ballast-sand, which has just been thrown out.

bottom was very evident on the occasion of the second journey, when the gas streamed out in great volumes under the diminished pressure. After Robert had landed, he had forgotten to take on board a corresponding quantity of ballast. At starting he had filled the car with as many sacks of sand as he could carry, but he forgot to give the matter further attention. It is impossible so to construct a balloon that the gas shall not be able to escape through the substance composing the walls. This is due to a property of gases called diffusion, of which mention will be made hereafter.

Charles' balloons, which were called the "Charlière," the "Charlotte," and the "Robertine," had been completely success-ful, and had altogether eclipsed the efforts of Montgolfier. The King of France ordered a medal to be struck on which Charles' head should figure beside those of the brothers Montgolfier, and

FIG. 13.—The "Rozière," constructed by Pilâtre de Rozier.

in this way he proposed to do honour to all the inventors simultaneously.

The balloons, called "Rozières," which were made by Pilâtre de Rozier, were even less successful than those of the hot air type. Rozier was anxious to have the distinction of being the first to cross the English Channel. But he was anticipated by Blanchard, whose flying car has been already mentioned, and who had since those days become a professional balloonist. A number of ascents had been made in different places on the Continent, and he now proposed to make the journey from Dover to Calais. A start was made at Dover on January 7th, 1785, in company with an American doctor named Jeffries. He took with him a variety of useless things in the shape of oars, provisions, and much else. The whole thing would have sunk in the water at the moment of starting if all the ballast had not been thrown overboard. With great difficulty they succeeded in covering half the distance, though they were obliged to throw away everything on which they could lay their hands, including a mass of correspondence and books, together with most of their provisions. They then sighted the French coast on the horizon, but the imminent collapse of their balloon made the outlook anything but hopeful. Blanchard now threw overboard the wings, which he had stated were necessary for the support of the contrivance and for guiding it in any given direction through the air. This did not produce the desired result, and they began to strip themselves of their clothing ; but it only sank further and further, till Dr. Jeffries proposed to lighten the load by jumping into the water. However, this plan proved unnecessary, as also was another scheme for cutting the car away from the balloon. Suddenly they rose in the air, and with great difficulty they effected a landing on the coast near Calais, where they were received with many rejoicings. A marble column with suitable inscription was erected on the spot, to convey to future ages the facts relating to the first crossing of the Channel by balloon.

Pilâtre de Rozier thought much over this adventure, and determined to repeat it at all hazards. The difficulties into which Blanchard and Jeffries had fallen were to be avoided by constructing a special form of balloon. He proposed to combine the ideas of Charles with those of Montgolfier, hoping to be able to balance the losses, due to the escape of hydrogen, against the lifting power, which he could generate, as required, by means of hot air. He therefore made a spherical balloon after the methods of Charles, and placed below it a cylindrical receiver, which could be filled with hot air. The rope for controlling the valve was brought down on the outside. He thought, by suitably regulating the heat of the fire, to be able to rise or fall, and the

careful study which he had given to this aspect of the problem
led him to think that this would constitute a very desirable
feature in the combination. He determined to start from the
French coast, but was obliged to wait a long time till there was
a favourable easterly breeze. At last, on June 16th, 1785, he
started with a friend in the " Aero-Montgolfière," as it was
called. The balloon rose rather rapidly, and remained stationary
for a short time in the air. It then fell suddenly on the cliff,
and both passengers lost their lives. According to the testimony
of those who witnessed the accident, a cloud was seen round the
balloon just at the moment when it fell. An explosion was
therefore the probable cause of the accident, and this seems very
possible, seeing that it is alleged there were slight leakages of
hydrogen, which were noticed before the start.

This accident had the effect of cooling the ardour of enthusi-
asts, and the number of journeys that were made decreased very
rapidly. Count Zambeccari, an Italian, had little better luck
than Rozier. He heated the hot-air balloon with a large spirit
lamp. At his first attempt he had the misfortune to fall into
the Adriatic, but was rescued by some sailors with the loss of his
balloon. At his second attempt, the heating arrangements worked
admirably, but as he was descending the lamp was upset, and the
car was set on fire. His companion displayed great agility and
reached the ground with the help of the anchor rope. But the consequence of this, and of the great heat, was that the car suddenly
rose to a great height, where Zambeccari succeeded in extinguish-
ing the flames. But this was no sooner done than the balloon descended suddenly into the Adriatic, as before, and Zambeccari was
rescued by some fishermen, though the balloon became a total loss.
He finally attempted an ascent at Bologna in 1812. The balloon
was blown by the wind against a tree, the spirit was upset, and the
car again set on fire. He met his death by jumping from the
balloon when it was at a distance of about 60 ft. from the ground.

This constitutes the last appearance of "Rozières" in the history
of aeronautics, and though schemes of this kind have since been
mooted, the danger attaching to work on these lines has always
prevented any practical outcome.

CHAPTER IV.

THE THEORY OF THE BALLOON.

ALL investigations into the theory of the balloon rest upon the principle of Archimedes. Years before the birth of Christ he enunciated the following law. " Every body, which is immersed in a fluid, is acted upon by an upward force, exactly equal to the weight of the fluid, which is displaced by the immersed body." A result of this law is that a body will rest in any position, if immersed in a fluid of equal specific gravity ; if the body has a greater specific gravity than the fluid, it will sink, and on the other hand, if it has a less specific gravity, it will float. This law can be extended so as to apply to all gases, and a balloon will therefore rise in the air, if its total deadweight is less than that of the air which it displaces.

A simple piece of apparatus is needed to show experimentally the truth of these assertions. Two spheres appear to have the same weight, when placed on an ordinary balance, the one being solid and the other hollow. If now the balance and the spheres are placed on the receiver of an air pump, and the air removed, the hollow sphere will appear to be the heavier. It is therefore evident that the hollow sphere is acted upon by a greater upward force when weighed in air than when weighed in a vacuum. The reason for this is very evident, when we consider that the weight of the gas displaced by the hollow sphere under the receiver of the air pump is much less than when it is weighed in the open air. It is therefore necessary to understand the properties of the air and of the gases used for filling balloons, before any adequate conception of the principles underlying their movements can be formed.

The air may be looked upon as a mixture of 79 per cent. of nitrogen with 21 per cent. of oxygen. Gases have a tendency to diffuse themselves on all sides ; they have therefore great elasticity and can be easily compressed. The weight of a cubic foot of the atmosphere at a temperature of 32° Fahr. and a pressure of 29·92 in. of mercury, is 0·0807 lb.; the weight of a cubic foot of hydrogen under the same conditions is only 0·0056 lb., and of a cubic foot of coal gas about 0·04 lb. on an average. The law of Archimedes therefore states that a cubic foot of hydrogen will be acted upon by an upward force of 0·0751 lb., and that the force acting on a cubic foot of coal gas will be similarly 0·0407 lb. Here we have assumed that the

FIG. 14.—The Baroscope.

hydrogen is chemically pure. In point of fact, the above figures are slightly too high, in so far as ordinary samples of hydrogen and coal gas are concerned.

But allowance must be made for the weight of the car, net, ropes, and other appurtenances, in calculating the effective upward force acting on the balloon. It will therefore be evident that the size must be considerable if it is to be capable of rising in the air. The following example will perhaps make this clearer. Let us suppose that the weight of a balloon with its appurtenances is a quarter of a ton, and that its capacity is 21,000 cubic feet. The weight of the air displaced by it is 1,700 lbs., and on the other hand, the weight of the contained hydrogen is only 118 lbs. Consequently the net upward force is 1,022 lbs. If the expedition is to be undertaken at a moderately low level, this force will probably be sufficient, and a reasonable number of passengers could be carried, together with instruments, maps, and a sufficiency of ballast. But if it is intended to rise to great heights, things become very different. According to the latest results, the atmosphere is supposed to be about 125 miles high ; consequently

FIG. 15.—Vienna. Photograph taken from a captive balloon by Captain Hinterstoisser.

the density and pressure of the air gradually decreases the higher we rise. The experiment which Toricelli carried out in 1643 with a glass tube, about 3 ft. long, filled with mercury, is well known, and on the facts which he then discovered, the construction of the barometer has been based. A mercury barometer is, however, very inconvenient for the balloonist, and is very liable to be broken during the landing. The aneroid type is therefore preferred. This consists of a very flexible metal tube, from the inside of which the air has been exhausted ; it is therefore more or less deformed by the external pressure of the atmosphere. A pointer on the front of the instrument is connected by an ingenious mechanism to the metal tube, and shows the amount of flexure or deformation which the tube has undergone at any moment. This pointer moves over a scale, and gives the pressure of the atmosphere in inches of mercury. Most of the aneroids, which are intended for aeronautical work, have a further graduation on the scale, showing the height, which is generally calculated with reference to some particular temperature, and is therefore liable to be very inaccurate. Hergesell gives a convenient formula which may be expressed as follows, viz.—

$$h = \frac{52500 \, (P - p) \, (0\cdot93 + 0\cdot0022\, t)}{P + p}$$

In this equation, h denotes the height to be calculated in feet; P is the barometric pressure at the earth's surface in inches of mercury; p is the pressure at the height h; t is the mean temperature in degrees Fahrenheit. Suppose, then, that P is 30 in., p is $25\frac{1}{2}$ in., t is 48° Fahr. Substituting these values in the formula, it will be found that the height in question is 4,400 ft.

The force with which the balloon is driven upwards will decrease as the pressure of the atmosphere decreases, seeing that the air which it displaces is less dense and therefore weighs less. The greater the atmospheric pressure, the greater will be the upward force. It will also be noticed, as a matter of experience, that the quantity of gas required by the balloon varies from day to day. Toricelli's experiments showed that the atmosphere exerts an average pressure equal to that of a column of mercury 29·92 in. high; the specific gravity of mercury is 13·59, and therefore the pressure of the air on a square inch is 14·706 lbs. Let us suppose the air to be contained in a cylinder, which is closed by an airtight piston, the cross section of the cylinder being 1 square inch in area. Let us further suppose that this little piece of apparatus is placed beneath the receiver of the air pump. It will then be found that, if the piston is to be kept in position without allowing the gas in the cylinder to expand, it will be necessary to load it with a weight of 14·7 lbs. If the piston is loaded with a weight of 29·4 lbs., the volume of the gas will be reduced by one half; the pressure of the gas will therefore be doubled, and its density similarly increased. Boyle and Mariotte have therefore stated that the volume of a gas is inversely proportional to its pressure or density.

It is now possible with the aid of Boyle's law to calculate the

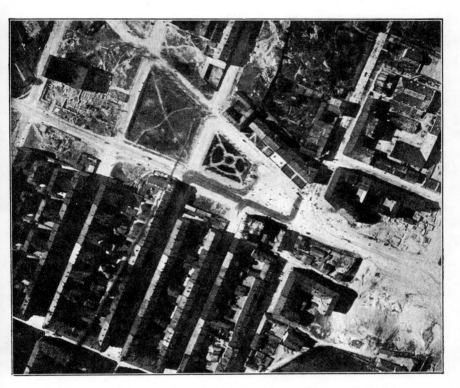

Fig. 16.—Stockholm, seen from a height of 1,600 feet. Photograph by Oskar Halldin.

"lift" which acts on a balloon at different heights, or with different atmospheric pressures. Let us suppose that the barometric pressure is that of 30 in. of mercury, and that the "lift" is 1,600 lbs. If the pressure sinks to 29 in., the lift will become $\frac{29}{30}$ of 1,600 lbs., *i.e.*, 1,550 lbs. The difference between these two forces is 50 lbs., and corresponds to the weight of about two sacks of ballast. At a height of 6,600 ft. a cubic foot of air

weighs only 0·064 lb., and a cubic foot of hydrogen would weigh
0·00396 lb.   It is therefore possible in this way to determine the
greatest height to which it is possible to ascend, if the dead-
weight of the balloon is already known.

Hitherto we have assumed the temperature to be constant, and
it is necessary to examine the effect produced by its variation.
The application of heat increases the volume of any gas.   A
simple experiment will make the matter plain.   Take a glass
tube, closed at the one end, and hold the open end below the
surface of some water.   If the glass tube is heated, it will be seen
that bubbles escape through the water, owing to the expansion of
the air within the tube.   If it is then allowed to cool, the contraction of the air still remaining in the tube will be made evident
by the rise of water, which is sucked up to take the place of the
retreating air, and Gay-Lussac has shown that all gases are equally
expanded or contracted by the same variations of temperature.

Finally, the diffusion of gases must be noticed.   Let us suppose
a closed vessel to be divided into compartments by means of a
porous partition, and the two halves to be filled with different
gases.   It will be found after a time that the two gases have
mixed completely with one another, even if the heavier gas
should have been put in the lower half of the vessel.   The speed
with which the mixture takes place depends on the specific
gravities of the gases in question ; for instance, hydrogen will
go more easily through a porous partition than coal gas or air.
As a general rule, it may be said that the diffusion-velocities are
inversely proportional to the square roots of the specific gravities
of the gases.   An obvious consequence of these facts is that the
enclosed gas in a balloon is always escaping through the walls of
the body, and being replaced by the intrusion of air.   No
substance can be used through which this diffusion does not take
place, however carefully it is made in the first instance.   Consequently the weight of the balloon is always gradually on the
increase, while the lifting forces acting on it similarly decrease.
A decrease of lifting force can only be met in one way, and that
is by throwing out a certain amount of ballast.   It is of course
possible to calculate the amount which must be thrown away.

but a little experience is far more useful than any amount of calculation.

It will now be evident that a balloon which is meant for great heights must be of great size. In order to make a steady start it is usually loaded with as much ballast as it can conveniently carry, and this is gradually thrown overboard as the journey proceeds. In consequence of diffusion a certain amount of the gas-contents is always lost, such losses obviously depending on the extent to which the leaks have been repaired, and ballast must therefore be thrown out in order to counteract the effects of diffusion. It has also been pointed out that an increase of volume is caused by a rise of temperature. The heat of the sun will cause an increase of the volume of the contained gas, and unless it is allowed to escape the internal pressure will rise. On the other hand, a fall of temperature causes a contraction in the volume. In this case a smaller amount of air is displaced by the balloon, and the upward force acting on it is therefore decreased. This too must be counteracted by throwing away some ballast. If this were not done it would gradually sink to the ground, because the increased atmospheric pressure would tend still further to decrease its volume. It is therefore extremely important to determine this loss of weight with some exactness, and not to throw away ballast unnecessarily. The result usually produced, if the temperature is at all variable, is to take the balloon steadily higher and higher, and a cloudy day with intervals of sunshine makes a very unsatisfactory combination for the aeronaut, who is apt to find his ballast disappear all too soon. Another peculiarity is shown by a balloon that has not been completely filled. As it ascends the gas expands, and consequently displaces a larger volume of the surrounding atmosphere. This has the indirect effect of sending it still higher, until at last it becomes completely filled. Any excess of gas is then driven off and escapes, a position of equilibrium being reached. It will therefore be easy to understand why a balloon which has made a descent will again rise to a height at least equal to that from which it has fallen.

It is now known that the heat of the sun will cause very

considerable variations of temperature within the balloon. This was first noticed by the brothers Robert during an ascent on September 19th, 1784, but it was not till much later that any exact measurements were made. Captain von Sigsfeld, who was fatally injured on the occasion of a descent at Antwerp in 1902, paid special attention to this matter, and concluded that the gases in a balloon might be heated to a temperature which was 80° or 90° Fahr. above that of the surrounding atmosphere. The effect of this on the "lift" will be evident when it is remembered that a difference of temperature of 1° Fahr. alters the weight of a cubic foot of coal gas by 0·0011 oz., and of hydrogen by 0·00016 oz. A balloon filled with hydrogen is much less affected by changes of temperature than it would be if filled with coal gas, and is therefore much simpler to manœuvre, especially at night time. It is also important to notice any tendency on the part of the balloon to sink. Otherwise, if it is only noticed after the sinking has continued for some time, it will be necessary to throw overboard a large amount of ballast, and the balloon may eventually rise to a much greater height than that from which it had fallen. A further trouble arises if the sinking is not noticed at an early stage, as the neck through which the gas is passed into the balloon at the bottom is usually left open, or in any case is only slightly closed. A descent causes a contraction in the volume, and there is a tendency for the air to enter by the neck. It then mixes with the gas, and as soon as the balloon rises again some of the mixture of air and hydrogen escapes, leaving the balloon in a less buoyant condition than it was before the sinking began.

It is therefore a matter of great importance to be able to detect at once any tendency to fall. For this purpose the most useful auxiliary is the barometer, more particularly one of the recording type. But such instruments are often sluggish in their movements, and fail altogether to show very slight variations. Even a very marked variation is often only shown after it has been in progress for some time, but to some extent this sluggishness may be avoided by gently tapping the instrument from time to time. These disadvantages have led to the development of instruments

which show at a glance any change of elevation. Of these, the
so-called statoscope, made by Gradenwitz, may be taken as a
type. It is contained in a metal case, somewhat similar to that
of a watch. Beneath the face is a circular opening, into which a
tightly-stretched rubber membrane is fitted, and a small rubber
tube communicates with the inside of the case. If now the rubber
tube is pinched, the outer air can no longer freely reach the
inside of the case. Supposing the balloon to be ascending, the
air enclosed within the stato-
scope will therefore expand, in
consequence of the reduced
external pressure; if it is descending, the opposite effect
will take place. The contraction or expansion of the enclosed air reacts on the rubber
membrane, which will be
sucked inwards during a descent, and blown outwards if
the balloon is rising. The
movements of the membrane
are communicated by very
delicate wheelwork to a pointer
on the face of the case, which

Fig. 17.—The statoscope, by
Gradenwitz.

therefore shows at a glance whether a rising or falling movement
is in progress.

It is not always necessary to throw out ballast in the case
of a momentary descent. The movements of overhead breezes
do not usually take place in straight lines, but rather partake
of the nature of wave motion. A balloon which is in a state
of equilibrium usually follows a path of this sort. Under such
circumstances one would merely be wasting ballast if it were
thrown overboard to counteract a fall; with a little patience, it
would soon be found that the balloon rises again of its own
accord. It is therefore rather a matter of determining the
relative motion between the aeronaut and the surrounding
atmosphere, and for this purpose von Sigsfeld has devised the

FIG. 18.—A parade on the Tempelhofer Feld. Photograph taken from a balloon by Major Moedebeck.

following simple method. Three different kinds of coloured papers are torn up into small pieces, the various papers having different thicknesses. Consequently each piece of paper begins to fall at a particular rate, which is known by its colour. For instance, let us suppose that the white paper falls at the start with a velocity of 18 in. per second, the blue at the rate of 3 ft. and the red at the rate of 6 ft. per second. By throwing out a handful of these papers, it is possible to tell at once what is the vertical movement. If the white pieces remain on a level with the balloon, then a fall is in progress at the rate of 18 in. per second. If all the pieces rise above the balloon, then the descent is more rapid than 6 ft. per second; if they all disappear below, then the balloon is either rising or at rest. Suppose that the barometer shows an increase of pressure, and at the same time it is noticed that the white pieces of paper remain on a level with the car; it will then be seen at once that the balloon has been caught by a descending breeze, because otherwise the great mass of the balloon would cause a much quicker descent. In this case, the ballast can be saved. The pieces of paper are also useful as an indication of the amount of ballast which it is necessary to throw overboard in any particular case, as much may be learnt by noting their apparent velocity. A simpler and more primitive method is to hang a feather at the end of a kind of fishing-rod over the side of the car. If there is no relative motion between the balloon and the surrounding air, the feather will remain at rest; otherwise it will rise or fall, and the deduction is obvious in either case. When a descent is noticed ballast must be thrown overboard; and though there is no precise indication of the moment when the operation can be stopped, the gradual sinking of the feather will show when the mark has been overshot. A further sign that may be noticed is given by the formation of folds on the body of the balloon, or by the collapse of the neck through which the gas is passed. We shall later have occasion to study the effect of meteorological conditions on ballooning, but for the moment we propose to consider in the following chapters the history and development of the dirigible balloon.

CHAPTER V.

THE eager restlessness of the human mind is well shown in the early history of ballooning. Long before the first practical successes were properly understood, countless suggestions were made on all sides with the object of constructing an airship which should be under control in so far as the direction of its motion was concerned. Many machines were actually built; but the number of suggestions was out of all proportion to their value. No idea seems to be too foolish to prevent it from being used by a succession of inventors, and it may be said that all the good and bad points of modern construction have been already used in some form or another in bygone ages. We are, however, little better than our ancestors. The most idiotic suggestions, which ever entered the mind of man, continue to arrive daily by post, until finally one ceases to be surprised at anything.

The Persian myth, according to which the King was presented with a throne harnessed to eagles, has been already mentioned, and it is rather amusing to find that an Austrian, named Kaiserer, published a treatise in 1801, entitled " A new method of steering balloons by means of eagles." Even nowadays the idea does not seem dead and buried, for in 1899 a German presented the Kaiser with a copy of a book, wherein he propounds a solution of the problem, which consists in harnessing a large number of pigeons to the balloon. His drawings showed the scheme carried out to the minutest detail, even including the reins, bridles and bits, proving him at any rate to be an expert on paper. It is a fact that a German patent was granted for this invention. Another absurd idea, which arose in the eighties, was to construct a balloon of such a size that it could rise to a height where it would no longer be acted on by the force of gravity, in which case a sail round the earth would be, at the outside, a matter of twenty-four hours.

It is now proposed to take a chronological survey of the development of dirigible balloons and flying machines, and to mention even some of those that did not directly lead to a successful issue. Many have contributed towards a solution of the problem, but it must at the same time be acknowledged that the progress, which was made in the course of some 120 years, was extremely small.

The first idea was taken from ships, and consisted in attempts to guide the balloon by means of sails, oars and rudder. Joseph Montgolfier showed much sense when he described this scheme, in a letter to his brother, as absurd. He pointed out that even if a number of men were to work something of the nature of oars, it would only be possible in perfectly calm weather to move at the rate of four or five miles an hour. In this connection it is necessary to bear in mind the small surface which can be exposed by the oars to the air, and to remember that the air offers an immense resistance to the motion of the balloon, in consequence of its enormous size. The only way to compensate for the smallness of the oars would be to move them very fast and to suitably design the shape of the balloon, and of the oars. But there is a limit to human effort, and since the resistance of the air increases with the square of the velocity, it soon becomes evident that even in gentle breezes the only method of overcoming the resistance would be by means of propellers, driven at high speeds. The effect produced by rudders is similar to that produced by them on ships, always supposing the balloon is under weigh. The proposals to use vertical sails betray a complete misconception of the laws underlying the movements of balloons. If a balloon, filled with gas, floats in the air, all its parts will move with the breeze, and at the same speed. A sail would therefore hang just as limply as it would do in a complete calm. It would be different if it were possible to give the balloon a smaller or greater velocity than the wind, and in such a case a pressure would be exerted on the sail. The explorer Andrée proposed to work on this idea in the simplest fashion. He

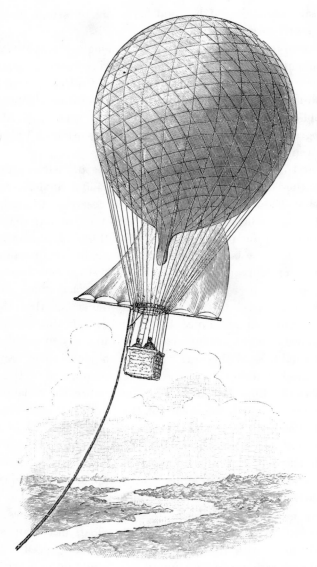

FIG. 19.—Balloon with sail, and with guide-rope fastened to the ring.

intended, with the help of the friction caused by a number of ropes dragged along the ground, to cause the balloon to go rather slower than the wind. A sail was then to be hung out, and placed in such a position that the force of the wind acting on it would drive the balloon in any desired direction. Tests have shown that with clever management it is possible to produce in this way a slight deviation from the direction of the wind. It is also known that surfaces slightly inclined to the horizontal will produce a slight movement of the balloon as it rises and falls. Stephen Montgolfier knew this and tried to utilise the idea in one of his models. Since his time many others have also worked on the same lines, but no practical success has been achieved.

In the year 1883, Professor Wellner, of Brünn, published his scheme for the construction of a sailing balloon. Seeing that

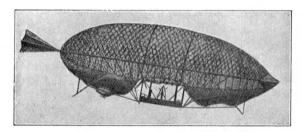

FIG. 20.—Scott's fish balloon.

surfaces inclined to the horizontal have a slight lateral motion as they fall or rise, he thought that by alternately raising and lowering such surfaces he would be able to move in any desired direction, and to produce the necessary vertical movements by increasing or decreasing the internal heat of the balloon. His calculations tended to show that a " fish-balloon," 150 ft. long, and 50 ft. in diameter, having a vertical surface in front and a horizontal one behind, might reach a speed of 10 miles an hour. As a matter of fact, his tests in Brünn showed that a single rise and fall moved the balloon over a distance of 3 miles in a direction opposed to that of the wind. There is no doubt as to the correctness of the mechanical principles involved, and Lébaudy has also worked on the same ideas, using several surfaces whose inclinations can be altered.

Guyot built the first sailing balloon in 1784, and naturally it was unsuccessful. The only noteworthy point about his design was that the body of the balloon was made of the shape of an egg ; the longer axis was horizontal, and the flatter end was at the front. Gradually it was recognised that any system which involved propulsion by oars was likely to be inadequate. Carra proposed to use paddle-wheels, which were to be mounted on a shaft, projecting over the sides of the car. This certainly was a move in the right direction, but even so the improvement was only slight. The effect produced by the shape of the balloon on the air-resistance was soon noticed, and they were consequently made rather longer than before. A start was made by the Academy of Dijon, who placed the matter in the hands of Guyton de Morveau. The front was to be wedge-shaped, so as to allow the air to pass lightly over it, while the steering was to be done by means of a vertical sail hoisted at the other end. This method of steering is still in use at the present day, and has been found to work well. Still the construction, which was proposed by the Academy, met with no success. It included a scheme for working with oars, in combination with a sail, which could be raised or lowered about a horizontal axis. Naturally it was found that forces of this order were much too small. Countless proposals of this kind were made in rapid succession, but all employed the same means of propulsion, and met with the same fate.

The *Montgolfières*, made by the priests Miollan and Janinet, were ingenious novelties. The balloon was to be 92 ft. broad and 105 ft. high, and according to an idea due to Joseph Montgolfier, it was to be driven forward as the result of the reaction produced by the escape of the hot gases. An opening, 14 in. in diameter, was therefore made in the middle of the balloon, and through this hole the hot gases were to escape, a fire being maintained, as usual, in the pan which was carried on the car. A further series of improvements occupied some time, until at last the exasperated mob, thinking that the start was likely to be postponed indefinitely, destroyed the whole concern.

The effect produced by the escape of gases and fluids is well known, and Barker's mill, which is nowadays used for watering grass lawns, is a familiar example of a reaction turbine. The idea, as applied to the propulsion of balloons, is still a popular one ; perhaps the most ridiculous form in which it has been expressed is to be found in the proposal to carry small cannons on the balloon, in the hope that the recoil would expend itself in driving it forwards.

General Meusnier introduced a great improvement by proposing the use of air-bags, to be carried inside the balloon. The air-bag plays even yet a considerable part in the working of captive and dirigible balloons. The first attempt that was made to test this idea on a practical scale nearly ended fatally. The brothers Robert, whose names have been already mentioned, placed the air-bag close to the opening by which any excess of gas was allowed to escape. It so happened that as they rose they came into a violent eddy, which tore away their oars and rudder, and broke the ropes which held the air-bag inside the balloon. An unfortunate result was that the opening became stopped up, and the gases, which expanded considerably on account of the ascent, were unable to escape. At a height of 16,000 ft. the Duke of Chartres, who was in the car, had the presence of mind to cut a hole in the balloon 10 ft. long with his sword. It was on the point of bursting, but now began to sink rapidly, and by throwing out a sufficient amount of ballast, they were able to reach the ground without injury. Although it seems obvious that the Duke's action saved the situation, his supposed lack of courage was the subject of much ridicule.

It may be useful to describe more exactly the design which was due to Meusnier, more especially seeing that he may be regarded as being to a great extent the forerunner of the modern inventor. He had great scientific and technical knowledge, and went very carefully into the question, basing his schemes throughout on the results of experimental work. In the first instance he studied questions relating to the resistance of the air, and the shapes which were likely to offer the least resistance. He found that an elliptical shape was the best, and in order still further to reduce the resistance, he proposed to use a boat-shaped car, pointing in the direction of motion. He was the first to

state that an absolutely rigid connection between the car and
the body of the balloon was an indispensable feature of a
dirigible machine. Even if the moving parts were to be housed
beneath the main body, they would necessarily be driven from
the car, and a rigid means of connection would therefore be
required. He used three propellers, which were supported mid-
way between the car and the body, and these were to be driven
by hand by means of pulleys. He well understood that the
result produced by one man would be very small, and calculated
that a crew of eighty would be required. At that time no other
form of motive power was available.

He also made careful investigations into the matter of gas
pressure, and by means of specially constructed models was able
to determine the exact force exerted on the envelope. His plan
also included the use of horizontal surfaces to increase the
stability, and this certainly foreshadows Lébaudy's inventions.
In addition, special arrangements were made to prevent the car
from sinking, in case an accident should plunge the balloon into
the sea.

But Meusnier's most important improvement is the use of the
air-bag, and this must be more fully described on account of its
importance. In his original memoir he described the object and
construction of a " special space, intended to enclose atmospheric
air." The importance of this arrangement lies in the possibility
of preserving the shape of the dirigible balloon. Every inventor
desires to reduce the resistance of the air to a minimum, and it is
therefore necessary that the balloon should retain a definite shape.
If the envelope were rigid, the matter would be simple enough ; but
we know that changes of temperature and external pressure cause
corresponding changes in the volume. An increase of internal
pressure can be relieved by an automatic valve, but a contraction
is at once noticed by the creases on the envelope. No doubt any
decrease in volume can be met by pumping air into the balloon ;
but this naturally dilutes the gas, besides gradually creating a
very explosive mixture. The best plan would be to pass more
gas into the balloon ; but owing to the weight of the cylinders
used for storage, it is impossible to take compressed gases on a

journey, though some method of storing gas in a liquid form may in the future be available. The use of air-bags is therefore the only solution; when the volume of the envelope tends to increase, the air is pressed out of the receivers, and when it contracts air is sucked in. These air-bags can be mounted in the balloon in three different ways. According to the first method, the envelope is made with two coverings over a portion of its length.

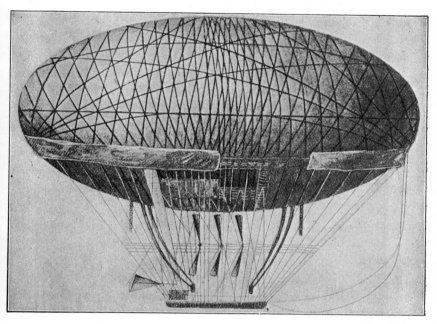

Fig. 21.—Balloon, designed by General Meusnier.

The two coverings lie tightly one upon the other when the balloon is full. But with a view to avoiding any unnecessary loss of gas, it is better to fill the outer space with a certain amount of air at the start, so that the volume of enclosed air corresponds to the increased bulk at the desired height. The valve will, therefore, only be opened when the balloon has risen to the proper level. The most ordinary method consists in simply putting air-bags inside the balloon. Their size depends on the height to which it is intended to rise, seeing that this determines the amount the balloon will expand. Such air-bags were used by the brothers Robert on the occasion of their ascent with the Duke of Chartres. The third method consists in having two separate envelopes, the inner one containing gas, and the space between the inner and outer ones being filled with air. Meusnier himself proposed the last form of construction.

But the air-bag is also used to serve other purposes. Meusnier intended to compress the air contained in it, and in this way to keep his balloon in a position of equilibrium. To a certain extent this is possible ; but the envelope is not capable of resisting any great pressure, and of late years this idea has been given up. But it has a more important use in regulating the height to which the balloon ascends. By compressing the air contained in it, the weight can be increased, and the balloon consequently sinks. The amount of gas which can be saved by these means in the case of a dirigible balloon is considerable. It is also possible to prevent the balloon from rising by the same method. Lébaudy was able to pump air at the rate of 35 cubic feet per second, and in spite of the fact that he threw overboard some of his ballast, he was able in a few seconds to make good the loss with the aid of his pumps. Meusnier's idea was to carry bellows on the car, and to work them by hand. He also proposed to have a third covering outside his balloon, and to bind it on with network, which was to be fastened to the car by means of ropes. His anchor was of a peculiar shape, consisting of a kind of harpoon, which was intended to bury itself in the earth.

Meusnier's scheme was the best that had been worked out by a single individual up to that time ; its probable cost, however, prevented it from being carried into execution. He was killed, fighting against the Prussians at Mayence, 1793. When the news of his death reached the King of Prussia, he ordered the firing to cease until Meusnier's body had been buried. After this time interest in the matter of dirigible balloons gradually waned, because it was recognised that the only driving power that was then known was wholly insufficient to meet the requirements of the case. So that after 1786, ballooning fell almost entirely into the hands of country showmen, who advertised excursions, and attracted attention in a variety of other ways. It cannot be said that there was an entire dearth of schemes relating to dirigible balloons, but at any rate nothing worthy of mention was published before the year 1852. The first half of the nineteenth century can therefore be passed over in silence.

CHAPTER VI.

THE HISTORY OF THE DIRIGIBLE BALLOON FROM 1852 TO 1872.

THE development of the dirigible balloon dates from the year 1852, when Giffard appeared on the scene. He subsequently invented the injector for steam boilers, and was already well known in the aeronautical world, having made ascents with Eugene Godard. In 1851 he succeeded in making a small steam engine of 5 h.p., which only weighed 100 lbs., and thought it might be useful in connection with balloon work. With the help of two of his friends, he built an airship, which was somewhat of the shape of a cigar with pointed ends. It was 144 ft. long, 40 ft. in diameter at the thickest part, and its capacity was 88,000 cubic feet. The envelope was covered with a net,

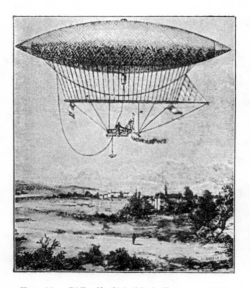

FIG. 22.—Giffard's dirigible balloon, made in 1852.

and a heavy pole, 66 ft. long, was carried below, being suspended in a horizontal position by means of ropes which connected it to the net. At the end of this keel, as Giffard called it, the rudder was placed, which took the form of a triangular sail. The car was carried below the pole at a distance of 20 ft., and contained the motor and propellers. The 3 h.p. motor together with its boiler weighed 350 lbs., and drove a three-bladed propeller, 11 ft.

in diameter, at the rate of 110 revolutions per minute. The total weight of the balloon, together with that of one passenger, amounted to 1½ ton, and it was reckoned that, when filled with gas, it could carry ¼ ton of coal and water. In the light of subsequent experience it is evident that the weight of the steam engine was too great, having regard to the effect which it was able to produce. Giffard himself saw this, but calculated that he would be able to attain a speed of 6 or 8 ft. a second. On one occasion this result was actually produced.

We must now examine the question of speed, and ascertain its value under ordinary working conditions. In other words, we must find out what speed it is reasonable to expect from a balloon that is to be used on and off the whole year round. Meteorological observations show that in Europe a balloon can move with a speed of 40 ft. per second on about 82 per cent. of the days in the year, and with a speed of 45 ft. on 90 per cent. This must of course be capable of being maintained for several hours. If the balloon has a speed due to its own internal energy of 40 ft. a second then it would be able to move at the rate of 3 ft. per second against a wind blowing at 37 ft. per second. It would thus have a resultant speed of two miles an hour, which seems no great achievement. But then it must be remembered that in stormy weather a sailing ship would remain in the harbour, and is only able to make headway against the wind by tacking. Moreover, the course of a balloon would not always be steadily in a direction opposed to that of the wind. Complaints are often made that a balloon caught in a storm is sometimes completely destroyed. But an aeronaut must be something of a meteorologist, and he ought to be able to form an opinion as to whether he is likely to encounter any serious storm. Naturally balloons are no more likely to escape the effects of rough weather than sailing ships.

After this short digression we can now return to the further consideration of Giffard's arrangements. He had a special contrivance to prevent the possibility of any explosion resulting from the escaping gases of the balloon. He placed a piece of wire gauze, similar to that used in safety lanterns, in front of the stokehole, and the gases from the boiler were taken to one corner of the car

A.   E

and discharged below.   These precautions were very important,
and it was only due to ignorance of these matters that Wölfert
and Severo lost their lives in later years.   In 1855 Giffard produced a second balloon, which he had made narrower and longer
with a view of diminishing the air-resistance.   It was 33 ft. in
diameter at the middle, and 230 ft. long, having a capacity of
113,000 cubic feet.   He stiffened the upper part of the envelope
with a special covering, to which the net was secured.   The car
was suspended by ropes, which were attached to its four corners.
He used the same engine as before, but the chimney was simply
taken to the side of the car and bent over at right angles,
explosions being avoided by placing the car rather lower.   In
company with a manufacturer, named Yon, he made a trial trip and

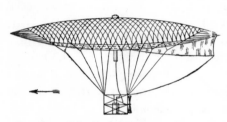

succeeded in moving
slowly against the wind.
When the descent began,
owing to some accident
the horizontal axis tilted
up, the weight of the car
broke the net from its
moorings, and the bal-
loon was completely

FIG. 23.—Giffard's second balloon, made
in 1855.

destroyed, the occupants escaping with slight injuries.   No air-
bags were used, and this accounted for the accident.

Giffard now planned a third balloon, which was to be 1,970 ft.
long, and 98 ft. in diameter at the middle.   Its capacity was to
be 7,800,000 cubic feet ; the motor was to weigh 30 tons, and the
speed to be 66 ft. per second.   The immense cost of this scheme
prevented it from being carried into execution, and Giffard then
devoted his attention to the design of small engines.   His subsequent invention of the injector put him once more in a position to
renew his work.   In 1868 he made a captive balloon for the exhibition in London ; its capacity was 424,000 cubic feet, and its cost
nearly £30,000.   A similar one was made in Paris in 1878, having
a capacity of 883,000 cubic feet.   In addition to all this, a dirigible
balloon was designed, holding 1,750,000 cubic feet, which was to be
fitted with two boilers, and to cost £40,000.   This scheme was

thoroughly worked out in every detail, but was never carried into execution. Giffard subsequently became blind, and died in 1882.

Nothing further was done till the siege of Paris. The French Government then commissioned Dupuy de Lôme to build a dirigible balloon, which, however, was only tested after the war in 1872. It is curious to find that this man, who was a marine engineer and therefore professionally acquainted with problems of this kind, proposed to employ a crew of eight men in driving the propeller. His method of construction was ingenious, and he succeeded in reaching a speed of 9 ft. a second, which was about the same as Giffard had done. His balloon had a cigar-shaped body; its length was 118 ft., its greatest diameter was 49 ft., and its capacity 122,000 cubic feet. The form which was given to the net was peculiar, and intended to prevent any displacement of the car, relatively to the body of the balloon, which might otherwise be caused by the working of the propellers. For this purpose some of the ropes were crossed in the space between the car and the

FIG. 24.—Dupuy de Lôme's balloon, 1872.

body, whereas the others were taken direct to the sides of the car, which was built in the shape of a boat. It carried 14 men, who worked the propeller, and also attended to the pumps used in connection with the air-bags. It is hardly necessary to give any further description of this scheme, seeing that it constitutes nothing of the nature of an advance on its predecessors.

In the meantime, Paul Haenlein (who died in 1895) constructed an airship in Germany. Its shape was that of a solid formed by the revolution of a ship's keel about an axis lying on the deck. Careful hydrostatic experiments led him to the choice of this curious shape, which in the middle is more or less cylindrical, and at the ends somewhat conical. Its length was 164 ft., the greatest diameter 30 ft., and the capacity 85,000 cubic feet. The car was placed close to the body, in order that the parts might be as rigidly connected as possible. For the first time in the

E 2

history of aeronautics it was proposed to use a gas engine, which was of the Lenoir type, and had four horizontal cylinders, giving 6 h.-p., with an hourly consumption of 250 cubic feet of gas. The gas for the engine was taken from the balloon itself, and the loss was to be made good by blowing out the air-bags. The car was made of beams running lengthwise, and was supported tangentially by ropes from the network. The envelope was made airtight by a thick coating of rubber on the inside, backed by a thinner one on the outside. Being filled with coal gas it

Fig. 25.—Paul Haenlein's dirigible balloon.

could not ascend to great heights, and the trials were therefore undertaken at a short distance from the ground, the balloon being kept in the captive state by ropes loosely held by soldiers. It attained a speed of 15 ft. per second, and this is an improvement of 6 ft. per second on the attempts of Dupuy de Lôme. Lack of funds prevented any further attempts from being made, and though the project promised well and had some notable improvements, it was unable to proceed further. If Haenlein's results are compared with those of Lébaudy, who has reached a speed of 40 ft. per second, we can hardly doubt he would have achieved more if he had filled his balloon with hydrogen, and if light motors, of the type now in use, had then been available.

CHAPTER VII.

Ten years later the brothers Gaston and Albert Tissandier produced a remarkable airship. During the Franco-Prussian war, Gaston Tissandier made many unsuccessful attempts to enter Paris by means of a balloon while it was in a state of siege. A model was shown during the Exhibition of 1881, and they were encouraged to proceed on a larger scale. The body was shaped, after Giffard's model, somewhat like a cigar. It was 92 ft. long, 30 ft. in diameter at the middle, and had a capacity of 37,500 cubic feet. It was made of varnished cambric. The car was in the form of a cage, constructed of bamboo rods, and contained a Siemens dynamo, together with 24 bichromate cells, each weighing 17 lbs. At full speed the dynamo made 180 revolutions per minute and the pull was 26 lbs. When the tests were undertaken it was found that a speed of 9 or 10 ft. per second was attained, when the motor gave 1½ h.-p. It cost £2,000, but there was nothing remarkable about the construction.

FIG. 26.—The basket of Tissandier's dirigible balloon.

So little success had attended the construction of dirigible balloons that it was gradually being regarded as likely to be impossible. Great astonishment was therefore caused in 1884 by the announcement that two French officers, named Renard and Krebs, had described a figure of 8 in a balloon, and had returned to the point from which they had started. Charles Renard had been studying the problem since 1878 with the assistance of one of his friends, named La Haye, and had hoped with the help of Colonel Laussedat, who commanded the Engineers, to obtain the necessary funds from the Minister of War. It was then pointed out that large sums of money had been wasted on similar projects in 1870, and their request was consequently refused. They therefore had recourse to Gambetta, who was much interested, and promised a sum of £8,000. In the meantime, La Haye had been succeeded by Captain Krebs, and with the help of the latter Renard proceeded

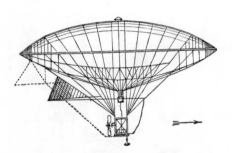

FIG. 27.—Tissandier's dirigible balloon.

with the work. The airship was of the shape of a torpedo, and was slightly larger in diameter at the front than at the back. It was 165 ft. long, and rather more than 27 ft. in diameter at the biggest part, and had a capacity of 66,000 feet. The car which was constructed of bamboo rods, was 108 ft. long, 6 ft. high, and 4½ ft. broad, being covered on the outside with silk. An electric motor, capable of giving 8·5 h.-p., was driven by an accumulator, and connected to a propeller, which was carried at the front, and made of wooden beams 23 ft. long. In order to prevent any injury to the propeller blades when a descent was made it was possible to slightly raise the axis on which they were mounted. Moreover, Renard intended to obviate any serious shocks on coming to earth by using a guide rope. The way in which such a rope is used becomes evident if the arrangements made for a descent are considered. Suppose a balloon to be falling. It will gradually reach a considerable velocity, unless measures are taken to prevent it, and a violent shock would

result from contact with the ground.   It is, however, difficult to
check this velocity by throwing out ballast, because the throwing
out of too little ballast might not be sufficient to prevent a
dangerous shock, and if too much were thrown out the balloon
might begin to ascend.   The following plan is therefore adopted.
A heavy guide rope, from 200 to 300 ft. long, is gradually paid
out shortly before the car reaches the ground.   This corresponds
to so much ballast, and the shock is consequently very much
reduced.   If for any reason the balloon begins to ascend again,
it drags with it some of the rope, and this increase of load tends
to bring it down again.   Automatic reactions of this kind play
an important part in bringing a balloon to the ground, or in
travelling at a low level.   The friction of the rope against the
ground is also useful in checking the speed, and allows an anchor
more time to fasten itself.   Renard also carried a so-called
" sliding-weight," and this could be moved into any suitable
position so as to counteract any shifting of the centre of gravity
that might be caused by movements of the passengers.   The
total weight, together with ballast, was 2 tons.   At the back
between the car and the body of the balloon a rudder was
mounted, which was rectangular in appearance, and trapezoidal
in cross-section ; any distortion of its shape was therefore
impossible.   It was moved about a vertical axis by means of ropes,
which were secured to beams projecting over the sides of the car.

The inventors waited nearly two months in perfectly calm
weather, but at last, at 4 o'clock in the afternoon of August 9th,
Renard and Krebs mounted the balloon, which they called " La
France," and made an ascent.   As soon as they had risen above
the level of the trees in the neighbourhood of Chalais, they set
the propellers in motion.   Immediately they noticed that the
speed was increasing, and as a further encouraging symptom it
was seen that small changes of direction could be effected by
means of the rudder.   The journey was therefore continued from
north to south till they crossed the road from Choisy to Versailles,
after which they turned to the west.   It had not been intended
to sail directly against the wind, which however only amounted
to a gentle breeze.   But their confidence increased, and at a

distance of 2½ miles from Chalais they turned round, completing
the bend in the small angle of 11 degrees at a radius of about
160 yards. After a slight deviation to the right-hand side, which
was soon corrected by the rudder, the balloon reached a spot
1,000 ft. above the starting point. The valve was slightly opened,
and the balloon was then manœuvred by means of the motor
into the most convenient spot for the descent, which was about
80 yards above the parade ground. The guide rope was caught

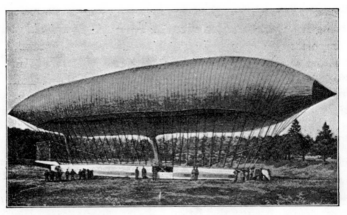

FIG. 28.—The balloon " La France," built by Renard and Krebs.

by the soldiers, and the balloon was safely landed, after having
covered rather less than 5 miles in 23 minutes.

A second expedition was less successful. The wind was rather
stronger, and drove the balloon before it. The arrangements
connected with the motor were injured, and a descent had to be
made at a distance of 3 miles from the starting point. The
balloon was then carried back to Chalais. On the third occasion
the course was directed N.N.E. against the wind towards
Billancourt. In order to determine the velocity of the wind,
Renard stopped the motor and let the balloon drift. He then
found that the wind was blowing at the rate of 5 miles an hour,
i.e., 7 ft. per second, while the velocity due to the motor was
14½ miles an hour, or 7 yards per second. The balloon was then
brought to land at the starting point. Out of seven attempts it

was possible to bring the balloon back to the starting point on five occasions. At the fifth attempt the wind was blowing with a velocity of 21 ft. per second, and it was consequently impossible to sail in the opposite direction. The sixth and seventh journeys were made to the city of Paris. It was therefore clearly demonstrated to all unbelievers that the dirigible balloon was now within the range of practical possibilities. In spite of its successes, the French have not adopted this type, partly because its speed was insufficient, and partly because it could only undertake a short journey. Renard made further attempts to construct one on a bigger scale, but they were unsuccessful.

FIG. 29.—Captain Renard.

In 1879 Baumgarten and Wölfert built a balloon in Germany that was fitted with a Daimler benzine motor, and the first ascent was made with it at Leipsic in 1880. It had a propeller for raising it in the air, and was fitted at the sides with things of the nature of wings, which were for the purpose of producing horizontal motion. Baumgarten almost came to grief during the first trial. The airship had three cars, and the result of carrying a passenger in one of the outer cars was that the load was unevenly distributed. In consequence the whole thing tilted over with the longer axis in a vertical position, and came with a crash to the ground. The occupants luckily escaped without injury. Baumgarten subsequently died, and Wölfert proceeded with the work alone. Successful experiments were said to have been made, and finally it was arranged to make an ascent on the Tempelhofer Feld, near Berlin, on June 12th, 1897. The balloon rose to a height of 600 feet and travelled with the wind. Suddenly a flame was seen to dart from the motor towards the main body of the balloon, a slight report was heard, and the whole thing fell to the ground, where it was entirely destroyed by the flames before it was possible to rescue Wölfert and his companion. The disaster was caused by the fact that no suitable precautions were taken in connection with the benzine vapour, which formed an explosive mixture with the air, and was accidentally fired. One would have thought an accident of this

Fig. 30.—Dr. Wölfert's dirigible balloon about to start.

kind was sufficient to put inventors on their guard, and it is therefore strange to find that Severo's death was caused a few years later by precisely the same defect in his arrangements.

An Austrian engineer, named Schwarz, made a balloon with a rigid envelope, but the ascent on the Tempelhofer Feld in 1897 was unsuccessful. Marey Monge and Dupuis Delcourt had already proposed in 1831 and 1844 to construct the body of metal and this was actually done. But their efforts failed in consequence of the insufficient rigidity of their design and the leaks

which occurred at the joints.   Schwarz's balloon was constructed
of aluminium, 0·008 in. thick, which was supported on a stiff
lattice-work, made of tubes of the same metal.   The shape was
peculiar, but it was probably owing to difficulties of construction
that it was impossible to use the form, which had been already
found, as the result of many experiments, to offer the least
resistance to the air.   The ascent was undertaken by a soldier
out of the Balloon Corps, and he was driven in the direction of the
wind.   The belts driving the propellers came off their pulleys,
one after another, and in consequence of serious leaks the

Fig. 31.—Schwarz's balloon after the accident.

balloon came to the ground in a short time at a distance of 4
miles from the starting point.   Great injury was done by the
shock on coming to earth, but the soldier escaped by jumping
from the car before it reached the ground.   Soon afterwards it
was completely destroyed by the wind.

The way in which rigid bodies of this type are filled with gas
must be here described.   It is not possible to pass the gas
directly into the balloon, as this would merely cause a mixture
of air and gas.   Schwarz's balloon was 156 ft. long, and contained 130,000 cubic feet.   It was filled by Captain von Sigsfeld,
who passed a number of bags into the balloon, and inflated
them with gas.   After it was filled the bags were pulled to
pieces and torn out again.   Another method consists in placing

a linen envelope within the aluminium casing. This linen envelope is first blown out with air, and the gas is then passed between the aluminium and the linen. The air is therefore gradually pressed out of the linen envelope, which is withdrawn at the end of the operation. It may be well to mention two methods which are unsatisfactory in practice. The one consists in passing steam into the body of the balloon, which condenses while the gas is passed in, and flows away in the form of water. The other consists in passing the gas while the balloon is submerged under water. In any case, under the most favourable conditions, it is a tedious and delicate operation.

If we glance back at the progress which has been described in this chapter it will probably seem as though little had really been done in these forty-five years. The speed which had been reached by these balloons was indeed lamentably insufficient. Still it must be admitted that many preliminary points of importance had been considered and solved. Not the least of their achievements was probably to be found in the fact that they had convinced the world that a dirigible balloon was likely to be a possibility of the immediate future, and one result of this was that there was no longer any insuperable difficulty in raising funds. France was certainly more lavish in this respect than most other countries, with the result that the French have succeeded in constructing a really serviceable airship.

CHAPTER VIII.

COUNT VON ZEPPELIN, who had distinguished himself over a well-known incident of the Franco-Prussian war, devoted his attention, after retiring from the army, to the construction of a dirigible balloon, a plan which he had long entertained. He formed a limited liability company for the purpose of raising the necessary money, and started on the work in 1898. His balloon was the longest and biggest which had been made. It had a strong framework of aluminium, which was covered with linen and silk, treated with pegamoid. Special compartments were built inside for holding linen bags, which contained nearly 400,000 cubic feet of hydrogen. From end to end it measured 420 ft., and its diameter was 38 ft. There were two cars, in each of which was a motor, giving 16 horse-power. These motors were altogether independent of one another, and worked propellers which were rigidly connected to the body of the balloon. Vertical and horizontal screws were used for movements in the corresponding directions. A " sliding weight " was used, if required, to raise or lower the front of the balloon and was moved by means of a winch along a steel support, on which it was carried. In this way it was possible to rise or fall over certain distances without loss of ballast or using the valves. Little was known about the probable results of the shock that would be experienced on coming to the ground in a rigid machine of this type. Schwarz's experiment was the only one which threw any light on the matter, and it was therefore considered safer to conduct the trials above the waters of the Bodensee. The construction of the outer envelope was a matter of great importance. It provided a smooth surface, and also protected the gas-bags from injury of any kind. Moreover a thin film of air came between the gas-bags and the outer covering, and served to protect them from undesirable variations of temperature. This is a matter of great importance, because the indirect effect of radiation would otherwise be to cause a rise or fall.

The first ascent was made in July, 1900, and it cannot be said that it was favoured by any unusual luck. The winch, which worked the sliding weight, was broken, and the whole balloon, together with the framework which connected the two cars, was

FIG. 32.—Count Zeppelin's dirigible balloon.

so bent that the propellers could not be properly worked. Consequently full speed could not be reached, the maximum that was actually attained being 13 ft. per second, and it was also impossible to steer, as the ropes that were used for this purpose became entangled. These mishaps, which could not be rectified in mid-air, made it necessary to descend to the lake, where everything happened as had been expected, and the only injury that was sustained was caused by running on a pile. The damage was repaired at the end of September, and on October 21st a further attempt was made on the original lines, and a speed of 30 ft. per second was reached. It was pointed out that a higher speed than this could probably be reached, but owing to the continual turns, it was impossible to get up full speed in any direction. Dr. Hergesell, the director of the Meteorological Institute in Alsace and Lorraine, undertook all the measurements. He determined trigonometrically the exact positions of three points, and from them continuous observations of the balloon were made. The speed of the wind was recorded on an instrument that was placed in a pilot balloon, and the figures so obtained may be confidently regarded as correct. The speed of the balloon was therefore greater than that of any of its predecessors, and exceeded that of Renard and Krebs by about 10 ft. per second.

At the end of another five years Count von Zeppelin had collected enough money to build a second airship. In the light of the experience that had been gained in 1900, the new model of 1905 was improved in all its details. The most important alteration was made by increasing the power of the motor

FIG. 33.—Count Zeppelin.

without adding to its weight. Each car carried a motor, weighing 8 cwt., and giving 85 horse-power. The body was about 6 ft. shorter than before, while the diameter was slightly increased, the length being 85 ft., and the diameter 38 ft. It had 16 gas-bags, which held 367,000 cubic feet of hydrogen, the capacity being about 32,000 cubic feet less than before. The total weight was 9 tons, which was a decrease of 1 ton. The four propellers were also somewhat larger. In front and behind were placed three vertical surfaces, constructed of linen, and intended to produce motion in horizontal directions ; between them and the cars horizontal surfaces were arranged, one above another, after the fashion of an aeroplane, in order to induce falling or rising movements. The steering was done by the occupant of the front car.

The first ascent took place over the Bodensee on November 30th, 1905. It had been intended to tow the raft, to which it was anchored, further from the shore against the wind. But the water was too low to allow the use of the raft. The balloon was therefore mounted on pontoons, pulled out into the lake, and taken in tow by a motor boat. It was caught by a strong wind which was blowing from the shore, and driven ahead at such a rate that it overtook the motor boat. The tow-rope was therefore at once cut, but it unexpectedly formed into knots and became entangled with the airship, pulling the front end down into the water. The balloon was then caught by the wind and lifted into the air, when the propellers were set in motion. The front end was at this instant pointing in a downward direction, and consequently it shot into the water, where it was found necessary to open the valves. Certain slight damage was sustained, and a delay of six weeks took place.

The next attempt was made on January 17th, 1906, when it was found that the lifting force was too great, and it rose at once to a height of 1,500 ft. When the propellers had been started at a lower level, it was found possible to move against the wind. But at a greater height a strong breeze was found to be blowing from the S.W., and the balloon was turned to face the wind. In consequence of lack of experience, it was found difficult to hit the mark, because the steering arrangements produced too strong a turning motion. In the meantime the balloon had reached the shore, and was carried with the wind, the motors having been stopped for various reasons. The descent was made without serious damage, although the anchor failed to hold in the frosty ground. A slight superficial rent was caused by rubbing against a tree. But during the night the wind did so much damage that Count Zeppelin was obliged to order it to be broken up. It is very difficult to form any decided opinion as to the merits of this design. At any rate it is certain that if the motors could produce a speed of 30 ft. per second, when working at 36 horse-power, the velocity would have been much greater if the full 170 horse-power could have been exerted. The latest news is to the effect that Count von Zeppelin has made a further attempt with a new balloon, and that this has been successful. Its stability is said to be very great, and it can be easily steered. According to Hergesell, a speed of nearly 50 ft. per second has been reached, which is far better than any previous record.

About the same time, a young Brazilian, named Santos Dumont, appeared in Paris, and proceeded to astonish the world with his feats, which soon made him the most popular hero in the ballooning world. He had great wealth, as well as courage and perseverance, and constructed altogether fourteen balloons, making ascents in all of them with greater or less success. He knew nothing about the work of his predecessors when he set himself, without any experience, to the task of constructing his first balloon.

List of Santos Dumont's Airships.

Number.	Shape.	Volume in cubic feet.	Length in feet.	Greatest diameter in feet.	Motor.
I.	Cylindrical ; conical at back and front.	6,350	82	11·5	3 h.p. Dion Bouton.
II.	ditto.	7,060	82	12·5	ditto.
III.	Cigar-shaped. Filled with coal gas.	17,650	66	24·6	ditto.
IV.	Cylindrical ; conical at back and front.	14,800	95	16·7	7 h.p. Buchet.
V.	ditto.	19,400	108	16·4	12 h.p. with four cylinders.
VI. Winner of the Deutsch Prize.	Elongated ellipsoid.	22,200	108	19·7	ditto.
VII.	ditto.	44,500	164	26·25	60 h.p., weighing 2¼ cwt.
VIII.	(Sold to an American ; only made one trip.)				
IX. "The Balladeuse."	Egg-shaped.	7,770	50	18	3 h.p. Clement. (26 lbs.)
X. "The Omnibus."	Ellipsoidal.	71,000	157	27·9	20 h.p.
XI.	ditto.	42,400	111	—	16 h.p. with four cylinders. (3¼ cwt.)
XII.	(Placed at disposal of military authorities.)				
XIII.	Egg-shaped.	67,100	62	47·7	—
XIV.	Cigar-shaped.	6,570	134	11·1	15 h.p. Peugeot. (57 lbs.)

A.

Perhaps he can hardly be said to have hidden his light under a bushel, and technically considered, his results constitute no great advance on account of the small speeds he reached. But, on the other hand, he succeeded, as no one else has done, in arousing enthusiasm for the sport of ballooning, especially in England and France. Zeppelin's balloon represented the rigid type of construction, whereas Santos Dumont favoured a flabby envelope with a slight amount of stiffening, and used an air-bag to keep the thing in shape. The measurements are also altogether different from those adopted by Zeppelin, though he gradually adopted larger sizes. This resulted from the fact that

FIG. 34.—Santos Dumont.

he was obliged to use larger motors, as he found that the speed was insufficient. Heavier motors meant an increase of weight, and this could only be met by increasing the dimensions generally.

It is extremely interesting to follow Santos Dumont on his expeditions. He succeeded in learning something on every occasion, and instantly proceeded to build a new balloon without giving a thought to the possibility of adapting the old one. He made very few expeditions in his first balloons, because he saw almost at once that they were unsuitable and that radical alterations were needed in the design. He went through all manner of accidents on his trial runs, but he also showed on many occasions that he well understood the art of guiding his ship through the air. He landed in trees, in the water, on the roofs of houses in rapid succession ; still his presence of mind always found a way of escape. His first attempt started very unluckily : the airship was at once dashed against the trees and torn to pieces. He said himself that the choice of an unsuitable starting-point was the cause of this accident. He made his ascent in a place that was surrounded by high trees. The force of the wind, which acted in the same direction as that produced by his propellers, drove him against the trees before he had time to rise above them.   He then took the precaution of starting always with the front of the balloon towards the wind.   The damage was repaired in two days, and after performing some evolutions at a low level, he gained such confidence that he sailed from Paris to Longchamps at a height of 1,300 ft.   At first all went well.   As soon as the balloon fell, the gas contracted and the air-bag was seen to be too small.   The balloon was no longer properly inflated, and it proceeded to fold up in the middle, like a pocket knife.   It then plunged downwards towards the ground,

FIG. 35.—Santos Dumont's second balloon breaks its back, May 11th, 1899.

but Santos Dumont did not lose his presence of mind.   He shouted to some small boys who were playing in a field, and told them to catch his guide-rope, and run with it as fast as possible against the wind.   They did as they were told, and the air-resistance was so great that the balloon came gently to the ground without causing any injury to the driver.

A new balloon was ready in the spring of 1899.   The air-bag was now to be filled by a small rotating fan, whereas in the earlier model a pneumatic pump, similar to those in use on motor cars, had been employed.   The whole thing snapped again in the middle, because the air-bag could not be filled quickly enough to counteract the decrease of volume caused by the cold.   It fell at once at a great rate, and the shock was luckily somewhat broken by rebounding from the trees in the Jardin d'Acclimatation. He proceeded to build a new machine, which was of a different shape, and intended to be filled with coal gas, as this had the advantage over hydrogen of allowing an ascent to be made almost at any spot. He thought to prevent the long body of his balloon from collapsing by stiffening it with a bamboo rod, which was placed between the car and the body, and acted as a connecting link between the two. The first ascent was made on November 13th, 1899, and was very successful. The start took place at the Champ de Mars, and the balloon made several circuits of the

Eiffel Tower before descending. It was not easy to make a descent at the same spot in the middle of the town on account of the chimneys, and he therefore came down in an open field on the very place where the first accident had occurred. In order

FIG. 36.—Santos Dumont's third balloon.

to have a more convenient spot for starting and landing, Santos Dumont built a shed in the grounds of the Aero Club, which was connected to the gas mains and was provided with an apparatus for generating hydrogen.

After he had made a few further trial runs with No. 3, he proceeded to build No. 4, which was shown in September, 1900, to the International Commission, then sitting in Paris for the investigation of scientific ballooning. The car of the new design had the merit of simplicity. The driver sat on an ordinary riding saddle, and his feet controlled the pedals connected to the motor. A tiller made connection with the rudder. The motor was joined rather less rigidly than before to the body of the balloon, and an important alteration consisted in placing the

propeller at the front instead of the back.   With No. 4, he made
several satisfactory ascents from the grounds of the Aero Club
at Saint-Cloud.   He is stated to have asserted that the Commission were satisfied that this balloon could make headway
against a strong wind, but on the day of inspection the breeze
could only be called moderate, although it may be admitted that
the standards by which the wind is judged are by no means well
defined, and allow for differences of opinion, according to the
point of view.   Still
he made no exact
measurements of
the force of the
wind, and con-
tented himself with
estimates.   Conse-
quently his state-
ments under this
head must be
received with
caution.   On the
other hand, it is
only fair to allow
that the instru-
ments at present
in use for the
measurement of

Fig. 37.—Gradenwitz anemometer.

the wind are not altogether satisfactory.   Perhaps the best of
them is the one made by Gradenwitz.   It depends on the gyrostatic principle involved in the construction of instruments for
determining the velocities of fluids.   If a glass cylinder is filled
with fluid, and rotated about a vertical axis, the upper surface of
the fluid assumes the shape of a paraboloid of revolution, and the
depression depends, as far as its magnitude is concerned, on the
speed of rotation.   If such an instrument is calibrated experimentally it is possible to determine the speed of rotation by noting
the extent of the depression, always assuming that the volume of
the fluid remains unchanged.   Gradenwitz's instrument consists

in the combination of a Robinson anemometer with a closed glass tube containing the fluid. The apparatus is set in motion by the wind, in the usual way, and it is then possible by noting the depression to tell the velocity at any instant. The calibration is carried out by means of the rotating apparatus used by the Meteorological Observatory at Hamburg. An instrument of this sort ought always to be used in trials of dirigible balloons. But even without taking into account any such measurements, the power given by the motor in Dumont's last balloon was much too small. He therefore changed it for one having four cylinders; it weighed much more, and it was therefore necessary to add to the size of the balloon by inserting a piece in the middle. At the same time he set to work on the making of a keel, which was 59 ft. long, and made of pine wood. It was triangular in cross-section, and covered with piano wire. Wire of this kind had been used by an American, named Rotch, for the purpose of holding a kite. A further novelty was introduced in the shape of a moveable guide-rope. The idea was that by moving the guide-rope either forwards or backwards, it would be possible to shift the centre of gravity of the balloon, and therefore to raise or lower the front end. He expected with the use of his propellers (which were placed at the back as in earlier models) to be able to rise or fall without the loss of gas or ballast.

The first ascent with the remodelled machine took place on July 12th, 1901. After passing ten times round the racecourse at Longchamps, a distance of twenty-two miles, the balloon was directed towards the Eiffel Tower. On the way, one of the ropes connected to the rudder was injured, and this was repaired in the gardens of the Trocadero. He then sailed round the Eiffel Tower, and returned to the Aero Club after a journey of one hour six minutes.

A prize had been offered by Monsieur Deutsch to the man who should succeed in sailing round the Eiffel Tower and returning to the starting-point at Saint-Cloud within half an hour, the amount of the prize being £4,000. Santos Dumont therefore notified the authorities that he was prepared to undertake the journey on the following day.   But the motor did not work satisfactorily, and the balloon fell on a chestnut-tree in Roth-schild's garden.   The attempt was repeated on August 8th, and again it met with a sudden end.   A serious accident was indeed only just avoided.   The balloon broke up, and the framework fell on the roof of a house near the Trocadero, and then plunged downwards into the courtyard.   Firemen rescued the aeronaut from his dangerous position by lowering ropes from the roof, but the balloon itself was torn to shreds.   Nothing daunted, his activity knew no bounds, and he set to work the same day on the plans for a new balloon.   After much hard work it was ready in twenty-two days, and the ascent was made.   In this model very special attention was paid to the valves, seeing that the last accident had been due to leaks.   The rigidity of the design was increased.   The air-bag was filled by a small fan, any excess being removed through a valve which opened automatically at a certain pressure.   After some unsuccessful efforts, Santos Dumont succeeded with No. 6 in circling the Eiffel Tower and winning the Deutsch prize.   He returned to the starting-point in 29 minutes 30 seconds, but the landing occupied another minute.   Nevertheless the prize was awarded to him by 13 votes to 9, in spite of the fact that, strictly speaking, the precise condi-tions had not been fulfilled.   He reached a speed of 22 ft. per second, which was very little better than the result obtained by Renard and Krebs in 1885.   The prize was divided into two parts : £3,000 was given by the winner for distribution among the poor of Paris, and the remaining £1,000 was distributed among his assistants.   The Brazilian Government sent him a gold medal, together with the sum of £5,000, which was allocated towards the expense of new balloons.

During the ensuing winter he continued his experiments at Monaco, where a large shed for housing his balloon was built for him by the Prince on the seashore.   After some successful ascents over the Mediterranean in good weather, the balloon tilted over on February 14th, 1902, because the air-bags were not filled quickly enough to make up the loss in volume.   It fell into the sea, and the aeronaut was safely brought to land.   The balloon itself was not recovered till later on, and it was then found to have sustained such damage that it was sent to Paris for repairs.

The later types were divided inside by partitions, which formed a series of chambers; diffusion of the gas was therefore still possible, but any sudden rush of gas to the one end or the other was prevented. Mention should be made of No. 13, which was a kind of *Rozière*. The envelope was egg-shaped, and below there was a pear-shaped appendage, which had a large tubular opening, stretching down to the car. It was expected that by the use of a special form of petroleum burner it would be possible to

Fig. 38.—Roze's double balloon.

rise or fall; but it failed altogether to come up to expectation. According to the laws of diffusion, which have been already explained, the gas from the main body would penetrate into the auxiliary receiver, and in this way an explosive mixture would be formed.

The tests with the last types led to no fresh results; the speed was always too small, and for military purposes they would have been useless. No. 9 was the most popular of the series. Santos Dumont went in this balloon to the racecourse at Longchamps, came down to the ground to watch the races, and then mounted again and went home. On another occasion he came down on the pavement in front of his own house, had breakfast, and then continued his journey. When the French troops were being reviewed by Monsieur Loubet, the President of the Republic, the balloon appeared opposite the grand stand and fired off a salute. He performed many other feats of a similar character, and though they may appear somewhat undignified, he succeeded in creating a widespread interest in the sport.

It will be interesting to notice the results of his experiments with different kinds of motors. He started by using the ordinary motor, carried by tricycles, and mounted two of these, opposite to one another, so that they worked on one crank, and could be fed by one carburretor. He called this a "motor-tandem," and found that an arrangement of this kind worked well, when driven along the streets. He then wished to know the amount of vibration which its working would be likely to cause, and the motor was therefore hung from the branch of a tree in the Bois de Boulogne. It was then seen that there was a slight amount of vibration when the motor turned slowly, but that this entirely disappeared when the speed was increased. With regard to the danger of an explosion, resulting from the mixture of the escaping gas with the air, Dumont stated that he had no fear on that score, seeing that the balloon would always be in motion, and consequently the escaping gas would never reach the motor. He said that he had seen flames 18 inches long dart from his motor, but that no accident had happened. He had more fear of a " cold " explosion, *i.e.*, of an explosion caused by expansion of the body of the balloon from any cause, supposing the valves to work badly. With petroleum motors, it is very necessary to be on one's guard against any accident, resulting in setting the petroleum reservoir on fire. On one occasion a fire of this nature occurred on board No. 9, but he luckily succeeded in putting it out with his Panama hat. His idea that escaping gases from the body of the balloon would not reach the motor, if in motion, is, however, incorrect. For instance, during the ascent it is quite possible that an accident might arise from this cause, and the necessary precautions must on no account be neglected. Another Brazilian, named Severo, met his death owing to an accident which was due to this very cause. His balloon, called the " Pax," was of a peculiar shape, and was sustained by an inner framework. Its capacity was 84,750 cubic feet.

A noteworthy point in its construction was the placing of the
two propellers at the ends of the longer axis.   The front propeller
was 13 ft. in diameter, and was intended to push the air aside,
the back one, 20 ft. in diameter, was intended to drive the
balloon forwards.   In addition to these, there was behind the
car a third propeller, 10 ft. in diameter.   Two Buchet motors, of
16 and 24 horse-power, were arranged symmetrically in the car,
which was built up of bamboo rods together with tubes of steel
and aluminium.

Severo made an ascent on May 12th, 1902, in company with
his friend Saché, having previously made three ascents in a
captive balloon.   The working of the propellers had been tested
while the balloon was held in a captive state by ropes.   Shortly
after the start, it was noticed that ballast was being thrown out,
and that the propellers only worked intermittently.   After a
quarter of an hour, flames were noticed at the back of the car,
and a violent explosion followed.   Immediately after this, a bright
flame was seen in the middle of the lower side of the main body,
and another explosion took place.   The balloon fell from a height
of 1,300 ft., and Severo and his companion were killed on the
spot.   It was subsequently found that the petroleum reservoir
showed signs of having been on fire, and the whole of the car was
more or less burnt.[1]

The fault lay in placing the car too close to the body of the
balloon ; the consequence was that there was always some of the
explosive mixture in the car, seeing that during the ascent the
hydrogen was escaping through a valve which was immediately
above one of the motors.   At the moment of starting, the speed
was too small to allow this escaping gas to be swept away, and
the explosion must have originated at the motor.   The flame
was then carried along the chimney, and came in contact with a
stronger explosive mixture, with the result that a second
explosion took place.   The balloon then crumpled up, and as the
outer envelope was not firmly secured, it did not act as a
parachute, the fall being in consequence very rapid.   Just before

---

[1] A full account of the accident is given by Espitallier, an officer in the French
balloon corps, in the *Illustrierte Aeronautische Mitteilungen* 3, 1902.

starting, Severo removed the pieces of wire gauze, which had been provided for the sake of security, thinking himself that they were unnecessary.   The Brazilian Government, which had already shown its interest in these experiments, has made provision for Severo's family, and paid £1,000 to Saché's friends.

The year 1902 was an unlucky one from the point of view of ballooning, and many fatal accidents took place.   Captain Bartsch von Sigsfeld of the Prussian balloon corps, who was well known from his work in connection with kites, was killed on the occasion of a descent at Antwerp on February 1st; soon

Fig. 39.—Severo's balloon about to start.

afterwards, a French naval officer, who was carrying out some evolutions at Lagoubran, fell with his balloon into the water and was drowned; Severo's death followed, and finally Baron von Bradsky was killed in Paris while making an ascent with a dirigible airship.   Baron von Bradsky-Laboun built an aerostat, which had an envelope just large enough to lift the dead weight of the balloon; any upward or downward movement was to be effected by means of a propeller, working on a vertical axis, while motion in a forward direction was produced by a horizontal screw, steering being, as usual, done by means of a vertical rudder.   No air-bag was used.   The balloon was 112 ft. long, and had a capacity of 30,000 cubic feet.   The gas was prevented from flowing to either end by means of partitions, which divided the interior into three compartments. A frame was built up parallel to the longer axis ; sails were mounted on it, having an area of 365 square feet, and these could be lowered when required. The car was connected with the framework by fifty lengths of piano wire, but very little lateral stiffening was used. Bradsky made an experimental ascent on October 13th, and a young engineer, named Morin, accompanied him ; both had previously made a couple of ascents as passengers in other balloons. Their plan was to sail towards the south-west against the wind, which only amounted to a light breeze. But they failed to do so, and were carried in a north-easterly direction. One of the propellers caused a tilt about the vertical axis, and they ascended to a much greater height than had been expected. Bradsky seemed to be about to give up the attempt, and began to descend. When he was about 300 ft. from the ground, he called out for information as to a suitable landing-place. As soon as he had satisfied himself about this point, it was noticed that Morin moved towards Bradsky, and the centre of gravity was shifted to such an extent that the car toppled over. Both aeronauts were thrown out and killed on the spot. General Neureuther's idea was that the accident was caused by the absence of sufficient rigidity, the result of which was that the piano wires became entangled and broke.

However successful Santos Dumont may have been, it cannot be said that he produced a balloon suitable for military purposes. This work was accomplished by Lébaudy, whose balloon has been introduced into the French army with very successful results. The construction of this airship deserves careful consideration. In 1899 the brothers Lébaudy commissioned an able engineer, named Juillot, to make investigations into the design of dirigible balloons. The actual work of construction was put in hand two years later, and the first ascent was made on November 13th, 1902. It was made of bright yellow calico, procured from Hanover, and was 187 ft. long, with a diameter of 32 ft., and a capacity of 80,000 cubic feet. It was fitted with a Daimler motor, giving 40 horse-power; the total weight, including two-thirds of a ton of benzine, water and ballast was $2\frac{1}{2}$ tons.

Twenty-nine ascents were made before July, 1903 ; on twenty-eight of these occasions, the balloon was able to return to its starting-place. The maximum speed was 36 ft. per second, though this statement has been disputed. The balloon had now been in use for seventy days, and its covering showed signs of wear : repairs were therefore carried out, and a fresh start was made in November. It was placed under the control of the aeronaut Juchmés, who was accompanied by a mechanic, and they brought it from the Champs de Mars to Meudon. As it descended, it was dashed against a tree and the outer covering destroyed. The motor was uninjured, and a new envelope was therefore put in hand at once.

The "Lébaudy 1904" must be described more fully, as it is similar to that at present in use. The unsymmetrical form of the first balloon was retained, but the pointed end at the back was somewhat rounded to an elliptical shape, and the axis was lengthened to 190 ft. Its capacity was 94,000 cubic feet, its surface 14,000 square feet, and the weight of the covering rather more than half a ton. The calico which had been brought from Hanover had turned out very satisfactorily, and it was therefore used on the new model. It was made airtight by coating with rubber both on the inside and outside. In France hydrogen is used which is prepared from sulphuric acid and iron ; in Germany chemically pure gas is ordinarily used, and prepared by the electrolytic decomposition of water. The former plan has the disadvantage of allowing minute quantities of sulphuric acid to be carried into the balloon, and therefore an inner coating of rubber is required in order to protect the calico from its effects. The air-bag was increased to a size of 17,650 cubic feet, and divided into three parts ; the fan was also arranged in a more convenient position, and placed closer to the main body. The air-chambers were so arranged in the first model as to be filled through a long neck which reached down to the car. This was found inconvenient, because at full speed the wind pressure was so great as to make it difficult to pass air into the neck. There was also the great danger which might arise if flames should break out in the neighbourhood of the motor, and be carried up by means of the neck. The fan was therefore driven by the motor; if the machine was at rest, an electric motor and a battery of accumulators were carried to supply the necessary power. Besides the main valve, there were also two safety valves, which allowed the gas to escape under a pressure of 1·4 in. of mercury. Two small

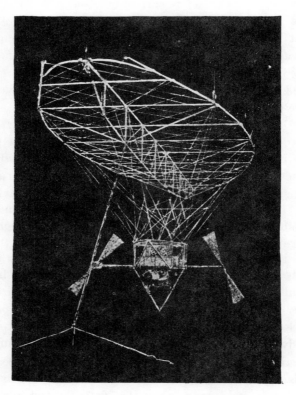

FIG. 40.—Framework and car of Lébaudy's dirigible balloon.

windows were provided for inspecting the inside of the balloon. Every possible precaution was taken to ensure the stability of the machine. A horizontal oval-shaped sail of blue silk, having an area of 1,055 square feet, was stretched below the stand; and beneath it there was a vertical sail, of much smaller dimensions, of the nature of a keel. At the back, which was elliptically shaped, surfaces having an area of about 240 square feet, and shaped like the tail of a pigeon, were arranged round the main body, and were crossed at the middle by a small vertical sail. Instead of having only one rudder, the new model had two, which were smaller and placed further back. They were movable about a horizontal axis, and of the shape of a V, with the pointed end towards the front. When at rest, it was in a state of stable equilibrium ; if one of the sails gave way before the wind, the other merely offered an increased resistance. The driver could also alter their positions according to requirements. A slanting horizontal sail could be stretched across the front, and helped to balance the whole. A movable vertical sail, having an area of 130 square feet, was provided for guiding the horizontal movements ; it could be turned about a vertical axis, slightly inclined towards the back. The car was boat-shaped with a flat bottom ; it was 16 ft. long, 5 ft. broad, and 3 ft. deep. The framework was of steel, and it was

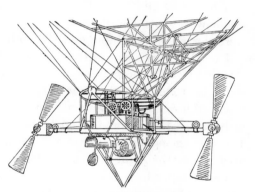

FIG. 41.—Car of Lébaudy's balloon.

covered with thin sheets of aluminium. In order to increase the rigidity and at the same time to diminish the shock caused by reaching the ground, an arrangement of steel tubes, shaped like a pyramid, was placed below the car, with the apex downwards. A guide-rope and an anchor were also carried. The car, which was only 10 ft. below the body, was more or less rigidly supported by steel ropes about 0·2 in. in diameter. The 40 h.p. motor made 1,200 revolutions per minute, and consumed 31 lbs. of benzine per hour, the reservoir holding 48 gallons. At the front of the car an acetylene lamp was mounted ; by daylight this was replaced by a photographic camera, which was worked electrically. The total height of the balloon from the apex of the pyramid to the upper surface of the main body was 44 ft.

The first experimental run was made on August 4th. However on the 28th of the month an accident happened. As the descent was being made, the balloon dashed into a tree, and was carried away by the wind, leaving its passengers behind. Four hours afterwards, it came to the earth, and it was found that little damage had been done. The "Yellow," as the first balloon was called, made 12 ascents in 25 days. In all it made 63 ascents. It had carried 26 different persons, among whom were the wives of the brothers Lébaudy, and altogether it took from first to last 195 passengers. The longest journey was made at Moisson on June 24th, 1903, when 60 miles were covered in 2 hours 46 minutes. The repairs necessitated by the above accident were completed on October 11th, 1904, and further tests were carried out, beginning on the 29th.

The "Lébaudy" had in the meantime been much improved. It was fitted with a horizontal sail, 12 ft. long and 5 ft. broad, which could be rolled up; this was carried in front of the car, and intended to produce movements up or down without loss of gas or ballast. Later it was found to be a very convenient device. The arrangements for lighting were also improved, and were used during the night of October 23rd. Each passenger carried a small lamp, which was fastened to his clothes, and two lamps, each of 100 candle-power, lighted the car and the lower side of the balloon. The candle-power of the acetylene projector was increased to 1,000,000. Eighteen journeys were made before December 24th, and the balloon was found to be completely under control. It was perfectly stable, and could always easily and safely be brought to the ground. The type of 1904 was, however, further improved. Among other things the cross-section of the main body was increased by 5 per cent. Calculations showed that this was likely to increase the air resistance by about 11 per cent. But at any rate it has had no effect on the speed, because the motor was increased to 50 horse-power, as an indirect result of raising the capacity to 105,000 cubic feet. The weight of benzine and ballast was at the same time increased by 75 per cent.

The French Minister of War paid much attention to the

progress of the work, and thought it desirable to find out how far such a balloon could be adapted to military purposes.   He therefore appointed a commission for this purpose, which consisted of Colonel Bouttiaux, who commanded the Balloon Corps, together with Major Viard and Captain Voyer.   A definite programme was proposed.   Lébaudy was to sail to the camp at Chalons, and there carry out certain experiments ; after that, it was to be

FIG. 42.—Lébaudy's dirigible balloon.

taken to Toul and Verdun.   The balloon was to remain in active service for three months, and always to be anchored in the open. Certain erections were made for the purpose of anchoring it, but they were not very successful in actual working.

On July 3rd at 3.45 a.m., the balloon started from Moisson in the direction of Meaux, having Voyer, Juchmés, and Rey on board.   Fifty-six miles were covered in 2 hours 35 minutes, and the balloon came to the ground at the precise spot where Lébaudy and his engineer were waiting.   The maximum height had been 1570 ft., and 2 cwt. of ballast had been thrown overboard.

A.   G

Another ascent was made on July 4th, when Major Bouttiaux
started from Meaux at 4.38 a.m., and sailed against a strong east
wind at the rate of 10 or 12 miles an hour.   He landed at
5.25 a.m., according to instructions, at a place called Sept-Sorts.
The balloon was somewhat damaged on the following night in
a thunderstorm; but he was able to make a further start on
July 6th.   At 7.59 a.m. he started from Meaux and passed over
Chateau Thierry to Chalons, where he landed at 11.20 a.m., after
a journey of 3 hours 21 minutes.   The distance, as the crow
flies, was 58 miles, but the balloon actually covered 61 miles. It
was then anchored to some trees, where it was exposed to a strong
wind.   It was soon torn away from its moorings, carried over
some telegraph wires to a height of 1,000 ft., and subsequently
dashed against trees with considerable violence.   The envelope
was completely destroyed, but three soldiers, who had been left
in the car to attend to it, escaped without serious injury.   The
Minister of War provided immediate facilities for the work of
repair.   It was astonishing to find how easily the repairs were
executed without having recourse to the factory at Moisson, and
without the provision of any special appliances.   This was due
in large measure to the energy displayed by Julliot, who showed
great ability in controlling the execution of the work.   A riding-
school belonging to the 39th Artillery Regiment was used as a
workshop.   Another riding-school was also placed at their disposal, and the ground was excavated so that the balloon, together
with the car, could be placed on the floor.   In addition to this,
a small installation was prepared to generate the hydrogen,
together with scrubbers, driers, etc.   The work occupied 150
men for 11 weeks, and on September 21st gas was again passed
into the balloon.   On October 8th, the Minister of War happened
to be in Toul on a visit of inspection, and though the weather
was windy and rainy, Julliot determined to make a start.   A
series of evolutions took place over the military hospital, and the
return journey was then made.   A further expedition was made
on October 12th, starting at 7.36 a.m., with 930 lbs. of ballast.
They passed over the fort of Gondreville, and all the fortifications in the neighbourhood of Nancy, returning to Toul, where

they landed at 9.50 a.m. In 2 hours 14 minutes they had covered 32 miles, the maximum height being 2,230 ft. On October 18th, the seventy-second ascent was made with five passengers on board. The instructions were to the effect that photographs were to be taken of the various fortifications, and a sack of ballast was to be thrown down at a given spot. Everything passed off according to the plan, and in spite of throwing out the ballast, the maximum height was only 1,800 ft. A fan was carried, which could pass 35 cubic feet of air into the air-bags in a second. The loss caused by throwing out 44 lbs. of ballast was quickly made good by pumping 635 cubic feet of air, and the further rise of the balloon was prevented.

A series of ascents were then made by some of the commanding officers, and took place without any accident, though the weather was not precisely calm. On the 24th of October the seventy-sixth journey took place, when the Minister of War, together with his adjutant, Major Bouttiaux, Captain Voyer, and others, made the ascent. On November 10th, the balloon was allowed to retire into winter quarters after having had a truly brilliant career. Reports state that other balloons of a similar design have been put in hand at Moisson and Toul, and that they are to be kept at the forts along the frontier. The cost of a balloon of this type is from £10,000 to £12,000, and cannot be considered unreasonable in view of the services which it could render in case of war. The cost of the experiments is not exactly known, but it is believed to have been between £100,000 and £150,000.

The successes of Santos Dumont and Lébaudy have spurred others on with the desire to rival their feats. Count Americo da Schio has a peculiar method of working without an air-bag, and alleges that he can rise without losing gas and descend without alteration of the shape of the envelope. His balloon has a cigar-shaped body, 130 ft. long, 20 ft. in diameter, with a capacity of 42,500 cubic feet. A broad band of rubber is placed inside, and as the gas pressure increases, it stretches from $4\frac{3}{4}$ ft. to 11 ft. A safety valve comes into operation before such pressure is reached as would be sufficient to burst the rubber band. Some trial trips were made at the end of 1905, and the arrangements

worked well, according to report. This sounds surprising in view
of the facts stated by Monsieur de Quervain, one of the Directors
of the Meteorological Institute at Zurich. He points out that a
rubber band offers the greatest resistance at the moment when
the extension begins, and that this resistance decreases during
the process of extension, gradually increasing shortly before it
breaks. From this it would seem that the automatic valve would
operate at the beginning of the extension; in fact, the rubber
would never be extended at all. This will be noticed on blowing
air into an india-rubber ball, when it will be seen that the
greatest lung power is required at the moment of starting. A
further peculiarity of this balloon consisted in coating it with fine
aluminium powder, which was intended to prevent it from being
heated by the sun to the same extent.

Much interest has lately been aroused in Germany by the
work done by Major von Parseval. He has invented a kind of
kite-balloon, and has built a motor-airship in the factory of
August Riedinger in Augsburg. The work is not yet complete,
but it has been possible to produce a speed of twenty-five miles an
hour even under somewhat disadvantageous conditions. One
advantage of this airship lies in the fact that there is an
absence of rigid connections, except in the car, sails, and
rudder. Consequently it can be packed up easily and put
on a railway truck. This adds much to its suitability
for military purposes. Lébaudy's airship is indeed capable of
being packed up, but it requires to be taken to pieces in consequence of stiffening of various kinds, and this work takes more
than a day. The shape of Major Parseval's design is also novel.
It consists of a cylinder with a spherical end at the front and an
egg-shaped end at the back. The length is 157 ft., and the
capacity 88,300 cubic feet. Two air-bags are placed inside the
envelope, one at the front and one at the back. These bags are
constantly filled by a fan, driven by a special motor, any excess
of air escaping through the safety valves. By a special arrangement of valves, the driver is able to adjust the amount of air
which passes to the air-bags. According as he wishes to raise
or lower the front end of the balloon, he adjusts the passage of

FIG. 43.—Major Parseval's dirigible balloon.

the air to the back or front air-bag, thereby causing a displacement of the centre of gravity. The surfaces, which are used for
steering and for adding stability to the balloon, are blown up
under pressure, and the shape which they thus assume is

considered to be more suitable for the purpose in view. A motor by Daimler is used, giving 90 h.p., at 1,000 revolutions per minute. It is placed at the back of the car, which is 16 ft. long. The car is hung by steel ropes about 26 ft. below the envelope, and is constructed for the most part of sheets of aluminium. Its weight, together with that of the motor, propeller, etc., is $1\frac{1}{4}$ tons. The propeller with its four blades is prepared from stiff canvas ; it assumes its proper shape when put in motion. The fan is placed above the motor, and a length of tubing connects

FIG. 44.—Count de
la Vaulx.

with the envelope. Tests have shown that the balloon keeps its shape well, that it is completely free from vibration when under weigh, and that it is well under control both with regard to movements in a horizontal and vertical direction. By altering the inclination of the axis of the balloon it is possible to rise or fall without loss of gas or ballast. The reaction produced on the upper cr lower surface of the balloon, when moving at full speed, is sufficient to give rise to forces of several hundred pounds. It is very important that a balloon, intended for use in the field of war, should be capable of being easily packed. Count de la Vaulx has therefore built a motor balloon which is capable of being taken apart with great ease, and packed in four parts. The first package contains the envelope, and occupies about 35 cubic feet of space ; the second contains the car, requiring floor space to the extent of 2 yards by 1 yard ; and the third and fourth contain the portions of the keel. Count de la Vaulx also uses yellow cambric of German make, because it is as yet impossible to obtain it of sufficiently good quality in France. The two thicknesses of cambric are usually separated by a layer of rubber, but there is a further coating on the outside. This is done with the object of preventing the absorption of any moisture. It is known that the covering of a balloon, having a capacity of 46,000 cubic feet, can absorb about

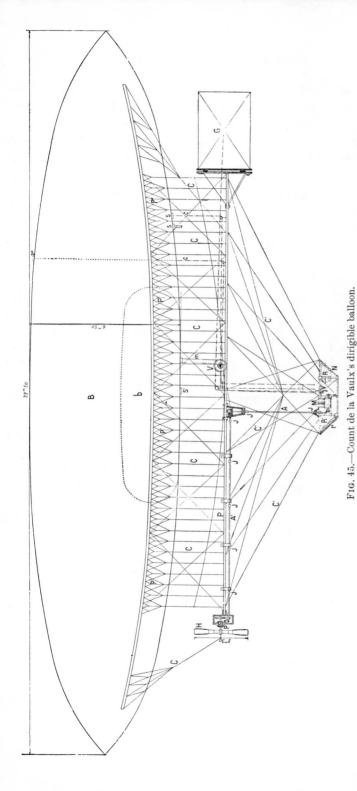

Fig. 45.—Count de la Vaulx's dirigible balloon.

B, balloon, capacity 25,000 cubic feet. b, air-bag, capacity 4,250 cubic feet. P, P′, P′, network. V, fan. A, A , shafting, connecting motor to propeller. M, motor. H, propeller. R′, water tank. S, S, S′, S′, valves, R, benzine reservoir.

2 cwt. of moisture, and it is evident that a dead weight of this order may have considerable effect on the length of journey which it is possible to undertake. A balloon of a capacity of 25,000 cubic feet has great advantages from the point of view of transport, and also takes a small amount of gas. Both of these matters are of importance from the military point of view. On the other hand, it has the disadvantage of being able to carry only one passenger. It is obvious that a man requires all his wits to manage a dirigible balloon, and would be unable to find any time in which to make observations in the capacity of a scout. Count de la Vaulx therefore proposes to increase the size of his airship, and the trial runs have turned out to his satisfaction.

Many other dirigible balloons have lately appeared, which have all met with their share of success and failure. A short table is added, giving particulars of the airships most frequently mentioned in the daily papers, together with some particulars as to their construction and performances. It must be admitted that the construction of a dirigible balloon is a difficult matter, but a combination of patience, skill, and money will generally lead a man to the goal. The problem is therefore not so much how to build the balloon as how to raise the money. Any government or any private person in possession of the necessary means can easily construct such things if they have recourse to men of technical experience.

PARTICULARS RELATING TO OTHER DIRIGIBLE BALLOONS.

Name of Inventor.	Shape.	Capacity in cubic feet.	Length in feet.	Maximum diameter in feet.	Motor.	Remarks.
Barton	Cylindrical with conical ends.	155,000	180	41	Three Buchet motors, each of 50 h.p.	Had thirty aeroplane surfaces, air-bag of 42,500 cubic feet. Unsuccessful.
Beedle	Shape of torpedo.	25,000	92	23	15 h.p. Blake.	Unsuccessful.
Danilewsky	Cylindrical with conical front: spherical at back.			Different Sizes.	No motor.	Fitted with wings. Tests safely carried out, but unsuccessful.
Deutsch de la Meurthe (Maurice Mallet). "La ville de Paris."	Ellipsoidal.	70,500	190	27	63 h.p. with four cylinders.	Two envelopes (Meusnier), air bag of 7,000 cubic feet. Shifting weights. One ascent in August, 1903, tests continued at end of 1906.
Albert de Dion	Cigar-shaped.				Two Dion Bouton motors.	A number of propellers, car at considerable distance from body. Results unknown.
"Français I."	Torpedo-shaped.	17,500	82	20	—	Sliding weights, intended for naval work.
François and Contour, built by Godard.	Ellipsoidal.	65,000	105	35	24 h.p. by Prosper Lambert.	Some inconclusive ascents were made.
Giuliani, "Aeronave".	Cigar-shaped.	33,500	85	20	16 h.p. electric motor.	Not constructed.
Goudron Beckmann	Fish-shaped.	13,000	66	17	One 5 h.p. motor and two 2·5 ditto.	No air-bag. Unsuccessful.
José de Patrocinio, "Santa Cruz," built by Louis Godard.	Cylindrical with pointed ends.	137,500	148	30	40 h.p.	Wings at the sides, nine compartments. Results unknown.
Pacini, "Aerovado".	Ellipsoidal.	28,000	82		—	Envelope in three parts. Result unknown.
Renard, "Aerovado".	Long and narrow.	106,000			Electric motors.	Built for military purposes. Results unknown.
Robert-Pillet, built by Surcouf.	Long and narrow.	70,500	36	9	35 h.p.	Tests to be carried out at Vincennes by the military.
Roze	Two cigar-shaped envelopes.	100,000	148	25	20 h.p. Buchet motor.	Framework of aluminium. Six compartments. Car between the bodies.
Steel balloon in Vienna	Cigar-shaped.	240,000	66	33	90 h.p. Körting.	Three compartments. Not tested. Ascent not allowed in Vienna.
Stanley Spencer	Cylinder with conical ends.	30,000	92	24	24 h.p.	Aluminium framework. Unsuccessful experiments at the Crystal Palace.
Stevens	Cylinder with conical ends.	28,000	85	18	Three motors successively used, of 7·5, 35, and 70 h.p. by the Regent Automobile Co.	Meusnier's system of air-bag, filled by fan. Rising and falling produced by inclined surfaces. Fairly successful.

CHAPTER IX.

FLYING machines include all such devices as enable a man to fly without the use of gas-bags, and to move in any direction with the help of such contrivances as are carried on board. Two forces are therefore needed ; the one to overcome the force of gravity, and the other to deal with the resistance of the wind. The oldest of these aerodynamic airships were worked by means of contrivances of the nature of wings. The flight of birds was the obvious example to be imitated. It would be merely necessary to provide suitable means for flapping some kind of artificial wing, and the thing would be done. Some devices of this

FIG. 46.—Degen's flying machine.

nature have already been described. In 1784 Gérard constructed a flying bird ; the wings were moved by mechanical devices, hidden in a box, but the details of his arrangement are not known. A man, named Meerwein, wrote a book in which he carefully investigated the subject of the flight of birds, and at the same time described a flying machine he had constructed. He is said to have made some unsuccessful experiments near Giessen, but he threw out the useful suggestion that experiments of this kind were best conducted over an expanse of water.

Blanchard made several ascents in Vienna, and this encouraged a watchmaker of Basle, named Degen, to construct a flying machine. With the help of some counterweights, he was able to fly short distances in a large hall. He made some unsuccessful experiments in Paris, and was so roughly handled by the mob that he afterwards preferred to do his work from the shelter of a balloon. All sorts of proposals of the most complicated kind were made in the course of time, but no success resulted. A man, named Buttenstedt, who was an ardent champion of winged machines, had curious ideas which he proposed to put into practice. He studied the position of the wings during the flight of storks, and developed a wonderful theory relating to " elastic tension." He pointed out that when the bird is at rest, the tips of the wings are pointed downwards and backwards ; when it is flying, they are pointed upwards and forwards. They reach the

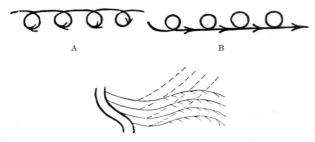

FIG. 47.—Diagrams illustrating Marey's theory with reference to the flight of a bird.

forced position, natural to flight, as a result of the reaction due to the upward pressure of the atmosphere on their bodies. This state of " tension " puts the bird in a position to exercise a certain pressure, which drives it forwards. The onward movement ceases when the pressure, exerted by reason of this tension, is no longer sufficient to overcome the resistance of the air. According to this view, the essential feature in the flight of a bird lies in the state of tension, succeeded by a corresponding state of relaxation. A bird can only fly forward, because the positions of its wings and of its centre of gravity do not admit of a backward movement. A Frenchman, named Marey, also made a special study of the subject, and found that a bird does not drive the air backwards as it flaps its wings in a downward direction, but flies in such a manner as to bring the tips of the wings towards the front. The tips of

the wings do not move as shown at A, but as shown at B.   As
the bird flies forward, it does not drive the air from under its
body, but throws it, from the side and from behind, beneath the
body ; at the same time the force of the downward blow alters
the shape of the feathers from a downward concavity into an
upward convexity.   These forces tend to drive the bird forward

FIG. 48.—Stentzel's flying machine.

in exactly the same way as a fish is propelled by the movement
of its tail.

    There was at any rate a better prospect of success as soon as it
was proposed to use some form of engine as the motive power.
Two attempts on these lines deserve mention.   An engineer,
named Stentzel, of Hamburg, constructed a gigantic bird ; the
distance between the tips of the wings was 20 ft. ; the wings
themselves were 5 ft. 6 in. broad, and formed a concavity of 1 in
12.   They were covered with silk, the main ribs being of steel

and joined by small connecting rods to a carbonic acid motor. It was intended to steer by means of a rudder, shaped like a cross. The surface exposed to the air was 87 square feet, and with an output of 1·5 horse-power, a weight of 75 lbs. was lifted from the ground. It was possible to make 84 flaps of the wings in a minute, and they were so powerful that a man was almost swept off his feet by them. Unfortunately this type was not found suitable for an extended trial. Flying machines with wings seem unlikely to promise great results, partly because questions of stability arise with which it is difficult to deal, and partly because a slavish imitation of bird-mechanism is hardly likely to be more successful than a human automaton.

The idea of using propellers was an improvement. This appears in its most primitive form in the scheme of Launay and Bienvenu, who used the tension produced by a stretched bow to produce rotation of the screw. Ninety years later, Pénaud improved on this design by proposing the use of rubber bands for a similar purpose. But here again it soon becomes evident that without some continuous motive power, little can be accomplished. For many years, nothing was done, but lately the problem has been further discussed in view of the great improvements which have been made in the art of building motors. The first idea was to revive the ancient models. A small machine was made by an engineer, named Kress, with rubber bands, on the lines proposed by Pénaud. On the occasion of a lecture, he succeeded in making it fly up to the ceiling. There is also a well-known toy which consists of a small screw, set in rapid rotation by pulling a string; the result being that the thing flies up in the air. A toy of this kind was common in France fifty years ago under the name of *Strophéor* or *Spiralifère*. It is still to be seen nowadays in the form of butterflies, etc.

A man, named Léger, has lately made some experiments with the help of the Prince of Monaco. He used two screws of 20 ft. diameter, which were driven by a motor, giving 6 horse-power, and produced a tractive force of 240 lbs. The same propellers can be used to produce vertical and horizontal movements. If the propeller works on a vertical axis, the apparatus will rise ; whereas if the axis is inclined to the horizontal at an angle of 45 degrees, a forward motion can be obtained. Dufaux worked at Geneva with a model which had propellers, weighing 37 lbs. It was fitted with a 3 horse-power motor, and produced a pull of 14 lbs. On October 28th, 1905, it is said to have flown over a distance of 500 ft.[1]

We seldom find a man imbued with the ideas of the balloon, adapting himself to the principles of the flying machine with any success. Yet it was done by the most popular balloonist of our time, Santos Dumont. On January 2nd, 1905, he announced

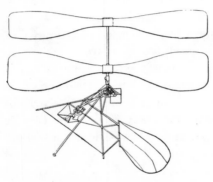

himself to the Aero Club as a competitor for the Deutsch and Archdeacon prize, after he had quietly built himself a flying machine. As shown in the appended diagram, the two upper propellers C C have a diameter of 20 ft., and produce motion in a vertical direction ; the propeller D. has a diameter of $6\frac{1}{2}$ ft., and drives the machine forwards.

FIG. 49.—Dufaux' flying machine with propellers.

Each of the propellers C has a total surface of 43 square feet, and together with the transmission gear it weighs 30 lbs. The one revolves in the opposite direction to the other, so as to prevent a rotation of the entire apparatus about a vertical axis. The car is constructed of bamboo, and contains a Levavasseur motor with eight cylinders, giving 28 horse-power. The weight of this motor together with the necessary supply of water is 1 cwt. At the back of the driver's stand is placed a vertical rudder. The preliminary trials are said to have been successful and each of the lifting propellers was found to be able to raise a weight of 200 lbs. ; the total lift was therefore 400 lbs., and this could raise the machine and

[1] See also " Proceedings of the International Conference on Aerial Navigation at Chicago," 1903, p. 284 ; and Lecornu, " La Navigation Aérienne," p. 397.

driver, besides about 30 lbs. of cargo. He used no sails, and this would add greatly to the danger of an accident caused by stoppage of the motor. In such a case he would scarcely get off so easily as he has done in the past. No doubt this fact weighed on his mind, for he proceeded forthwith to build himself a kite, intending to drive it by propellers placed at the sides of the sails. The rudder is in the shape of a cross, and capable of being turned about both horizontal and vertical axes. The sails are of silk, stretched over bamboo, and are 50 ft. long and 26 ft. broad, with an area of 237 square feet; the weight of the whole machine together with the driver is only 310 lbs. He has already made two ascents in this airship. On the first attempt, it rose in the air, but after a short distance it came to the ground with rather severe injuries. Santos Dumont immediately built another, and in this he is stated to have travelled a distance of 200 ft.

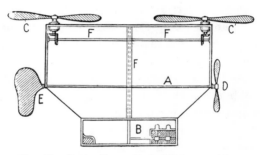

Fig. 50.—Santos Dumont's first flying machine.

at a height of 12 ft. from the ground. This aeroplane is of a totally different nature from the original design of flying machine adopted by Santos Dumont; and it cannot be doubted that it is the thing of the future. It would be exceedingly dangerous to propose to do without sails of any kind; a motor is capricious enough, even when standing on solid earth; in mid air, it is likely to be more so. The weight of kites or aeroplanes is small, and they have the further advantage of presenting a small surface to the wind, in consequence of their horizontal motion.

A kite may be defined as a flying machine, carrying sails, which support the weight of the apparatus. The sails may be large or small, flat or concave, and are for the most part slightly inclined to the horizontal. The forward motion may be produced indirectly by gravity, as, for instance, in the case in which it is allowed to fall slowly from a height with its sails slightly inclined to the horizontal.   Or on the other hand it may be moved forward by the action of propellers.   Motion in a vertical direction may be induced by a propeller arrangement of the sails or by moving a horizontal rudder.   Steering in the ordinary sense depends on the position of vertical sails, and the possible arrangement of sails is almost infinite, as will be seen from the following examples.

The first aeroplane, driven by motive power, was the work of an Englishman, named Henson, in 1843.   A light framework of wood was constructed, 100 ft. broad, and 30 ft. long.   It was covered with silk, and slightly bent upwards at the front.   A rudder, shaped like the tail of a bird, and 50 ft. long was used to steer in a vertical direction.   The car was placed below the main sail, and contained the steam engine and passengers.   Two screw propellers were placed on either side of the driver ; the speed of these could be regulated, and by suitable adjustment it was possible to turn to the right or left.   The steam engine gave 20 horse-power.   The machine was built on correct principles and caused great excitement ; but Henson only succeeded in making it work over a downward path.   The air is always compressed beneath the sails of an aeroplane, and this exerts a lifting or supporting force.   Generally speaking, it is impossible to maintain a position of equilibrium, because motion is necessary for the continued compression of the air.   Henson's propellers were probably insufficient to generate the requisite lifting power ; but it was generally admitted that patience would bring success. Consequently a multitude of proposals were made, for the most part of no great importance.   Perhaps mention ought to be made of a lieutenant, named de Temple, who prepared very careful plans for the construction of a kite, to be driven, as before, by propellers and steam engine.

Phillips made a curious form of flying machine in 1862.   It somewhat resembled a Venetian blind, supported on a wooden frame.   The height was 9 ft. 3 in., and the breadth 21 ft. 8 in. The whole thing was mounted on a carriage, shaped like a boat, and running on wheels, 24 ft. 6 in. long.   It was driven round a

circular track, 600 ft. long, by a small steam engine connected
to propellers, making 400 revolutions per minute. The weight
of the whole was rather less than 3 cwt. It was anchored by a
rope to the middle of the track. The tests showed that a dead
weight of 72 lbs., placed on the front wheels, could be lifted
30 ins. into the air, and this proved that the principles of construction were correct. It seems curious that after such
preliminary success nothing further should have been done.
But the difficulty is to determine the right position for the
centre of gravity, and to ensure a reasonable amount of stability

Fig. 51.—Phillips' flying machine.

when in motion. These points can only be settled after the
expenditure of much time and money.

Some of the most interesting experiments were carried out by
Sir Hiram Maxim in 1888, with the assistance of the late Professor Langley. The aeroplane cost over £20,000, and was
designed on a large scale. It consisted of a big sail with a
number of smaller sails to the right and left of it, having
altogether an area of 3,875 square feet. They were connected to a
platform, 40 ft. by 8 ft., by means of a framework, built up out
of thin steel tubes. The platform contained a seat for the
driver, together with the boiler, engine, etc., and the boiler was
fired by a gas-burner, which was fed with naphtha. The burner

A.   H itself consisted of a cylinder with a number of horizontal tubes and about 7,650 jets. The diameter of the propellers was

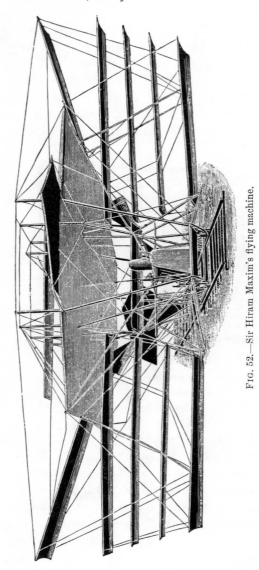

FIG. 52.—Sir Hiram Maxim's flying machine.

17 ft. 6 in. The vertical movements of the machine were controlled by two horizontal sails, one at the front and one at the back. Horizontal movements were regulated by two sails, inclined to one another at an angle of 7·5 degrees, and arranged on either side so as to be capable of being hoisted or lowered, the result being to shift the position of the centre of gravity and consequently to alter the direction of motion. The machine weighed $3\frac{1}{2}$ tons, and for the purposes of the trial runs it was mounted on four wheels and put on a railway track. An overhead rail was placed a few inches above the top of the machine with a view to controlling the upward motion. With a steam pressure of 22 atmospheres, the machine rose off the lower rails and came in contact with

the upper one. During a later test, the overhead rail was broken by the force of the impact. The machine flew away across the field, and was partially destroyed. A dynamometer showed that a dead weight of 4½ tons would have been lifted, and as a result of these tests it is safe to affirm that it is possible to design aeroplanes of great weight.

During the Exhibition in Paris in 1900, a peculiar form of flying machine was to be seen, which looked like an enormous bat. A Frenchman, named Ader, had built it, with the assistance of the Minister of War. The sails were of the nature of wings, and could be folded up at the back. In addition there were two propellers, each with four blades, driven by power. The whole apparatus weighed nearly half a ton, but it managed

FIG. 53.—Ader's flying machine.

to lift itself off the ground. It soon toppled over, and was much injured in consequence. An engineer, named William Kress, living at Vienna, also distinguished himself by making a flying machine. He had been interested for many years in the sporting features of the problem, and finally began to study the matter in its scientific aspects. The model which he made with rubber bands has already been noticed. His designs received their final shape in June, 1901, when he started his trial runs on a reservoir near Vienna. The machine was mounted on two narrow boats, made of aluminium. The boats served a double purpose. They were useful in case of unexpected descents into the water, and on the other hand they could be used to slide it over snow or ice, as he had an idea that a flying machine of this kind might be useful on polar expeditions. A frame of steel tubes was mounted over the boats, and on this the sails were fastened. The design took the form of a keel with the sharp end pointing forwards, and with its lower surface acting as a sail. Above this were mounted three other sails, one behind the other, inclined at different angles, the total area of the sails being 1,000 square feet. They were slightly concave, to the extent of 1 in 12, with the view of offering more resistance to the wind. The original intention was to use a motor weighing 13 cwt., but the boat was built before the motor was ordered. Some preliminary experiments were made with a 4 horse-power motor, treating the machine as a sailing boat. He was able to sail about in any direction on the reservoir, and even to make headway against a slight wind. A Daimler motor of 35 horse-power was then ordered, and it was stipulated that it should only weigh 530 lbs., but when delivered it was found to scale 840 lbs.

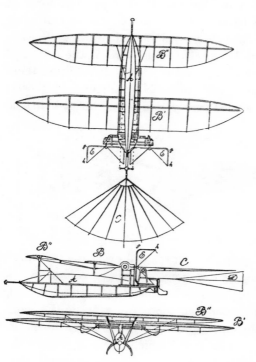

FIG. 54.—Kress's flying machine.

However, this motor was used in spite of the fact that it was nearly 4 cwt. heavier than the weight allowed for in the design. The money had been spent, and it was not possible to make great alterations at this stage. Kress brought the boat on rails down to the water's edge, and then very carefully performed certain evolutions. Gradually his courage increased, he ran the motor a little faster, and found that at 18 horse-power there was a tendency for the boat to be lifted out of the water. He

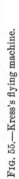

Fig. 55.—Kress's flying machine.

reached the end of the lake in 20 minutes, and then proceeded to turn back. At this moment the boat swayed first to the left and then to the right, and as a result of these vibrations it got into such a position that it was unable to right itself. A gust of wind added to the difficulty, and there was nothing to be done but to jump into the water. A man had been deputed to be ready with a boat in case of accident. But he was so overcome by the dangers that stared him in the face as to be obliged to get further assistance before making a start. Kress was finally rescued as he was on the point of being drowned. The remains of the kite were found after some days; the motor was uninjured, but everything else was a confused mass of wires and tubes.

Experiments on the water, conducted after this fashion, give a totally wrong impression of the probable behaviour of a kite in the air. On water, the point of support is below the centre of gravity; in the air, it is just the other way round. Therefore those contrivances which are likely to increase the stability in the air will only tend to upset it on the water. Attempts have been made to raise money in Austria in order to help Kress to make further progress with his work; but up to the present little appears to have resulted from these efforts.

Professor Langley has also carried out his experiments in America over the surface of water. He was director of the Smithsonian Institute at Washington, and died in March, 1906. He tested his first model over the Potomac River in 1896. His " aerodromes " Nos. 5 and 6 gave satisfactory results. He had a special arrangement for starting, which consisted in sliding it off a swinging table into the air. A barge was used as the starting-point. Mr. Frank Carpenter stated that the best result was obtained on December 12th, 1896, when a distance of a mile was covered in 1 minute 45 seconds. Langley conducted his work in the greatest secrecy, and Mr. Carpenter was indeed present at this test quite by accident. Dr. Bell reported in *Nature* (May 28th, 1896) that to his knowledge two successful trials had taken place. A drawing in the *Aeronautical Annual* for 1897 shows that Langley's "Aerodrome No. 5" had the following measurements, viz., length without rudder 8 ft. 6 in., total span 15 ft. The bearing surfaces consisted of four sails, the length of each sail being 30 in. Two propellers were driven by steam in opposite directions, the steam pressure being 150 lbs. per square inch, and the diameter of the propellers 3 ft. The weight of the entire machine was about 28 lbs. The only information to be had about " Aerodrome No. 6 " was to the effect that it came to grief on its trial run, and the same thing happened to its successor. The last kite had two immovable sails on each side, which were rigidly connected by a steel framework to

FIG. 56.—Starting arrangements for Professor Langley's flying machine.

the boat, the breadth of the machine being about 46 ft., and the depth 33 ft. It was driven by two propellers arranged at the sides.

Professor Manley, who helped Langley, is said to have made a trip along the Potomac River in the following fashion. The workshop had a horizontal platform 30 ft. above the level of the water. The aerodrome was mounted on a car, which was pushed rapidly forward by means of strong springs. The movement of the car was stopped as soon as it reached the edge of the platform ; the aerodrome then slid off, and after dipping down for a short distance, it turned upwards and continued its flight. This at any rate was the intention; but according to the reports of the Smithsonian Institute, there was a slight hitch in the proceedings, which resulted in the sudden immersion of the airship. It was prevented from sinking by certain hollow cylinders, which had been thoughtfully fixed to it at different places, and Manley was eventually rescued from the water.

The arrangements for starting are of great importance. It has been already pointed out that a certain amount of kinetic energy

must be created in order that the air may be sufficiently compressed beneath the sails. The machine can then hover in the air. The motors have then their work to

FIG. 57.—Professor Langley's flying machine at the moment of starting.

do in the shape of driving it forward. As a start, it would be satisfactory to make the machine work with special arrangements for launching it; but it ought to be understood that this is only a temporary expedient. Otherwise the area over which it would be possible to fly such a machine would be very limited. This point has been borne in mind by another inventor, Herr Hofman of Berlin, who uses the kinetic energy generated by the fall to start his machine. It is built on legs or stilts. When ready to start, the legs are laid against the body, and the wings folded together in the middle. Just before the flight begins, the wings are unfolded and the legs placed more upright. The centre of gravity is therefore raised, and the machine is started in this position, so that the propellers can be set to work. A considerable speed is soon reached,

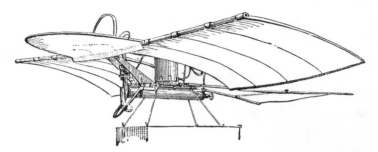

Fig. 58.—Hofmann's first model with carbonic acid motor.

because the sails are carried in a horizontal position. The legs are then jerked up against the body, and the whole thing begins to fall. In doing so, it turns over so that the sails are no longer parallel to the ground, while the motor continues to drive it

Fig. 59.—Hofmann's working model.

forwards. But this upward movement is only intended to last an instant. The wings soon get into such a position that they are able to take the whole load, and as the machine moves forward, fresh quantities of air are successively compressed beneath the wings. The upward reaction becomes so great that the machine not merely floats but soars higher, continuing its flight steadily under the influence of the propellers. If a fall should take place, the speed of falling is much reduced by the reaction of the exposed surfaces, exactly in the same way as with parachutes. The correctness of the inventor's ideas is probably shown by the fact that he has often publicly exhibited a small model, reduced in the proportion of 1 to 10, which flies successfully in a large hall.

FIG. 60.—Herr Hofmann and Mr. Patrick Alexander in the workshop.

The machines which have been described were intended to be worked by motors, and even in the smallest designs, such was always the case. Many, however, believe that this is wrong in principle, in so far as experiment is concerned. Their idea is that the first step should be in the direction of floating, and that when sufficient is known to deal with the niceties of that art, it will be reasonable to talk about working with motors.

The man who first started on these lines was a German, named Lilienthal. His methods have been much imitated in France and America, and require to be fully described in order to understand the problem of floating motion. When he was a schoolboy, he tried the most primitive methods. He fastened wings to his body, and tried to get sufficient impetus for the start by running down a hill. Later on, with the help of his brother, he used sails, which were distended to represent the wings of a bird, and made of calico, supported on a frame of wickerwork. He sat with the lower part of his arms resting on the frame; in this way he controlled the movements of his machine. In a strong wind, he would soar above the heads of the astonished spectators; under other conditions, he would appear to float, almost at rest. This simple type of sail led Lilienthal to develop other designs, with a view to having greater control over the force of the wind.

FIG. 61.—Lilienthal on his flying machine.

Sudden gusts were particularly dangerous and might cause the whole machine to turn over. He found a maximum area of 150 square feet to be suitable for his sails, with a span from tip to tip of 23 ft. Anything bigger than this only caused loss of stability. Landing was also a difficult operation; he said that he was often obliged to perform a kind of wild dance in order to keep his equilibrium. Still he generally came without accident to the ground, though he felt to have very imperfect control over his movements. He started by thinking he could do what was necessary by shifting the position of his body, and in this way he altered the position of the centre of gravity. This worked well so long as the sails were small, but he was driven to increase their size. He therefore made an apparatus, which had a sail both on the left and on the right; the area of each was 97 square feet, and the span from tip to tip was 18 ft. In this case, the old method of shifting the position of the centre of gravity worked well. If the wind lifted the wing on the left side, a slight change in the position of the body at once restored it to its original position. He was also able to rise to much greater

FIG. 62.—Lilienthal starting from the hill on his flying machine.

heights, and to float over the spot from which he had started, if the speed of the wind was greater than 30 ft. per second. In order to land in a gentle breeze, the machine was pointed upwards by allowing the body to fall backwards. Just before reaching the ground, the legs were thrown out, as if about to make a spring. In this way a very unpleasant shock was generally avoided, but if the wind was stronger, the apparatus would fall to the ground gently of its own accord.

On his many trips Lilienthal always noticed the decided tendency of the wind to raise his machine. He also believed that the wind induced an eddying motion, similar to that noticed in the flight of birds, but the hill from which he started was too close to allow him to indulge in the execution of any such manœuvres. His practising ground was generally in the neighbourhood of Berlin. He always started from a hill, and finally constructed one for his own purposes near Gross-Lichterfelde, 50 ft. high and 230 ft. in diameter at the bottom. He gradually reached a certain proficiency in the art of flying, and thought he might safely try the effect of a small motor, which was to be used to flap the wings. He had a further scheme by which he altered the position of the rudder through a movement of the head, but unfortunately on August 9th, 1896, some mistake was made in one of his adjustments. When at a height of 50 ft. the whole thing turned over and fell to the ground, Lilienthal being killed on the spot. Two years previously he had had an accident on the same spot, owing to the breakage of one of his arm supports; at that time he escaped without serious injury. But the fate of this indefatigable man has in no wise discouraged his successors; his work is being continued in many parts of the world.

Percy S. Pilcher made many machines of this kind, and was very skilful in their management. He employed the methods of a child's kite, and employed men to pull him by a rope in a direction opposite to that of the wind. In this way he often rose to heights of 60 feet. But he met with the fate of Lilienthal, and, falling from a height of 30 ft., sustained fatal injuries. Chanute and his assistant Herring made many attempts with aeroplanes in Chicago. Chanute introduced an improvement in the shape of an elastic rudder. This consisted of an arrangement by which the inclination of the sails was adjusted to meet the pressure of variable gusts, and he made a great number of trips in aeroplanes of this description. Herring continued the experiments and added a motor. This was placed between two of the exposed surfaces of the machine, and with its aid he actually succeeded in flying, but the flight only lasted a few seconds, as the air was not sufficiently compressed.

Hargrave was the inventor of a peculiar but excellent type of kite, somewhat of the form of a box. But the brothers Wright far outstrip everybody else, if the reports of their doings are true. The world was lately astonished at the news that they had formed a company in Paris, which was to buy their invention for the sum of £40,000, and place it at the disposal of the French War Office. The Wrights then stated, in answer to enquiries, that they were proposing to sell it for the sum mentioned in the report; but as a condition precedent to the sale, a trial run was to be made in the neighbourhood of Paris,

Fig. 63.—Starting an aeroplane.

and was to show a speed of 30 miles an hour. Wilbur and Orville Wright are natives of Dayton, Ohio, and having enjoyed a good technical education and started a successful bicycle factory, they turned their attention to the problem of flight. They had the help of Chanute, and followed Lilienthal's plan of mastering the art of floating before trying the effects of a motor. With a wind blowing at the rate of 26 ft. a second, they were able with their apparatus to maintain themselves for a while in the air. The experiments were carried out on the dunes along the shore of the Atlantic, where a steady wind blows the whole year round.

They first directed their attention to three points : (1) whether it is better to let the driver stand or lie down ; (2) whether stability is better ensured by special steering devices or by shifting the position of the centre of gravity ; and (3) what effect is produced by a rudder placed at the front of the machine. The experiments were always carried out in the same order, and the machines were first tested like kites at the end of a rope.

Fig. 64.—Aeroplane in flight.

(From the *Leipziger Illustrierte Zeitung*.)

After any necessary changes had been made and a certain modicum of stability seemed assured, one of the brothers laid himself at full length in the machine. The work then continued in the same keen and determined way ; neither the expected nor the unexpected was sufficient to upset their mental balance. The form of the aeroplane was almost exactly the same as that of Chanute and Herring. Two surfaces of the nature of sails were arranged, the one above the other. At first they were slightly concave ; but this was abandoned in favour of flat surfaces. The driver lies at full length on the lower sail in a space arranged for this purpose. In front of him is the rudder controlling the elevation. The vertical rudder for directing the horizontal motion is behind him. The design used in 1900 had a sail area of 172 square feet; in 1901 and 1902 this figure was increased to 312, and finally, in the year 1903, when the motor was first introduced, it was again raised to 625 square feet. In 1902 the length of the sails in the direction of motion was 5 ft. 3 in., and their breadth 35 ft. The vertical rudder for horizontal movement had an area of 14 square feet, and was placed at the back and shaped like a bird's tail, the total weight of the machine being 117 lbs. The course was inclined at an angle of 7 degrees to the horizontal, but a slight accident led to an alteration of the back rudder. This was reduced to half its former size, and the stability was then found to be all that could be desired. The angles of flight varied from 5 to 7 degrees, the longest distance travelled being 200 yards in 26 seconds.

They then made an important step forwards and turned their aeroplane into a flying machine by using a motor, which was built in their bicycle factory from their own designs. It was then arranged so as to drive two propellers at the back, and the weight of the whole machine amounted to $5\frac{1}{2}$ cwt. The first trial was made against a wind blowing at the rate of 33 ft. per second, and the start was made from a railway track with the motor going at full speed. It rose upwards to a height of 10 ft., and after some irregular movements came to the ground. The longest distance travelled in 1903 was 850 ft. in 59 seconds. The trials were continued in the following year, and distances of 300 and 400 yards were covered. In September, sufficient progress had been made to enable them to turn round slight bends, and on the 20th they succeeded in returning to their starting point. All these journeys were naturally undertaken with a driver on board; latterly small loads of iron rods were also taken, which gradually rose to 2 cwt. The following is a statement of the best results obtained in 1905. On September 26th, a distance of 11 miles was covered in 18 minutes 9 seconds. The length of the journey depends on the amount of benzine carried ; in this case it had been supposed to be capable of lasting 40 minutes. On September 29th, 12 miles were covered in 19 minutes 55 seconds ; on October 3rd, with a larger reservoir for the benzine, 15 miles were done in 25 minutes 5 seconds ; on October 4th, 21 miles in 33 minutes 17 seconds, and on the following day, 24 miles in 38 minutes 3 seconds.

Captain Ferber, of the Balloon Corps, and the editor of *L'Aérophile* put themselves in communication with the

Fig. 65.—Archdeacon's experiments on the Seine.
(From Moedebeck's " Die Luftschiffahrt.")

Wrights in order to find out the exact position with regard to these trials. The answer which Ferber received tended to show that there had been much exaggeration in the reports. Chanute, however, stated in a letter that he had witnessed a trial trip over a distance of 500 yards, and had heard that great distances had been covered ; but a journey, which was to cover 40 miles in an hour, had been abandoned on account of the strong wind blowing on the day of his visit. In so far as the outsider is concerned, not the least mysterious part of the affair seems to be the proposal to sell the invention to the French Government.

The work done by Professor Montgomery in California does

not seem to have been so successful.   He built an aeroplane for the Jesuits of the monastery " Santa Clara." His intention was to raise it to a height of about 2,500 feet by means of a *Montgolfière*, and then to cut it adrift.   On July 19th, 1905, after a series of successful experiments, one of the sails broke after the machine had started from the balloon.   The apparatus fell directly to the ground and the driver was killed on the spot.

Mention must also be made of the work done by Archdeacon in Paris.   His aeroplane was towed by a motor-boat, travelling at 25 miles an hour, in a direction opposed to the wind, which was blowing at 4 miles an hour.   It was constructed after the

FIG. 66.—Langley's flying machine on the Potomac.
(From the *Illustrierte Aeronautische Mitteilungen*.)

fashion of a Hargrave kite in Surcouf's balloon factory.   At the front there were two sails, 33 ft. by 6 ft. 6 in., and at the back two other sails with an area of 220 square feet; the rudder, with an area of 32 square feet, was placed at the front.   The weight of this machine without driver was 6 cwt., and it was mounted on two small boats after the manner adopted by Kress. Generally speaking, it turned out to be very stable, and rose to heights of 150 ft.   But it often fell into the river, over which the flight took place, and on one occasion it turned over completely, sustaining serious damage.

Lately a good deal has been heard of another type of flying machine.   It is proposed to run the machine along the level by the aid of a motor until such a speed is reached that the

compression of the air suffices to lift it upwards. All these experiments tend to show that the crux of the problem lies largely
in the creation of sufficient kinetic energy to give the machine a
start. For the sake of completeness, two other types ought to
be mentioned, viz., the paddle-wheel and the sail-wheel. Koch
of Munich advocates the former ; the propulsion is effected by
paddle-wheels, placed below the sails of the machine. Professor
Wellner advocates the latter, which consists in mounting the

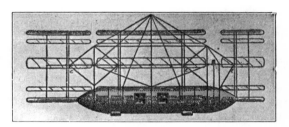

FIG. 67.—Wellner's flying machine.

sails on the surfaces of revolving drums, and thereby causing
them both to support and propel the load.

Even if the reports from America about the Wrights are
largely discounted, it is quite certain that substantial progress
has been made of late years in the design of flying machines.
It therefore does not seem to be unduly optimistic to suppose
that the twentieth century is likely to solve this problem and to
produce a flying machine, capable of doing work of a really useful nature. The difficulties mainly lie in producing flight in
the direction of the wind, and still more, in a direction at right
angles to that of the wind. It is far easier to move against
the wind in a machine of this kind than in a dirigible
balloon.

CHAPTER X.

KITES.

THE kite was probably invented at least 200 years before the birth of Christ, and seems at that time to have been used for military purposes. The Chinese general, Han Sin, brought his forces to the relief of a beleaguered town, and by means of kites he is said to have signalled to the inhabitants, showing them the direction in which he was making an underground passage into the town. The peculiarities of kites must therefore have been understood at that time.[1] Some 800 years later another Chinese general used them to help him to effect a junction with his allies. He was besieged in the town of King-Thai, and sent out a number of kites with a request for speedy relief, the position of the kites showing the most convenient side of the town for an attack. In later years the English and the Spaniards are said to have used them for similar purposes.

FIG. 68.—The Japanese " May Carp."
(From the *Illustrierte Aeronautische Mitteilungen*, 1905.)

Moedebeck made enquiries as to their use in Japan. It appears

[1] Lécornu, " Les Cerfs-Volants," Paris, 1902.

that a fish-shaped kite, called a " May carp," is hoisted on the tops of the houses on May 5th, if the father of the family has been blessed with a son during the preceding year. This takes place during the observance of the May festival, which was founded about 500 A.D. Curiously enough, a very similar device has been invented

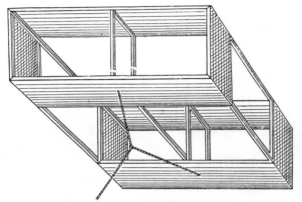

FIG. 69.—Hargrave kite.

by Mr. Patrick Y. Alexander during the last few years, and is called by him an aerosack. It may be described as consisting of a pillow-case, into the mouth of which a hoop has been inserted. If it is hoisted on a stick and kept with its mouth towards the wind, it behaves in exactly the same way as the Japanese carp.

The ordinary kite must have been well known at the time when Benjamin Franklin applied them for electrical purposes. He had proved that long insulated metal rods were able to collect electricity

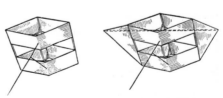

FIG. 70.—Other shapes of Hargrave kites.

from the atmosphere, and proposed to conduct it from the clouds to earth. In 1752 he constructed kites, such as were used by children; he covered them with silk and added a metal point at the top. About the same time Romas did likewise. The metal tip was connected in one way or another with an insulated conductor, from which it was possible to extract sparks 10 ft. long. Many scientific men followed in his footsteps, and applied his methods to the study of atmospheric electricity, and in Philadelphia a club was founded for the purpose, called " The Franklin Kite Club."

The first scientific investigation into the problem of the kite was published by the celebrated mathematician Euler in 1756 ; and lately the American meterologist Rotch, director of the Blue Hill Observatory at Boston, has made further publications on the subject, with the help of his assistant, Marvin. The part which is played by kites in meteorology at the present day will be discussed in a later chapter, and they are also usefully applied for military purposes in a variety of ways. It has been thought

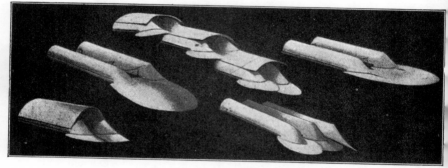

FIG. 71.—Various forms of kites.

that it might be possible to use it as a substitute for the captive balloon in windy weather, and if this should be possible, it might displace it altogether. Kites would be far cheaper, and have the further advantage of being independent of gas generators and of the nature of the country in which the ascent is made. They are also used by the military for the transmission of signals, and for photographic purposes. The progress that has been made has been largely due to the fact that there has been little difficulty in raising funds, and successful experiments have been carried out by Rotch, Marvin, Fergusson, Clayton, Eddy, and Wise.

From the modern point of view there are three main forms of kite ; firstly, the Malay kite, as improved by Eddy ; secondly, the Hargrave kite, which appears in all sorts of shapes ; and thirdly, the keel-kite, invented by Clayton. The first two types are fairly well known, but the keel-kite is not in the same position, and therefore requires to be more fully described. A framework, built up out of wood and phosphor bronze wire, is covered by cambric and used as a keel. It is mounted on a piece of pine wood, and the rest of the kite is constructed in the usual way. The only difference lies in the possibility of slightly altering the angle of inclination of the sails. By means of a spring, it is possible to lessen the inclination of the exposed surfaces to the wind, so that it flies along more

FIG. 72.—Cody's kite.

easily under a diminished pressure. This is a real improvement. On the one hand, the vertical position of the kite is more stable, and on the other, a serious accident is rendered more improbable.

In mounting to great heights it is necessary to use a light kite. In consequence, it is not likely to be very strong. It has often happened that a kite of this kind has been destroyed by the wind, which may be blowing strongly at a great height without being very noticeable at the ground level. This is a common occurrence in meterological work. As it is not possible to reach great heights with one kite, it is usual to put several on the same cord, one behind the other, and sometimes as many as nine are joined together in this way.   A kite of this kind is quite able to support the weight of the rope and recording instruments.

The Americans have applied them to many military purposes, and Lieutenant Wise has carried out a great deal of work with this object in view.   It is particularly well adapted for signalling.

FIG. 73.—Cody's kite used as a captive balloon.

An absolutely calm day or night is a very rare occurrence; and it is nearly always possible to send up a string of kites to a height of a few hundred feet.   Signalling can therefore easily be carried out, either by hoisting flags in the daytime, or lights at night. With regard to lights, the simplest plan is to use different colours, and to vary their position with regard to one another.   Bengal lights of different colours could also be used to convey intelligence.

Doubtless the best thing in this respect is the electric light, which can be switched on and off from below. If electric lights are arranged, one above the other in separate compartments, and shaded by glasses of different colours, a message can be signalled. The Morse code could always be used by showing the lights for longer and shorter intervals. Tests have shown that the electric light is clearly visible over a distance of 12 miles, so that signals of this type would be useful over that range.

Attempts have been made in America as well as in England

FIG. 74.—Kite for signalling.

FIG. 75.—Signalling by means of lights from a kite.

and Russia to hoist an observer in a kite. The first load was a dummy of suitable weight, and on January 27th, 1897, an American officer went up. The velocity of the wind was 23 ft. per second. Four Hargrave kites were used, of different sizes. The top one had a surface of 20 sq. ft., the next of 39 sq. ft., the next of 86 sq. ft., and the lowest of 155 sq. ft. The total area was about 300 sq. ft. To the lowest kite a very primitive seat was attached, made of bamboo rods. The kites weighed 58 lbs., the cord 20 lbs., and the passenger 148 lbs. On this occasion Lieutenant Wise rose to a height of 50 ft., and could see over the tops of the houses. He thought he could have risen still higher, but contented himself with this as a first attempt.

Millet has proposed an arrangement by which the basket for the passenger is fastened to a single kite of curious design. The advantage of his scheme lies in the possibility of converting the apparatus into a parachute, in case the rope should break or be shot away. For this purpose it would be necessary to close down the sails at the side, and so create an enclosed space capable

of compressing the air in its fall. The driver is also able to regulate the height of ascent. The basket is hung from a pulley and can be drawn up by ropes so as to come nearer to the kite. In this way the position of the centre of gravity would be changed, and the inclination of the sails to the wind would be correspondingly altered. The reaction due to the wind would therefore change, and would tend to produce a rise or fall, according to the circumstances.

Similar kites have been invented by Major Baden Powell, Lieutenant Uljanin, and Captain Bolscheff. In August, 1825,

FIG. 76.—Lieutenant Wise making an ascent in a kite.

a man, named Pocock, is said to have driven three passengers from Bristol to London in a carriage drawn by two kites. The main one was made of muslin covered with paper ; it was 20 ft. long, and rose to a height of 160 feet. Above this was a smaller kite that could be so steered as to help the other to surmount trees and obstacles. With a favouring wind, Pocock was often able to cover twenty miles in an hour, and to beat all other vehicles that competed against him.

Much interest was taken in the performances of Cody, otherwise known as Buffalo Bill. He had a light folding boat, 13 ft.

long, and 3 ft. broad, which was covered with cambric, and had
a space in the middle to accommodate the passengers. A kite,
flying at the height of 560 ft. was fastened to the top of the
mast, and pulled the boat along. On November 6th, 1903, he
succeeded in crossing from Calais to Dover in 13 hours. A
rowing boat accompanied him, with a crew of five men, but the
pace was too great for it to keep up with him.

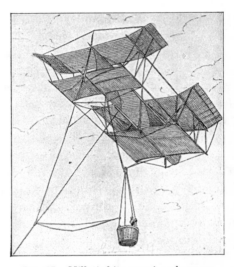

FIG. 77.—Millet's kite carrying observers.

Kites have often been proposed for the purpose of saving life at
sea. They have been used for the purpose of throwing lines on
board a wreck, or from the ship to the land, and many cases are
on record where they have served a useful purpose in such
emergencies. It may also play its part in Polar expeditions.
Quite apart from its use for meteorological observations, it might
be used to drag sledges, and so take the place of dogs. There
are few things capable of such varied application as the kite. It
may assume almost any shape, and every fresh enthusiast seems
to evolve something new in the way of design.

CHAPTER XI.

PARACHUTES.

THE first mention of parachutes is to be found in the writings of Leonardo da Vinci, and Fauste Veranzio seems to have risked his life at the work. Joseph Montgolfier also made similar experiments at Annonay before turning his attention to the balloon. Sebastian Lenormand made a descent from a tree in a parachute in 1783; but his later experiments were confined to dropping animals, which were placed in a basket attached to the parachute. Blanchard took up the matter professionally, and made a good deal of money by inviting the public to witness his performances. Garnerin was taken up by a balloon on October 22nd, 1797, and after the supporting rope was cut, he fell 3,000 ft. to the ground. In 1836, Cocking used an inverted form of parachute. He was taken up by Green in a balloon to a height of 3,000 ft. and then cut adrift. The framework of the parachute collapsed under the pressure of the air, and Cocking was killed on the spot.

For balloon work, parachutes are of no use; they are merely suitable for country shows. Balloonists are often asked whether they take parachutes with them in case of unforeseen disaster. The fact is that any such precaution is unnecessary. Suppose a balloon were to lose its gas suddenly. It would fall at the rate of about 20 ft. per second, because the balloon itself would behave after the manner of a parachute, and if the velocity should rise to 30 ft. per second, as happens occasionally in stormy weather, this is due to the fact that a downward wind helps to increase the speed.

Professor Koeppen has collected some figures from which he concludes that too low an estimate has generally been put on the time occupied in falling. Robertson is said to have fallen 10,000 ft. in 35 minutes, which is at the rate of 4 ft. 9 in. per second. Frau Poitevin fell 6,000 feet in 45 minutes; her husband took her up in a balloon, and when she reached the ground, he was in the act of packing it up. Dr. Bräuler has

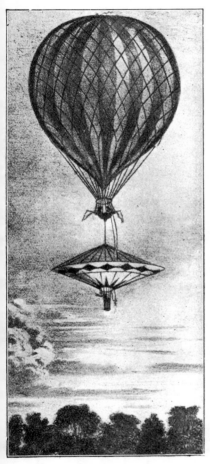

Fig. 78.—Cocking's parachute.

shown that with pressures on the surface of the parachute of 0·2, 0·4, 0·8, 1·6 and 3·2 lbs. per sq. ft. respectively, the correspondingly final velocities will be 7·87, 11·5, 16·4, 22·6, and 32·8 feet per second. It is very important to provide a small opening at the top of the parachute, so that the compressed air

has some chance of escaping.   Otherwise a vibratory motion,
like that of a pendulum, may be set up, and in an extreme case,
the parachute may be turned over.   Poitevin's parachute had a

FIG. 79.—Fräulein Käthe Paulus preparing
to descend in her parachute.

FIG. 80.—Fräulein Käthe Paulus with
her double parachute.

diameter of 40 ft., with an opening 6 ins. across at the top; its
weight was 66 lbs.

The latest novelty is a double parachute, invented by the
balloonist Lattemann, and used on her many descents by
Fräulein Käthe Paulus.   They are rolled up, the one under the
other, and hang from the balloon.   The upper one opens as soon
as the spring has been made, and the lower one comes into
operation as soon as the motion becomes steady.   If a double
parachute is used, it is necessary to make the descent from a

great height. Fräulein Paulus has made sixty-five descents in the parachute without serious injury; but it must be admitted

FIG. 81.—Fall of a parachute.

that the journey has not always been a very smooth one. A certain amount of grim determination is necessary for this kind of work, and the profession is never likely to be overcrowded.

CHAPTER XII.

THE DEVELOPMENT OF MILITARY BALLOONING.

GIROUD DE VILLETTE made an ascent in one of Montgolfier's captive balloons in 1783, and pointed out the obvious advantages which must result from its use in war. Meusnier was induced by these considerations to devote much time to the study of dirigible balloons; his work has already been noticed in an earlier chapter. In 1792, the Committee of Public Safety was urged by Guyton de Morveau to consider the question of using balloons in the defence of the country. He had already built a dirigible aerostat for the Academy of Dijon, and was able to convince his colleagues as to their probable value. Indeed in the next year at the siege of Condé, attempts were made to communicate with the besieged by means of pilot balloons. But they were badly constructed and fell into the hands of the enemy.

The experiment was not repeated exactly in the same form. It was now proposed to use captive balloons, and Guyton de Morveau was instructed to proceed in the matter. It was, however, laid down that no gas was to be used that required sulphuric acid for its production. In those days, sulphuric acid was comparatively a rare product, and the making of gunpowder absorbed all the sulphur that was available. Guyton de Morveau turned to the chemist Lavoisier, who had discovered a new method of making hydrogen. With the help of a physicist named Coutelle, they proceeded to construct an oven, which was to be used for preparing hydrogen by passing steam over red hot iron. This was soon ready, and a balloon, 30 ft. in diameter, was filled with the gas in the gardens of the Tuileries. The experiments succeeded so well that Coutelle was sent on a mission to General Jourdan, who was commanding the armies on the Sambre and Maas, with a view to inducing him to make use of a captive balloon. It so happened that when he arrived in Belgium, he was received by a member of the National Assembly. To him the idea of a military balloon appeared so ridiculous that he threatened to shoot Coutelle. General Jourdan, on the other hand, was much struck by the plan, and instructed Coutelle to return to Paris and procure the necessary materials. The castle at Meudon, which served as barracks for a division of artillery, was utilised as the first regular balloon factory. Great skill was shown over the work, and the requirements of a military balloon were very carefully considered. The size was calculated on the assumption that it was to carry two passengers. A very light material was used for the envelope, and it was made airtight by

a special kind of linseed oil varnish. This varnish turned out to be excellent, and it is therefore a misfortune that the mode of its preparation should be one of the lost arts.

In a few months Coutelle was able to invite the committee to inspect the first war balloon ever made. It was held captive by two ropes. Com-

FIG. 82.—Methods of transporting a captive balloon. On the left is shown a means of protecting the balloon from the wind.

munication with the ground was by means of a speaking-tube, or by flag signals. A long message was written on paper and then sent down in a small sand-bag, along one of the ropes. It is curious that drawings are nowadays sent to the ground in the same way, the only difference being that small bags are used to which lead plates are attached; they are allowed to slide down the telephone cable, because the connecting rope is too far from the basket. The committee was so well satisfied with the performance of " L'Entreprenant," as the balloon was called, that Coutelle was appointed a captain, with instructions to form a balloon corps. At the same time he received the title of Director of the Aerostatic Experimental Station, with Conté for his assistant. The first balloon company on record came into

A.   K

existence on April 2nd, 1794, and consisted of a captain, a
lieutenant, a sub-lieutenant, a sergeant-major, 4 non-commissioned officers, and 26 men, including a drummer-boy.   The
uniform consisted of a blue coat with black collar and facings,
finished off with red braid.   Their buttons bore the inscription
"Aérostiers."   A special uniform of blue colour was provided as
a working costume, and they were armed with swords and
pistols.   The lieutenant, named Delaunay, was a builder by trade,
and turned out to be a very useful and practical man.   Within

FIG. 83.—Landing of a balloon in the streets of Strassburg.

a week of the formation of the company they marched against
the Austrians at Maubeuge, unaccompanied by their balloon, and
came off with flying colours.   Coutelle reported that his men
were looked upon with contempt by the rest of the army, because
they were mere artizans, and nobody understood in the least the
nature of their work.   He therefore begged the commanding
officer to allow his men to have some opportunity of distinguish-
ing themselves.   The result was that the sub-lieutenant was soon
killed, and two of the men grievously wounded, but their bravery
was now established beyond all dispute.   The balloon soon arrived,
and was filled with the gas from an oven that had been got ready

in the meantime. The construction of the furnace will be described later.

Coutelle undertook the first ascent in company with an officer amid the booming of cannon and the applause of the soldiers. They were able to report at once as to the movements of the enemy, with the result that an officer of the general staff was ordered to make an ascent with Coutelle twice daily, and General Jourdan himself made several trips in the car. The Austrians objected strongly to this method of waging war. Not only were their plans known to the enemy, but their whole army had a superstitious dread of the new methods. Orders were therefore given that two 17-lb. howitzers were to open fire on it. This was done on June 13th, and for the first time in history cannons were directed against the aerial battleship. Coutelle greeted their efforts with the shout of "Vive la republique"; but noticing that their artillerymen were making good practice, he cautiously withdrew to a higher level out of range.

Still it could be hardly said that the firing was wholly ineffective. It greatly annoyed the men who held the ropes of the captive balloon, and also did more material damage. Jourdan therefore sent for an experienced gunner from Lille, who declared that he would soon silence the fire of the enemy. However, the Austrians knew nothing of the moral effect produced by their guns, and thinking that they were producing no result, withdrew them in another direction. But the balloon did not altogether escape injury. It was blown by a strong wind against the church tower of Maubeuge, and somewhat damaged. Moreover the gas-oven was out of order, owing to damage to some of the retorts.

On June 18th Coutelle received orders from General Jourdan to join the army at Charleroi. In order to avoid loss of time in packing the balloon and building a new gas generator at Charleroi, he determined to send the balloon up in the air and have it towed over the distance of twenty miles, which separated him from his destination. Twenty guide-ropes were fastened to the balloon, halfway down the net; all the instruments were put in the car together with the signalling flags. Coutelle then mounted the car, and the march began on a dark night through the outposts of the Austrian army. It was necessary to avoid interference with the rest of the French troops ; the rope-holders were therefore obliged to march on opposite sides of the road, and this added greatly to the fatigue of the journey. Orders were given through the speaking tube from the car ; and the balloon was kept at such a height that it just passed over the heads of the horses. After almost superhuman efforts on a scorching day

Fig. 84.—Belle-Alliance Platz, Berlin, taken from balloon by a member of the Prussian Balloon Corps.

the balloonists arrived in fifteen hours at Charleroi, where they were received with open arms. On the same evening an ascent was made, and on the next day Coutelle had General Morelot as a companion in the car, where they remained for eight hours under the continuous fire of the Austrians. Morelot was able to see that it would be impossible for the town to hold out much longer, and therefore was on the point of ordering it to be taken by storm when the garrison capitulated.

The balloonists were now ordered to proceed to headquarters

at a place called Gosselie. This formed the middle of the French position, and an important battle was impending. On June 26th General Morelot went up in the balloon with Captain Coutelle before the beginning of the battle; they rose to a height of 1,300 ft., and in consequence of the clearness of the atmosphere they were able to report to General Jourdan as to all the movements of the enemy. The Austrians tried to dislodge the observers by heavy firing; but they failed, although one or two shots passed between the car and the envelope of the balloon. In the afternoon they were ordered to attach themselves to the right

Fig. 85.—Helping to land a balloon.

wing of the army, and to lead the way by means of signals. The battle was finally won, and the generals expressed themselves as thoroughly satisfied with the work of the balloonists, to whose efforts the result of the day was largely due.

The Austrians, on the other hand, were much disconcerted by the new methods, and recognised that the balloon was an insidious form of attack. They therefore announced that all balloonists, who fell into their hands, would be treated as spies. And after the battle of Fleurus they fell upon evil times. Coutelle marched with the army against Liège, but after reaching Namur, he was obliged to fall back on Maubeuge. A gust of wind had dashed the balloon against some trees, and it was found impossible to execute the repairs with the means at disposal. Coutelle there-fore returned to Meudon, where he made a new cylindrical balloon, called the "Céleste." It was immediately put to the test at Lüttich, but turned out to be very unstable in a light breeze. It was therefore unsuitable for observations, and the old balloon, which had in the meantime been repaired, was once more brought into the field. It was put in a boat, taken across the Maas, and sent along the road to Brussels.

Fate then overtook it a second time, before the gates of the town, where it was much damaged through being driven by the wind against a pole. The repairs that were carried out in Brussels were unsatisfactory ; it had therefore to be sent to Meudon, and the balloonists were left without employment for many months at Aix-la-Chappelle. The time was not, however, entirely lost, for improvements were made in methods of housing the balloon, and a kind of tent was built to shelter it from the force of the wind.

In March, 1795, Coutelle was recalled to Paris, in order to carry out the formation of a second balloon corps in accordance with the decree of the National Convention of June 23rd, 1794. In addition to this, an "École nationale aérostatique " was formed in consequence of the successes already achieved in actual warfare, and Conté, who was Coutelle's assis-tant, was placed in charge of it. The school was intended for the instruction of officers and men in the art of ballooning, and it was also proposed that it should undertake investigations into any suggested novelties. Conté set about his work with great zeal, and an efficient factory was soon organised, where six balloons were built. Two were sent to each of the existing corps, one was despatched to Italy, and the other was kept at Meudon for purposes of instruction.

Trustworthy reports show that the material used for construc-tion was as good as that in use nowadays. A balloon intended to carry two persons to a height of 1,600 ft. had an envelope weighing between 180 and 200 lbs. The covering was made tight with five coats of varnish, and held so well that it was possible to use the same balloon for ascents, even after it had been filled for two months. The men were trained to the work of holding the balloon and pulling it in, and the school soon had a sub-director, a storekeeper, a clerk, and 60 men in training. The latter were divided into three divisions, each of which consisted of twenty men. One division was sufficient for holding a balloon ; each man had his own special rope to hold, which was fastened to the main rope, the same method being still employed at the

FIG. 86.—A balloon about to land.

present day. As the balloon was pulled down, the rope was wound round a drum.

Conté also paid attention to improvement of the signalling arrangements. He introduced a system by which cylinders, made of black calico, stretched over rings, could be used to convey information. This was done by hanging the cylinders at a greater or smaller distance from the car, but this method was not very serviceable, as the wind was apt to scatter the cylinders in all directions with many entanglements. The gas generator was also improved, as the result of experience.

The Balloon Corps was quite independent of the school. Coutelle received the title of "Commandant," and in virtue of his office commanded both companies. Each company had a captain, two lieutenants, one lieutenant acting as quartermaster, one sergeant-major, one sergeant, three corporals, one drummer, and forty-four balloonists. The second company was sent with the repaired "Entreprenant" to join the army on the Rhine. It was placed under the command of General Lefevre, who besieged the town of Mayence for eleven months, and reconnaissances by balloon were made daily till towards the end of the year. The aeronauts showed great skill on these occasions, which eventually received recognition even from an enemy who had declared that they would be treated as spies. On one occasion the Austrian generals sent word to the enemy to the effect that their observer was being sadly bumped by the heavy wind, and they thought it would only be reasonable to consult his feelings by pulling him in. But perhaps the advice was not altogether disinterested. Coutelle further states that he was sent under a flag of truce to the commander of the fortress, and that he was allowed to examine the fortifications as soon as it was understood that he was commander of the Balloon Corps. But the continual exposure did its work, and Coutelle had to be invalided home after recovering from typhus.

With the loss of its leader came also the loss of good luck for the balloon. In the spring the "Entreprenant" was on duty before Mannheim, when it was badly injured by the fire of the enemy. It was sent to Molsheim to be repaired, and then followed the army through Rastatt, Stuttgart, Donauwörth and Augsburg, being hauled about from place to place while full of gas. Finally the return journey was begun, and the balloon was packed up and sent to Molsheim. Morelot's successor, General Hoche, took no interest in the balloon, and left it behind at Strassburg. He also sent a letter to von Wetzlar, the Minister of War, on August 30th, 1797, to the following effect :—

"CITOYEN MINISTRE,—I beg to inform you that the army on the Sambre and Meuse has a company of balloonists, for which it can find no use ; perhaps it would be better to let it join the seventeenth military division, where it would be nearer the capital, and so in a better position to do useful work. I therefore ask permission to be allowed to dispose of the services of this corps in the manner suggested.

"L. Hoche."

No notice appears to have been taken of this letter, and the corps therefore remained at Molsheim.

It is now necessary to describe the fortunes of the first corps, which had joined the army on the Sambre and Meuse, and had the balloons "L'Hercule" and "L'Intrépide" under the command of Captain l'Homond. There was much work to be done. They were used at the sieges of Worms, Mannheim, and Ehrenbreitstein. After the defeat at Würzburg the corps retired within the fortress, and was imprisoned after it had surrendered to the enemy. At the end of the

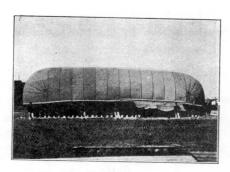

FIG. 87.—Kite-balloon at anchor.

campaign they withdrew to Meudon, where the corps was enlarged and fitted out afresh. Conté persuaded Napoleon to use the company on his expedition to Egypt. But the first detachment had the misfortune to encounter a British man-of-war, and was duly sent to the bottom; the second was similarly captured. No feats of valour were therefore performed on the plains of Egypt. Conté was, however, appointed to the general staff, where his sound sense and technical ability were much appreciated. On the occasion of a fête given by Napoleon at Cairo the balloonists sent up a *Montgolfière*, 50 ft. in diameter, and adorned with the "tricolore." This was supposed to be likely to instil a feeling of dread in the native mind, but it was largely without effect.

On his return in 1798 Napoleon closed the ballooning school,

and on January 18th, 1799, he disbanded the two companies.
The balloons and their appurtenances were sold, with the
exception of some things that were sent to Metz for storage. It
has been already mentioned that Napoleon ceased to take any
practical interest in ballooning after the day on which a balloon,
sent up in his honour, was said to have fallen on the tomb of
Nero. Forty years were to elapse before the Balloon Corps was
revived. In 1812 a plan was mooted in Russia to use the balloon
for military purposes. A German mechanic, named Leppig,
proposed to the Russian Government that he should be allowed
to construct a dirigible balloon. It was to carry fifty soldiers
and a quantity of explosives, which were to be conveniently
dropped on the heads of the enemy. It was intended to carry
on the work with the greatest secrecy, and to place the factory
in the village of Woronzowo, near St. Petersburg, which was to
be isolated from the rest of the world by a kind of blockade,
organised by 160 foot soldiers and 12 dragoons. Eventually
two small balloons were got ready, each carrying two men; it
took six days to fill them instead of six hours, as the inventor
had promised. The trials failed miserably, and the inventor
was cast into prison. Thus ended an experiment, which had
cost £10,000, and no further work on ballooning was done in
Russia till the year 1870.

In 1815 Carnot caused observations to be made from a balloon
during the siege of Antwerp, but nothing is known as to the
results. During the campaign in Algiers a private balloonist,
named Margat, was engaged to follow the army, but his balloon
was never put on shore. In 1848 the insurgents in Milan
devised a new use for pilot balloons, which they placarded with
a proclamation of the Provisional Government, and in the
Franco-Prussian war the French dropped a number of pro-
clamations on the heads of the Prussian soldiers by the same
means. During the siege of Venice the Austrians, in 1849,
loaded small balloons with bombs, which were to be fired by a
time-fuse and fall on the heads of the enemy. These balloons
were naturally sent up without passengers, and it was expected
that the wind would carry them in the desired direction. But

this it failed to do, with the result that the bombs were discharged in their own ranks. Experiments on these lines were therefore discontinued till 1854, when a similar attempt was made in the arsenal at Vincennes with negative results.

In 1859 Napoleon III. procured a large silk *Montgolfière* from Italy, holding 28,500 cubic feet. It was handed over to a man named Nadar, who had done much photographic work from a balloon, and he made an ascent at Castiglione, accompanied by Godard, the balloon manufacturer. But they failed to accomplish anything noteworthy, and the same result attended their efforts on another hydrogen balloon, specially sent from Milan.

Balloons were, however, largely employed during the American Civil War, when Professor Lowe, of Washington, went to the seat of war, and placed himself under the orders of General MacClellan. A man named La Mountain went up in one of the balloons, and drifted away in the direction of the enemy's camp. After making his observations, he rose higher in the air, and found a current which brought him back again. An aeronaut, named Allan, went up in the other balloon, and reported telegraphically to headquarters. Lowe also sent telegrams direct to Washington by making connection with the overhead wires, and the artillery also received signals from the balloon. Lowe was able to give them useful information as to the position of the enemy's batteries, and also as to the effect produced by their own firing. Strong winds often prevented ascents, and sometimes it was not possible to reach a sufficient height to see all that was wanted. Still, MacClellan was well satisfied with the results, and requested the War Office to despatch four more balloons. On the retreat from Richmond to the James River the General lost all his baggage, together with the balloons and gas-generators. The balloonists' occupation was therefore gone.

In England similar work was done in utilising the balloon for scouting purposes. Much was done at Aldershot, but no special corps was formed at that time.

In 1866 balloons were used in the war between Brazil and Paraguay. General Caxias sent up a balloon to reconnoitre on the road leading through the marshes of Neembucu ; it was under

the guidance of a French aeronaut, but was accidentally burnt.
It has generally been assumed that fires and other mysterious
forms of explosion must be caused by flames coming in contact
with the main envelope.   But it has lately been found that this
was not always the case, and further investigation seemed
necessary.   It now appears that electricity is the most probable
cause of these disasters.   A balloon descending from a height is
charged with electricity, which may be discharged through the
iron parts around the valve.   The spark which follows may
set fire to the explosive mixture which would collect near the
valve, and in this way many accidents of a mysterious nature
may very possibly be explained.   Soon after the above incident,
Caxias discharged the French aeronaut, as it was said that he
was in the pay of the enemy.   An American balloonist from Rio
de Janeiro was therefore pressed into the service, and several
balloons were placed at his disposal.   Information of a useful
nature was soon received, and a practicable path through the
marshes was then found.   But General Caxias found the balloons,
and more especially the gas-generators, very awkward in active
campaigning, and soon dispensed with their services.

In France attempts were made in 1868 and 1869 to use
balloons for signalling purposes at some of the naval stations.
At Cherbourg small cylinders were hung from the balloon as
signals, and at night projectors were used.   But the results were
rather unsatisfactory in windy weather.   Lights were used to
signal from balloons during the siege of Paris, and according to
report the method gave satisfactory results.

CHAPTER XIII.

THE English balloonist Coxwell was entrusted by the Germans with the formation of two balloon detachments with all the necessary tackle. Colonel Josten and a lieutenant commanded the two companies, each consisting of 20 men, and Coxwell supplied two balloons, having capacities of 40,000 and 23,500 cubic feet respectively. They were put to work in the neighbourhood of Cologne, and did well, except in rough weather, when it was evident that 40 men were insufficient to hold them. It was therefore determined to form the men into one company, and to send them to the front at Strassburg with the smaller balloon. It was filled with ordinary coal gas, and one of the officers proceeded to make reconnoitring expeditions up to a height of 1,200 ft. Orders were then received to forward the balloon to Suffelweiersheim. In consequence of the strong wind, it was necessary to empty the balloon after it had travelled a few miles, and the problem of refilling it then arose. This was by no means an easy task in the neighbourhood of Strassburg, and the necessary barrels were not to be found without great trouble But after four days' search in the enemy's country Lieutenant Josten succeeded in getting together 75 wine-casks of different sizes. Of these, 60 were used for generating hydrogen from sulphuric acid and zinc, 12 served for washing the gas free from impurities, and the remaining three for drying the gas. The balloon was filled on September 24th in five hours, and in the afternoon an ascent was made by the two officers, who were later joined by an amateur from Cologne, named Dr. Mehler. The wind was too strong to allow of very exact work, and the balloon was consequently secured by a grapnel. Although every possible precaution was taken to shelter it from the force of the wind, it was nevertheless much damaged, all the gas escaping.

Before it was refilled Strassburg had capitulated, and orders were received to move forward to Paris.

The march to Paris was a laborious operation. All available vans were placed at the disposal of the commissariat department, and so none were left for the balloonists. As soon as they arrived in the neighbourhood of Paris it was found to be impossible to refill the balloon, and the company was therefore disbanded on October 10th, 1870, the balloon being sent back to Germany.

FIG. 88.—Steam winch for pulling in a captive balloon.
(From " Die Geschichte der Luftschiffer-Abteilung.")

The French also found them to be of doubtful value. At the beginning of the war all proposals to employ aeronauts were refused by Lebœuf, the Minister of War. Even the offers of assistance from the celebrated scientific balloonist, Wilfrid de Fonvielle, were rejected, and it was not till after the fall of Sedan and the old régime that the experience of the beginning of the century was turned to account. During the battle of Valenton, on September 17th, 1870, four balloons were sent up. Several captive balloons were used in Paris, but they did little good, owing to the winter fogs. On one occasion useful information with regard to some trenching work done by the Germans at

Pierrefitte was received. But on the whole the results were negative, and the military authorities sold their balloons to the Post Office.

Paris was soon completely surrounded, and it became a matter of necessity to organise means of communication with the Provisional Government at Tours, and with the troops in the provinces. A postal service by balloon was therefore arranged by Rampont, who was at the head of the Post Office. Balloon workshops were constructed under the control of Eugene and Julius Godard at the Orleans Railway Station in Paris ; another was similarly organised at the Northern Station by Yon and Camille Dartois. The balloons were to have a capacity of 70,000 cubic feet, to be made of the best varnished cambric, to be provided with a net of tarred rope, and a car capable of seating four persons. All accessories were to be provided by the contractors in the shape of grapnel, valves, ballast, etc., the whole to be handed over ready for actual work. They were to be delivered on appointed dates, and a penalty of £2 a day was to be paid for any delay beyond the fixed time. Each balloon was to cost £160, which was afterwards reduced to £140 ; the driver was to be provided by the contractor for a payment of £12, and this was subsequently reduced to £8. Gas was to be charged as an extra, and payment was due as soon as the balloon was out of sight. Godard's balloons were coloured blue and yellow, or red and yellow ; those of the rival contractor were white. Drivers were found in the shape of marines ; but the cars for their accommodation were of the most primitive kind, supported by iron carriers. The working of the valves and instruments was explained to them, and they were also instructed in the art of emptying ballast and throwing out the grapnel. Altogether 66 balloons left Paris. They contained in all 66 aeronauts, 102 passengers, 409 carrier pigeons, 9 tons of letters and telegrams, as well as 6 dogs. Five of the dogs were sent on the return journey to Paris, but nothing more was heard of them. Fifty-seven carrier pigeons were all that reached the besieged city, and they carried 100,000 messages. Fifty-nine balloons did their work as arranged, five fell into the hands of the enemy, and two disappeared altogether, having most probably fallen into the sea.

Some of the voyages deserve special mention. On September 30th Gaston Tissandier threw down 10,000 copies of a proclamation, addressed to the German soldiers. It contained a demand for peace, stating at the same time that France was prepared to fight to the bitter end. Gambetta left Paris on October 7th, with the intention of organising a fresh army in the provinces, and intended to march to the relief of Paris. The balloon was unskilfully managed, and came to the earth close to the German outposts. At first it was supposed to be a German balloon, seeing that it was known that one was expected to arrive from Strassburg. This delay allowed them to throw out some ballast. They then managed to escape, but not before Gambetta had been wounded in the hand.

On December 2nd, 1870, the celebrated astronomer Jansen left Paris in the balloon " Volta," taking his instruments with him. He was anxious to reach Algiers before December 22nd, in order to observe an eclipse of the sun. The English had offered to endeavour to get him a permit to pass through the German lines, but this he had refused. The quickest and longest journey was made by the "Ville d'Orléans" on November 24th. It left at 11.45 p.m., and reached Kongsberg in the province of Telemarken in Norway the next day at 1 p.m. On December 15th "La Ville de Paris" landed at Wetzlar in Nassau, and the "General Chanzy" on December 20th at Rothenburg in Bavaria. The remains of the latter balloon are now in the Army Museum at Munich. Naturally these sorties were not at all to the taste of the Germans, and Krupp was ordered to make a cannon suitable for bringing the balloons to earth. It was to be capable of being tilted almost into a vertical position, and to have a special gun-carriage fitted to it. But it was not a success and was soon relegated to the Zeughaus in Berlin. The outposts, however, were constantly on the look-out, and the result of their firing was to drive the French to start their balloons by night.

The German artillery knew the diameter of these balloons to

be 50 ft., and were therefore able to tell the distance approximately. In this connection it may be well to explain the principles on which aim is taken at balloons. The difficulty in hitting a captive balloon is not great; it consists in determining the distance and the range of the gun. The distance can be

Fig. 89.—Gun constructed by Krupp for firing at balloons.

estimated if the size is known. In that case it must be examined through a telescope provided with spider lines, and the angle at which a non-spherical balloon would be standing must be taken into account. For instance, a French spherical balloon has a capacity of 19,000 cubic feet, and a diameter of 33 ft. With the telescope, its apparent size would be measured in sixteenths, and with the aid of a table (which,

by the way, is very easily remembered), it is possible to
estimate the distance. The table is as follows, and gives
the distances corresponding to known diameters, on the
supposition that they subtend one-sixteenth on the spider lines
of the telescope :—

A diameter of 3·3 yards corresponds to a distance of 3,000
yards.

A diameter of 4·4 yards corresponds to a distance of 4,000
yards.

A diameter of 5·5 yards corresponds to a distance of 5,000
yards.

A diameter of 6·6 yards corresponds to a distance of 6,000
yards.

A diameter of 11 yards corresponds to a distance of 10,000
yards.

Wherefore, if the French balloon measures one-sixteenth on
the spider lines, its distance would be about 10,000 yards. It is
merely necessary to compare the apparent with the known
diameter to get the distance of the balloon.

Another very simple method is to take observations of the
balloon from two points at known distances apart. If the results
are graphically transferred to paper the distance can be measured
off. Experience shows that this method is very simply applied,
and gives results of value both for field batteries and for heavier
guns.

Still it must be admitted that observations of this kind require
a certain amount of time, and regulations are therefore laid
down, prescribing a method which is applicable, even if the
distance is unknown. Firing is to begin either with shrapnel or
with shells at the longest possible range, in order to find whether
the balloon is within range of the guns.[1] In order to determine the precise spot where the shell bursts, a number of
observers must be sent out, and range themselves on either side
of the path of the projectile. These observers report whether
the shot appears to have gone to the right or left of the balloon.

---

[1] "Mitteilungen über Gegenstände des Artillerie- und Geniewesens," Vienna,
1905. *Militärwochenblatt*, 1906, No. 11.

The precise position can then be easily fixed, with the exception of one doubtful case. This will be made clearer by a study of the diagram. The following cases may arise :—

(1) From the point of view of the battery (B), of the left observer (L), and of the right (R), the smoke hides the balloon (1, 2, 3). The shell has fallen short of the mark, and the range must be increased, if possible.

(2) The smoke appears to all the observers to be in a line with the balloon, but partly hidden by it (4, 5, 6). Then the gun has been set for too long a range, and the shell has fallen behind the balloon.

(3) The shell appears to L to have fallen on the right, and to R on the left of the balloon (10). Then it has fallen short.

(4) The shell appears to L to have fallen on the left, and to R on the right (5, 9). Then the range has been too long.

(5) Both observers report that it has fallen on the left or on the right. This is a doubtful case, and must be marked as such.

In cases (3) and (4), the more the shot appears to one of the observers to lie to the one side, the greater is its actual distance from the mark. The tangent sight must then be put

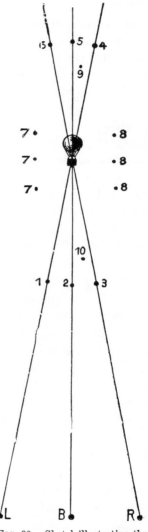

Fig. 90.—Sketch illustrating the method of aiming at a balloon.

in position, and special attention must be given to the direction of the aim. Therefore as soon as it is found that the balloon is

within range of the gun, the sights must be so set as to continually diminish the range, till it is found that successive shots
fall, the one in front and the other behind the balloon.   It is thus
possible to get the range within 100 yds.   Care must also be taken
to see that the shells burst above the balloon; otherwise they
would not produce any effect.   To judge from trials that have
been carried out in time of peace, it seems likely that a balloon
would be hit within 10 minutes.   Still, in dealing with one that is
moving rapidly, it would not be quite so simple.   Rifle fire would
probably be harmless to a balloon.   Up to a range of about
1,600 yds. a volley might produce some effect; but the balloon
would hardly be likely to be so near the lines of the enemy.

After this digression, it may be well to describe further the
events connected with the siege of Paris.   The successful
organisation of the post naturally drove the professional
aeronaut to attempt greater feats, by returning to the
beleaguered city from the outside.   Gaston Tissandier therefore
built a balloon in Tours, having a capacity of 42,500 cubic feet.
With it he intended to return to Paris when the wind provided a
suitable opportunity.   Before it was ready, he heard that his
brother had reached Nogent-sur-Seine in the " Jean Bart " from
Paris.   He immediately went to meet him, and brought his
balloon to Chartres.   Unfortunately serious injury was done by
a violent storm, and he had much difficulty in preventing it from
falling into the hands of the Germans.

Gambetta and Steenacker gave the brothers much assistance.
Everybody was convinced they would succeed.   One man indeed
went so far as to give the key of his house to Tissandier, asking
him to be good enough to go round and see that everything was
in order.   But unfortunately they failed.   At Le Mans, the wind
was for a long time from an unfavourable quarter; when at last
it seemed suitable, they were not ready to make a start.   They
finally left Rouen in foggy weather; but soon came to the ground,
and found they had been driven far out of the course.   They
tried again the next day, but with the same result.

The Government in Tours had meanwhile determined to place
some balloons at the disposal of the troops in the provinces.   The

FIG. 91.—Waggon carrying gas cylinders for one division of the Balloon Corps.

(From " Die Geschichte der Luftschiffer-Abteilung.")

"Ville de Langres" had been got ready in Tours, and was sent
with the aeronauts Duruof, Berteaux, and some marines to join
the army on the Loire at Orleans. The Tissandiers followed in
the "Jean Bart." Révilliod and Mangin were sent to Amiens,
and shortly before the declaration of peace, Wilfrid de Fonvielle
with two balloons was ordered to join General Faidherbe. Many
accidents happened in the storms of December, 1870, the balloons
being often torn to pieces by the wind. The work of marching
with the balloons, filled with gas, was very laborious, and superhuman efforts were required to meet emergencies of various
kinds. Still, it must be admitted that the value of the observations made in this way was not great, though the possible value
of military ballooning under favourable conditions was thoroughly
recognised. It was therefore determined to form a balloon
corps, and Steenacker was authorised to make the necessary
arrangements.

In consequence, two divisions were formed. The one was
placed under the command of the Tissandiers with the balloons
"La Ville de Langres" and "Le Jean Bart"; the other was
under Révilliod and Poirrier, and had two balloons, each with a
capacity of 70,000 cubic feet. Accommodation was provided in
Bordeaux, and each division had the assistance of 150 soldiers,
when necessary. General Chanzy took much interest in the
work and even made some ascents, though his adjutant had
declined the offer of a seat in the car on the ground of unnecessary risk. When peace was declared, there was no further
need for ballooning in its military aspect, and the corps was
disbanded.

CHAPTER XIV.

THE great advantage which France had derived from the balloon postal service during the war was thoroughly appreciated both in Paris and the provinces. Moreover, the journey of Gambetta to Amiens in " L'Armand Barbès " was an event of great importance. The war would undoubtedly have ended some months sooner if he had not succeeded in his work of organising resistance, and Gambetta's feat would of itself have been sufficient to justify the existence of military balloons, even if the history of the war had no other successes of the kind. The message delivered by an officer of the General Staff to General Chanzy on December 22nd, 1870, was also a matter of importance, seeing that it stated on good authority that Paris could only hold out for a month longer, unless very energetic measures were taken.

It is as well to remember that there are no means of preventing the departure of a balloon by night, whereas most other methods of communication are easily interrupted under the conditions of war. Even with a full moon, a yellow balloon is almost invisible at a short distance, a fact which has been frequently noticed. But in order to derive the full benefit from ballooning, it is very necessary that the organisation should be complete even in times of peace. It is precisely the kind of work that cannot be developed to a state of efficiency during a war. There is much to be learnt which requires long and careful practice. During the siege of Paris, sixty-six balloons were sent up, but of these only about a dozen were in the hands of really experienced aeronauts.[1] All the others were in the charge of marines, who worked with a right good will, but without any special knowledge. Towards

---

[1] The figures here given are more accurate than those which have been given by other authorities, and embody the results of the latest investigations.

the end of the siege coal was almost exhausted, coal gas was an unknown commodity, and there was a general dearth of all suitable appliances.   These things were taken into account in organising the arrangements subsequently, and in 1874 the "Commission des communications aériennes" was formed.   Colonel Laussedat presided over its deliberations, and was well acquainted with all the technical requirements of the problem.   He was assisted by Captain Renard and Captain La Haye, whose work has been noticed in an earlier chapter.   The members of this committee met with an unfortunate accident in December, 1875, while

Fig. 92.—Old method of generating hydrogen.

engaged on their duties in a balloon, built by Tissandier, which fell from a height of 750 ft. in consequence of a defective valve. Laussedat, Mangin, and Renard escaped with broken legs, while the remainder of the eight passengers had more or less severe contusions.

Soon afterwards Laussedat reported his proposals to the Minister of War, and asked for the necessary funds to be placed at his disposal.   Money was, however, forthcoming only to a very limited extent.   Hitherto they had been allowed the sum of £32 a year, and they were probably surprised to find that they were now to be allotted the sum of £240 to meet immediate requirements.   Still much good work was done.   Renard had carefully considered the question of generating the gas, and had constructed an apparatus for generating hydrogen from sulphuric acid and iron, which worked well.   In 1877 the castle at Chalais was placed at their disposal.   Nearly a hundred years had elapsed since it was first put to a similar purpose, and Renard now equipped it with all the necessary appliances.   He arranged a workshop, chemical and physical laboratories, gas generators, testing machines, and a meteorological observatory.   It is astonishing to find what he was able to do.   He had the assistance of a professional aeronaut, a sergeant, four sappers, and a ropemaker, and between them they soon managed to construct a balloon.   Laussedat indeed considered that he was too energetic, and proposed to apply to other purposes the sum of £8,000, which

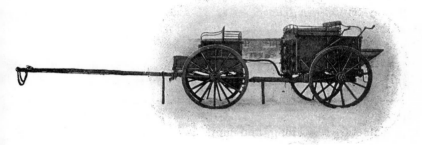

FIG. 93.—Modern gas waggon.

the Government had now allotted at Gambetta's suggestion. But Renard contrived to resist this pressure, and it was then arranged that he was to be allowed to proceed independently on his own lines.   After an inspection by Gambetta, the Government voted money for the further development of the work. The establishment at Chalais-Meudon was enlarged, and Captain Paul Renard was ordered to give his brother such assistance as he required.   Gradually the work proceeded, each company having three balloons ; the two main ones were to be suitable for use either as captive balloons or otherwise.

    The ordinary balloon, now employed, has a capacity of 19,000 cubic feet and a diameter of 33 ft.   It is intended to be filled with hydrogen, and to take two passengers to a height of 1,650 ft.

The so-called auxiliary balloon has a capacity of 9,200 cubic feet, carrying one person ; but it has the advantage of being more easily worked.   In addition there is a gasometer, with a capacity of 2,120 cubic feet, for the storage of hydrogen.   However, in most cases cylinders containing compressed gas are taken with the balloon in carts, and this dispenses with the use of the gasometer. For use in the forts, balloons with a capacity of 34,500 cubic feet are used, and can be filled with coal gas in case of need, though ordinarily they are intended to be used with hydrogen.   The methods of construction will be described later.

Since 1880 the balloonists have always taken part in the manœuvres, and it was soon seen that the waggons were too cumbersome.   It also required three hours to fill the balloons, and this would make them practically useless in an emergency. The system of gas generators was therefore abolished, in so far as their use in the field was concerned, and the English method was adopted, which consists in taking cylinders with compressed gas for the purpose.   By these means it is possible to fill the balloon in fifteen or twenty minutes.   Sufficient gas to fill four balloons can be carried on eight waggons.   Each waggon takes eight cylinders, weighing in all two tons ; a cylinder is one foot in diameter, 15 ft. long, and contains 1,250 cubic feet of gas under a pressure of 300 atmospheres.   One waggon, with a total weight of rather more than three tons, will carry 10,000 cubic feet of gas, which is sufficient to fill an auxiliary balloon.   This new apparatus was brought into use during the manœuvres of 1890, and was divided into two columns.   The first consisted of the balloon, winches, and gas waggons, while the second was composed of other gas waggons, together with the generators and compressors. General Loizillon mounted the car, and examined the position of the enemy from a distance of eight miles, giving all his orders from the balloon.   At the manœuvres of 1891, General Gallifet also made an ascent, and issued his orders in the same way, remaining in the car for two and a half hours.

Experiments were also made to test the use of balloons in the navy.   These were successful, and installations were consequently set up at Toulon, and at Lagoubran, near Brest, where a certain number of officers and men go into training every year. Balloons were also used to search for submarines, and in June, 1902, Lieutenant Baudic was drowned near Lagoubran while engaged on a work of this kind. The ascents were generally made with a captive balloon, secured to the stern of the vessel, and in August the approach of the submarine " Gustave Zedé " was discovered in this way. However, in 1904 the marine corps was disbanded, a measure which called forth a certain amount of disapproval, but was doubtless justified by the results of experience. Still the advantages to be derived from the use of balloons for reconnoitring purposes along the coast seem fairly obvious. It would thus be possible to detect the approach of the enemy at a much greater distance than would be the case if observations were only made from the ground level, provided, of course, that the weather was reasonably clear.

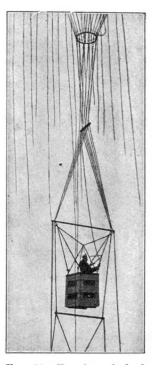

FIG. 94.—French method of suspending the basket for an observer.

Various alterations have lately been made in the general organisation of the French Balloon Corps ; and, in particular, a great improvement has been introduced by making it altogether independent of any experimental work. Consequently all their attention is devoted to instructing the men and increasing their smartness in the field. A special laboratory has been erected in Paris for the study of problems directly or indirectly connected with ballooning, and for carrying out experimental work. The central offices are at Chalais-Meudon, where instruction is given to all grades in the service, and where the main workshop is situated. Four companies are stationed at Versailles with the usual number of officers and men, and there are also companies at Verdun, Epinal, Toul, and Belfort, with all the necessary appliances.   At Versailles, Montpellier, Arras, and Grenoble the organisation is subject to the general control of the engineers, and would only become an independent unit in the case of mobilisation.   In all these places manœuvres on a small scale take place every year.

The equipment in the field is rather different from that used in the fortresses.   In the latter, compressed gas in cylinders is

FIG. 95.—One of the balloons is pegged down in the open field, and the other is sunk in a specially prepared pit.

not used; it is generated from time to time as required.   But waggons are also provided in the forts, and could easily be used in case of emergency.   The provision of skilled aeronauts is also a matter of importance, and this is part of the work done at Chalais-Meudon, where every year a certain number of men, principally from the educated classes, are instructed practically and theoretically in the art.   They receive the title of "Aéronaute breveté" after passing an examination, and are instructed to place themselves at the disposal of the authorities of a given fortress in the event of mobilisation.   The French Balloon Clubs also receive assistance from the Minister of War with a view to placing the services of their members at the disposal of the country in case of need, and they receive lessons in the art of construction for this purpose. The French army therefore disposes of the services of a large number of experienced men, who could, in case of need, do much useful work in the fortresses and elsewhere. It has both a civil and military organisation to procure a number of skilled aeronauts, and under these conditions there should be a sufficient supply.

The balloonists, enrolled by Captain Renard, had their first experience of actual warfare in 1884 in Tonkin. General Courbet took a detachment with him under the command of Captain Cuvelier, consisting of two officers, 13 non-commissioned officers, and 23 men. The appliances were designed with a view to easy transport,

FIG. 96.—Front and rear waggons of a modern gas equipment for use in the field.

(From " Die Geschichte der Luftschiffer-Abteilung.")

and the gas was generated by heating granulated zinc with bisulphate of potash. The balloon, which was not of the normal type, took 9,200 cubic feet of gas, and a hand-winch for controlling its movements was carried on the tool-waggon. The commanding officer reported that the detachment had been strengthened by the addition of some artillerymen and some coolies, and that good work had been done. They were particularly useful in finding a way through more or less track-less marshes, where the cavalry were unable to penetrate, and where small reconnoitring parties were very liable to be ambushed in the dense bamboo forests. At the bombardment of the town of Hong-Hoa the firing of the guns was directed from the balloon, and in the same way the retreat of the enemy was signalled, with the result that the order was given to advance to the attack. In the following year, they were attached to the reconnoitring party under General Negrier, who frequently mounted the car for purposes of observation. In all subsequent colonial wars the balloonists have been employed in the French army, as, for instance, in Madagascar in 1895, and Taku in 1900.

Cases often arise in which there is no immediate use for the balloon on an expedition, and the time is therefore employed in photographic work, so that the country may be mapped out and the salient features of the landscape recorded in case they may be of service at a later stage of the operations. The photographs can also be carefully developed into maps, or they may be merely stuck together on a sheet of paper as a kind of rough guide to any detachment that may have to pass along the road. This work has been found very useful in countries of which no maps exist.

The Minister of War is said to be satisfied with the results produced by balloons in colonial wars, and in spite of the cost of their operations (which is by no means small) the work is likely to be still further developed and brought to a higher state of efficiency.

GERMANY.

In Germany a Balloon Corps was organised in 1884, although experiments made in 1872 by a regiment of Engineers had turned out unsatisfactorily. The German Balloon Club had been founded in Berlin in 1882, and was busily occupied with the study of the question, having many officers among its members.[1]

[1] " Die Geschichte der Kgl. Preussischen Luftschiffer-Abteilung," 1902. Published by Meisenbach, Riffarth & Co.

The original detachment consisted of thirty-three men and four officers, viz., Captain Buchholz, and Lieutenants von Tschudi, von Hagen, and Moedebeck. Their first task was to arrange an experimental station for captive balloons, to be used for artillery purposes. They had the assistance of a professional aeronaut, named Opitz, and settled down to work at the Eastern Railway Station in Berlin, which was placed at their disposal. In this way they had a large hall as a kind of drilling-ground, the waiting-rooms, etc., being turned into workshops and barracks, and the platforms into ropemakers' runs. It was thought necessary to exercise the men without delay in the work of practical ballooning, and arrangements were therefore made to have the use of a balloon for this purpose. This was done by agreement with a professional aeronaut who made ascents at Schöneberg on Sundays; the corps had the use of his balloon on the other days of the week, until such time as they should have constructed one for themselves. Within three years they had already made eleven balloons, and gained much useful experience with regard to materials, varnishes, ropes, gas, etc. The ordinary gas from the mains was used; but for active warfare it was intended to follow the example of the French, and to generate hydrogen either by the dry or wet way. However, it was found that the inflation took too long, and lasted for three or four hours; consequently the English method was adopted, and compressed gas in steel cylinders was used. Waggons were built for holding

FIG. 97.—Waggon carrying tools and appliances, the balloon being packed on the top.

(From " Die Geschichte der Luftschiffer-Abteilung.")

twenty cylinders, each of which contained 250 cubic feet at a
pressure of 200 atmospheres.   A steam winch was made in order
to wind up the rope holding the captive balloon; but this was
soon found to be a clumsy arrangement, as steam was often not
available at the moment when it was wanted.   It was therefore
replaced by a hand-winch, which would be always ready for work
and could be driven by the men on the spot.   Gradually the
detachment increased.   In 1886 it consisted of five officers and
fifty men; in 1893 there were six officers and 140 men; and in
1901 it formed a battalion of two companies, together with a
team of horses.   Horses are provided specially for the corps in
order that they may be able to carry out such tactical movements
as may be required in manœuvres or in war.

The corps were mainly regarded as being for the purposes
of the Intelligence Department, and were consequently directly
under the control of the·General Staff; but in so far as uniform
and discipline were concerned they were regarded as being part
of the Railway Regiment.   In order to distinguish them from
the engineers of the Railway Regiment the men had the letter
" L " on the shoulder-straps, and also carried a rifle.   Barracks
were provided for them on the Tempelhofer Feld.

In 1890 a military school for ballooning was started by the
Bavarian army in Munich, and consisted of three officers and
thirty men.   They were attached to the Railway Regiment, and
subject to the control of the engineers and the authorities of the
fortresses.   The division was afterwards made into a company.
The non-commissioned officers and men have the letter " L "
on their shoulder-straps, and wear the uniform of the Railway
Regiment, whereas the officers retain the uniforms of the regiments to which they were previously attached.   A number of
officers from other regiments also receive instruction, both of a
theoretical and practical kind.

The balloonists have a many-sided activity in Prussia and
Bavaria, and are always present at the manœuvres.   They
also take part in summer in various artillery exercises.   At
Heligoland and Kiel experiments have been carried out with
balloons on the men-of-war.   At the manœuvres a signalling

FIG. 98.—Balloons used for wireless telegraphy on the Tempelhofer Feld.

(From "Die Geschichte der Luftschiffer-Abteilung.")

balloon is placed directly under the control of the commanding officer, and has the duty of conveying in all directions
the orders that have been issued. The signals are conveyed
by inflated spherical or cylindrical air-bags, which are kept

A.   M in position in windy weather by means of a load of ballast. The Kaiser took much interest in the arrangements of the signalling balloon, and was present at the first successful trials.

The Balloon Corps has rendered help in the matter of scientific investigations, particularly in the meteorological department. It has assisted in the exploration of the upper layers of the atmosphere by means of the " Humboldt " and the " Phœnix," a work which also received much encouragement from the Kaiser. Captain von Tschudi, one of the officers of the corps, superintended the preparation and inflation of the balloon " Prussia," which was filled with hydrogen, and had a capacity of nearly 300,000 cubic feet. It subsequently rose to a height of 34,500 ft., which is the greatest altitude yet reached. The battalion also takes part in the ascents organised by international agreement for the purpose of meteorological observation. The expedition to the South Pole started from Kiel on August 11th, 1901, under Professor von Drygalski, and here again valuable help was given by the military authorities in the arrangements for the balloons, which were made from their designs, and have since proved of great assistance amongst the ice-fields of the Antarctic Ocean.

When Marconi developed his system of wireless telegraphy orders were received that it was to be tested by the Balloon Corps, so as to find whether it was likely to be suitable for military purposes. This added a new field to their activities, demanding much study, and a great deal of experimental work. Captain von Sigsfeld was the moving spirit in the matter, and thanks to his efforts, a system was developed which, since his untimely death, has been extended throughout the army. Lately this work has been removed from the balloon section, and has more fitly taken its place in the Telegraph Department. But, for the purposes of the war in South-West Africa, a division was sent out that was wholly recruited from the balloon section, and succeeded in giving useful help.

ENGLAND.

Experiments with captive balloons were made in England in 1862. A military school for ballooning was started at Chatham

FIG. 99.—Barracks for the Prussian Balloon Corps at Tegel.

(From " Die Geschichte der Luftschiffer-Abteilung.") .

in 1879 under Captain Templer, and in the following year the
24th company of the Royal Engineers was instructed in the

necessary field-work. Manœuvres took place at Aldershot every
year, in which the ballooning section played their part ; and a
factory with a school for ballooning was consequently erected
there. It has been already mentioned that the English were the
first to introduce the use of hydrogen, compressed in steel
cylinders, which has greatly simplified work on the field of battle.
Military balloons, as used in England, have very light and airtight envelopes. They are made out of goldbeater's skins, and
their size ranges from 7,000 to 10,000 cubic feet. These sizes
are much smaller than those in use in other countries, but the

Fig. 100.—A collection of exploded gas cylinders.

cost of making them is very great. The gas is mostly prepared
by the electrolytic decomposition of water, and is stored in steel
cylinders, 8 ft. long and $5\frac{1}{2}$ ins. in diameter. In consequence of
the low pressure, a cylinder weighing 80 lbs. only contains
127 cubic feet of gas. In addition to this there are also the
usual generators, which employ sulphuric acid and iron.

England has greater experience in colonial wars than any
other nation, and balloons have always been taken on such
expeditions. They have thus been used in Egypt, Bechuanaland,
and China, as well as in the Boer war. Four balloon sections
were employed against the Boers, and the following instances of
their useful services may be recorded. A balloon for observation
purposes was used in Ladysmith for twenty-nine days, and the

positions of the Boer guns were often discovered by its means. Several times they were struck by shells during the siege. At Spion Kop it was considered, as the result of balloon observations, that the Boer position was impregnable. A section under Captain Jones formed part of Lord Methuen's column, and was used for several days in the neighbourhood of Magersfontein, the balloon being finally destroyed in a storm. It was also of service to Lord Roberts at Paardeberg in discovering the precise position of Cronje's force, and in directing the fire of the guns. Another section was sent to Kimberley and Mafeking, and did a fortnight's scouting work at Fourteen Streams. Laborious marches were also made with inflated balloons for survey purposes. At the beginning of the war there was a great dearth of reliable maps, and the want was gradually supplied by means of photographs, taken from balloons. In places high mountain ranges had to be crossed, and the height to which the balloons would rise in such places was naturally found to be much reduced, a result of the physical laws which have been expounded in an earlier chapter. The gas was at first sent out from England to Capetown, but at a later stage of the war, gas generators and compressors were used.

In China the balloons were not used for discovering the positions of the enemy, but for the preparation of maps, and in this useful service the English were ably assisted by the French. The general experience of many colonial wars has convinced the English of the importance of the services which a balloon section can render, and in case of mobilisation the corps will be found to be in good working order.

AUSTRIA.

A civilian was the first to introduce the balloon to military circles in Austria. Some isolated experiments had doubtless been made, as in the case of Uchatius, who tried to drop bombs into Venice from balloons, but only succeeded in endangering the lives of his own comrades. Again, in 1866, a captive balloon was built to assist the forts round Vienna; but on the first

occasion that it was taken into the field it escaped from the
soldiers who were holding the ropes.

In 1888, an extensive exhibition of all things relating to
ballooning was arranged by Viktor Silberer, a well known
amateur, who took great interest in the sport. The success of
the exhibition was very great, and it attracted general attention
to the subject. The inevitable committee was of course formed,
with instructions to visit London, Paris, and Berlin in order to

find out all that was known.
Voluminous reports were presented
in due course, and in 1890 a
.military course of aeronautics was
started. It was placed under the
direction of Silberer, who had
constructed a ballooning establishment for himself in the Prater at
Vienna. Practical instruction was
given both with captive and free
balloons, and the theoretical aspect
of the matter was also considered.
The value of the instruction was
considered evident, and it was
continued during the next year and

Fig. 101.—Captain Hinterstoisser,   attended by a larger number of
of the Austrian Balloon Corps.
                                        men and officers.

In 1893 a corps was organised for the special work in hand,
and consisted of two officers, four non-commissioned officers, and
twenty-six men, who were placed under the control of the
artillery stationed at Vienna. Buildings for the purpose were
erected, and the whole organisation was placed under the command of Captain Trieb. It was considered advisable to study
the methods used in Prussia, and Lieutenant Hinterstoisser was
therefore sent to Berlin to make all necessary enquiries and to
acquaint himself with the methods there adopted. He subsequently took command of the corps, and the development of its
activity and efficiency has lately been very marked. The numbers are still small; but in case of pressing need, such as would

arise in time of war, recourse would probably be had to the Aero Club, of which Silberer is president.

RUSSIA.

The experiments made by Leppich in 1812 have already been mentioned ; they were entirely unsuccessful, and it was not until 1869 that the matter was further mooted. General Todleben then formed a committee for the study of the military aspects of ballooning, the main idea being that it might probably be possible to introduce some improvement in the signalling arrangements. The work was mostly done by the navy ; and signalling balloons were constructed which displayed flags by daytime and electric lights by night. In September, 1884, a special detachment was formed, consisting of one officer (who later became Colonel von Kowanko) and twenty-two men. The Russians bought their entire outfit, including gas generators, from French manufacturers, nearly all of them receiving orders in due course, viz., Brisson, Yon, Godard, and Lachambre.

It is curious to remember that the Russians ordered a dirigible balloon from the firm of Yon in the year 1886, but when it was tested, they refused to take it on the ground that it appeared to be useless. Experiments were also made with a *Montgolfière*, constructed by Godard ; its capacity was 110,000 cubic feet, but the tests, which were made at Brussels, were also unsatisfactory. A great deal of work was done by the navy, about 1894, with balloons in connection with the unsuccessful attempt to discover the warship " Russalka," which had been sunk in the Gulf of Finland.

The organisation of the corps was gradually evolved. A school for aeronauts was started at Wolkowo Polje, near St. Petersburg, after the French model, instruction being given both for the purposes of the army and navy, and extensive workshops being constructed. The establishment included seven officers and eighty-eight men, from which the detachment for the manœuvres was selected. They also provided any officers that were required for ballooning purposes. The apparatus used in the field was

extremely inconvenient, owing to the fact that the Russians had
not adopted the system of compressed gas in steel cylinders.
At the manœuvres of 1903 no less than 150 waggons were
required by the Balloon Corps, and this had the result of interfering greatly with the movements of the troops. Consequently
General Dragomiroff expressed himself as being very dissatisfied
with their arrangements. But the outbreak of the war with
Japan changed the system ; the spherical balloon was given up,
and a number of kite-balloons were ordered in Germany. The
method of generating hydrogen from sulphuric acid and iron
was abandoned. It was considered necessary that everything
should be capable of transport either on mules or in two-wheeled
carts, and the gas was therefore generated by the reaction
between aluminium and caustic soda, all the materials required
to inflate one balloon being carried on twenty mules. A battalion
of the East Siberian Balloon Corps was formed for the campaign,
consisting of two companies, which reached the front in
September, 1904, and another company was already with the
first army under Linevitch. The reports which have been made
public as to the results of the campaign from the point of view
of ballooning experience are very meagre. Reconnoitring work
of various kinds was often done under the heavy fire of the
Japanese, and to judge from the number of decorations that
were afterwards bestowed it would appear that the second company must in some special way have distinguished itself. The
balloon which had been intended to be used in the forts of Port
Arthur was loaded on board a ship and subsequently captured ;
and the same fate probably overtook a German steamer, named
Lahn, which was intended to help in the service, but disappeared
mysteriously. At the present moment Russia is devoting herself
to the reorganisation of the service in the light of the experience
gained from the war. It may also be mentioned that kites have
been used, principally in the navy, for purposes of observation ;
but the results have not been altogether encouraging. Reference
will be further made to the matter in a later chapter.

CHAPTER XV.

THE balloon disappeared from the army of the United States for thirty years until a fresh effort was made in 1892. The material then employed was goldbeater's skin, and a balloon of this kind, together with net and basket, was shown at the Exhibition at Chicago. In the following year English methods were adopted, and storage accommodation was supplied at Fort Logan. Experiments were also carried out by Lieutenant Wise on the use of kites, which have been already described.

In the war against Spain, Major Maxfield with his company did good work in the field. At Santiago de Cuba the observations which were made of the arrangements of the forts were of great value, and it was also similarly known that Admiral Cervera's fleet was in the harbour. Later in the campaign the Spaniards succeeded in chasing the balloon through the dense brushwood with their cavalry, and in bringing it to earth with some well directed rifle fire. This was merely the result of a lack of caution, and helps to emphasise the fairly obvious fact that the balloonist must be on his guard against surprises of this kind. It is insufficient for him to direct his telescope towards the horizon, more especially as it is also a part of his duty to report to the commanding officer as to the movement of any of his own troops which may no longer be in touch with headquarters.

After 1890 a disposition was shown to imitate German models in America. Gradually the organisation was completed both for the employment of balloons in forts and in the field. Most countries started by copying French methods, but lately there has been a decided tendency to follow German practice. The following notes give brief particulars of the various countries in alphabetical order.

In Belgium the necessary materials were ordered from

Lachambre, of Paris, in 1886, and a company of an engineering regiment in Antwerp was allotted for ballooning work. A school was started in the following year, and trials were made of hot air balloons on the Godard system, as well as of others for signalling purposes of the dirigible type. Lately the kite-balloon has been introduced.

During the exhibition in Philippopolis a small company was organised by Eugene Godard in Bulgaria; but it can hardly be said to have resulted in any real military organisation.

China claims for itself the credit of having invented *Montgolfières* centuries before Montgolfier was born; but it has since somewhat failed to keep in the van of modern progress. It must, however, be admitted that in 1886 Yon, of Paris, was instructed to deliver two balloons, with all necessary appurtenances, in Tientsin, and several months were spent in inducing them to rise in the air. This delay was caused by the fact that the varnished silk melted into a slimy mess on account of the tropical heat. Meanwhile suitable storage accommodation was provided, together with a ground from which the ascents could be made, and the various exercises carrried out. Naturally enough the plans included the erection of a magnificent pagoda, from which the presiding viceroy could conveniently follow the manœuvres. After all the preparations had been completed, it was found that the balloons were completely useless, and more were therefore ordered with all haste from the same contractors. These arrived in time to fall into the hands of the Russians at the capture of Tientsin in 1900, and nothing further is known about the state of the art in China.

Unsuccessful experiments were made in Denmark between 1807 and 1811 with a dirigible balloon; but it was not till 1886 that an officer was sent to Belgium, England, and France, to study the question. This journey resulted in the giving of an order to Yon, of Paris, for a complete equipment for one balloon. When this arrived it served for various exercises till it was eventually worn out. Nothing further has been done in the matter.

In 1885 a complete ballooning outfit was ordered by the

Italian Government from Yon, of Paris, and a company was formed, which has done much work in the field. English methods were, however, followed in 1887, goldbeater's skin being used as a material, and steel cylinders being introduced for compressed gas. At the same time French methods were not entirely discarded; silk balloons and gas generators were employed to some extent. A company was sent to the front at

FIG. 102.—After a landing.

the time of the war in Abyssinia, the balloons being transported on mules and camels. The German kite-balloon was employed in the navy in 1900, and in 1901 the system was still more widely adopted.

A legend is still told of a Japanese soldier who mounted in a kite during the siege of a fortress in 1869, and threw bombs on the heads of the enemy. This may be true, but it has a slightly mythical sound, not altogether out of keeping with the air of mystery which veiled Japan at that time from the gaze of the outer world. The first fact which is definitely known about

Japanese ballooning activity in its military aspect is that the firm Yon, of Paris, supplied them with the necessary materials in 1890, though it was supposed at the time that the Germans might have received the order owing to the known partiality of Prince Komatzu for their products. However, the Japanese had the same experience as the Chinese, and found the varnished silk balloons useless for their purpose. Many enquiries and experiments were therefore made with a view to finding suitable material, varnishes, etc., and finally a kite-balloon was ordered from the firm of Riedinger, in Augsburg. Experiments were still being made at the time of the outbreak of the war against the Russians, and balloons and kites of all shapes and sizes were soon to be seen on the field of battle. In particular they did good work in directing the fire of the Japanese guns at Port Arthur, so that several Russian magazines were exploded by the shells.

Morocco ordered balloons from Surcouf, of Paris, in 1902, and at the same time a steam-winch for captive balloons was delivered by Schneider, of Creusot.

The Netherlands procured their supply from Lachambre in 1886, and this was handed over to a regiment of engineers stationed at Utrecht. A company was also formed in Batavia, and the German kite-balloon was introduced in 1902. Norway has a corps provided with German material. In 1893 Godard instructed some Roumanian officers in the art of ballooning, and an order was afterwards given to the firm for the supply of balloons to a regiment of engineers stationed at Bucharest. In 1902 an officer was sent to Germany and Austria to study their methods, and this led to the introduction of the " Sigsfeld-Parseval " system of captive balloons into the Roumanian army.

Sweden had a similar experience to that of Roumania and the Netherlands. In 1897 a corps was formed in the fortress of Vaxholm, and material was supplied by the firms of Godard and Surcouf, in Paris. In 1900 an officer was sent to Versailles to study the French methods of instruction. A year later Lieutenant Saloman was sent to Vienna for a similar purpose, and in 1905

Lieutenant von Rosen was attached for several months to the corps stationed at Berlin. A balloon-ship was introduced in the Swedish Navy in 1903, intended for purposes of coast defence. It carried a German kite-balloon of a capacity of 25,000 cubic feet, which is filled with hydrogen, produced electrolytically, and compressed in cylinders.

In Switzerland a corps was formed and stationed at Berne. It was originally fitted out with French supplies, but in 1901

FIG. 103.—A balloon ready for inflation.

orders were given in Germany for further requirements. Servia has used balloons since 1888 for signalling purposes, and has lately proposed to introduce them for reconnoitring work.

Spain has also been very actively engaged on the work. In 1884 it was proposed to furnish their own supplies, but five years later orders were given to Yon, both for balloons and generators. On June 27th, 1889, the first and only Royal ascent that has ever been made took place, when Queen Marie Christina mounted the car in Madrid. Lately officers have been sent to all parts of Europe to study the latest improvements, and in 1900 the kite-balloon, due to Sigsfeld and Parseval, was introduced into the corps, which was stationed at Guadalajara. It is now under the command of Colonel Vives y Viches, who has furthered the development of its efficiency in many directions. His interest in scientific work was shown by the assistance he afforded to the meteorologists and astronomers on the occasion of the last eclipse of the sun, and he has also encouraged his men to do photographic work and train carrier pigeons.

It will therefore be seen that almost every civilised nation is developing its ballooning capacities, and lately there has been a tendency towards the adoption of German models, evidence of which is to be found in the fact that within the last nine years the firm of Riedinger, in Augsburg, has supplied more than 500 spherical and kite-balloons.

CHAPTER XVI.

BALLOONS can be filled either with hydrogen, water gas, or coal gas. The preparation of hydrogen can be effected in various ways. The method originally suggested by Charles is probably the simplest, and consists in the addition of dilute sulphuric acid to iron. But practically it leads to difficulties. The newly-generated gas is very hot, and adulterated with a certain amount of acid vapours. It must therefore be cooled and washed free from impurities. This is done by allowing it to pass through flowing water, after which it is dried by coming into contact with substances which easily absorb moisture, such as calcium chloride. It is then ready to be passed into the balloon. This method is still employed with various modifications; iron can, of of course, be replaced by zinc, and sulphuric by hydrochloric acid.

The chemical formula showing the reaction is as follows, viz. :

$$H_2SO_4 + Fe = H_2 + FeSO_4,$$

i.e., the addition of sulphuric acid to iron forms hydrogen and ferrous sulphate. From this formula it is possible to calculate the amount of gas that is formed. The atomic weights are $H = 1$, $S = 32$, $O = 16$, $Fe = 56$. A cubic foot of hydrogen weighs 0·09 oz. Suppose it is required to know how much iron and sulphuric acid will be needed to generate sufficient hydrogen to fill a balloon of 20,000 cubic feet capacity. We find, first of all, the weight of the hydrogen, which is $20,000 \times 0·09$ oz., *i.e.*, 1 cwt. The amount of iron will be 28 times the weight of the hydrogen, and will therefore amount to 1 ton 8 cwt. ; the weight of sulphuric acid will be 49 times that of the hydrogen, and is consequently 2 tons 9 cwt. In the process of the work losses of one kind or another are sure to arise, added to which the iron will probably be rusty, and the sulphuric acid will certainly

contain impurities. It will therefore be found that in actual
working about 20 per cent. more sulphuric acid and iron will be
required than is allowed for in the calculations.

If hydrogen is generated on this system it starts very fast,
but gradually the evolution of the gas becomes slower, until it
finally ceases altogether, owing to the formation of a film of

FIG. 104.—Ascent of a captive balloon in calm weather.

The car contains Colonel Vives y Viches, of Spain, Lieutenant von Corvin, of
Austria, and Captain Sperling, of Germany.

ferrous sulphate on the surface of the iron. The so-called
circulation system was therefore introduced as an improvement, by which the fluids are kept in a state of circulation,
and the iron sulphate is steadily removed in consequence.
It is very important to use pure sulphuric acid, because the
cheaper kinds contain arsenic. The use of impure acid has led
to several fatal accidents, and the smallest amount of arsenic

produces such an effect on the red corpuscles in the blood that death quickly results.   The vats or barrels must be lined with lead, which is the only common metal not attacked by sulphuric acid.   If suitable arrangements are made, it is possible to generate a large quantity of gas in a very short space of time.   In 1878, Henry Giffard prepared nearly 900,000 cubic feet of gas in

FIG. 105.—Ascent of a captive balloon on a windy day.

three days, using in the process 180 tons of sulphuric acid and 80 tons of iron turnings.

It has been already mentioned that the first military use of the balloon took place soon after the French Revolution, and that one of the conditions was that sulphuric acid was not to be used for the generation of the hydrogen, seeing that all available sulphur was required for making gunpowder.   Coutelle therefore devised an arrangement by which Lavoisier's method of passing

A.   N steam over red-hot iron was used for the generation of hydrogen. Some iron retorts (old cannons were actually used) were built into a furnace and kept at a red heat. They were then filled with iron turnings, and steam was turned on. Hydrogen was therefore generated, as shown by the following formula—

$$Fe_3 + 4\,H_2O = Fe_3O_4 + H_8.$$

If this method is used, a cubic foot of hydrogen will require 1·881 oz. of iron, and 0·806 oz. of water. Improvements were also made in this arrangement, but the main principle remained the same.

The purest gas is obtained from the electrolytic decomposition of water. A little sulphuric acid is added to the water in order to make it conduct. On passing an electric current, the water is decomposed into its constituents, which are hydrogen and oxygen, the hydrogen going to the negative and the oxygen to the positive pole. In Germany the ordinary way is to produce hydrogen as a bye-product in the soda works, as, for instance, at Bitterfeld, near Halle, and Griesheim, near Frankfort. The cost of carriage is considerable, so that it is worth 14s. per 1,000 cubic feet, whereas at the works it might be had almost for the asking. The cost of the gas, if prepared from sulphuric acid and iron, would probably be nearly twice as much.

Water-gas is obtained by passing steam over red-hot carbon, and consists of a mixture of hydrogen and carbon monoxide.

A large number of other reactions can be used to generate hydrogen, but they are either dangerous or costly or cumbrous. Amongst these may be mentioned the reaction between slaked lime and zinc, between steam and fused zinc, between sodium and water, or potassium and water, and between zinc or aluminium and either of the caustic alkalis.

In any case the generation of the gas on the field of battle would be out of the question, and the English method of using the compressed gas in steel cylinders is now everywhere employed. A cylinder with walls 0·187 in. thick weighs about 88 lbs. and contains 140 cubic feet under a pressure of 120 or 130 atmospheres. A military waggon carries 35 cylinders, and the gas is allowed to pass into the balloon by opening the valve at the top of the cylinder. When a balloon is to be inflated, several waggons are drawn up at the side, and the various cylinders are all connected to a tube, which conveys the gas to the interior of the balloon. The inflation occupies from 15 to 20 minutes.

FIG. 106.—Steel cylinder for containing hydrogen.

Coal gas is only used for free balloons, and was first proposed by Green in 1818. The "lift" due to the use of the hydrogen or coal gas has been already studied in an earlier chapter, and it was there shown that the size of the balloon depends on the amount of lift that is wanted. Therefore captive balloons, which are generally filled with hydrogen, are much smaller than free balloons filled with coal gas. If it were not for the matter of expense the use of coal gas would certainly be discontinued.

The sphere is the body which combines the smallest surface with the greatest volume, and therefore all free balloons are spherical in shape. The size is obviously dependent on the weight of the load to be lifted. Generally speaking, a balloon to carry 3 or 4 persons would have a capacity of 45,000 cubic feet or thereabouts. The higher the balloon is to rise, the greater

Fig. 107.—Section through steel cylinder.

must be its capacity, and, of course, with hydrogen, much greater heights can be reached than with coal gas. If long journeys are to be undertaken, large balloons are necessary. This arises from the fact that leakage is continually occurring, and it must be possible to neutralise this by throwing out ballast. In other words, the balloon must be capable of carrying a considerable load of ballast, and must therefore have a large capacity. The materials used for the construction of the envelope are very numerous. Dirigible balloons may have a framework of aluminium sheets, but it is better to use some kind of woven material. Paper and rubber are only used for pilot balloons; they are also useful for meteorological purposes, and are sent to great heights in the manner suggested by Assmann. But they have very small power of resistance, and have generally done their work after making one ascent. The Italian balloonist, da Schio, put a rubber band inside the envelope, for purposes that have been already explained.

Goldbeater's skin, which is so called owing to its having been used for beating gold into thin sheets, is used in England for making the envelopes of balloons. These skins are about 36 inches by 10 inches; they are very light and hold the gas well without needing to be specially varnished. They are laid in layers, one upon the other, sometimes as many as eight being used. Twenty-five square feet of the skin weigh about 1 ounce, and would probably be used in layers of five. Unfortunately they are extremely expensive, and not very suitable for continuous exposure to the weather. There is, however, an advantage in using balloons of this type in colonial wars, partly because they are very light, and partly because the tendency to develop leaks is slight. Seeing that under such conditions the generation of gas, to make good any leakage, would be a difficult matter, it will be evident that this advantage is worth paying for.

Of woven materials, the most important are silk and cotton. Linen is sometimes used in forts in time of war, but seldom otherwise. Silk is both light and strong, but also expensive, and little capable of resisting the weather. Vegetable substances withstand atmospheric influences better than those of animal origin. In France, the military balloons are made of the so-called "ponghée" silk, which is of an inferior quality, and therefore cheaper. One layer is sufficient on account of the great strength of the material. When cambric is used, it is necessary to have two layers, which are placed diagonally, one on top of the other, so that the pattern of the one is at an angle of 45 degrees to that of the other. This much increases the strength of the covering. It is necessary that it should be very closely woven throughout, and that it should be in all places of the same strength, special machines having been designed for testing its resisting power. All envelopes made of silk or cotton require to be varnished in some way. The oldest method was to coat it with rubber solution, as proposed by Charles, applied by hot rollers. This is also vulcanised with sulphur, which helps to preserve it. However, light has the effect of gradually disintegrating rubber, and this can to some extent be prevented by

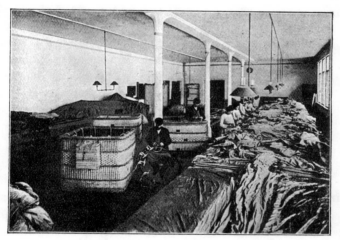

FIG. 108.—Making balloon envelopes in Riedinger's factory, in Augsburg.

colouring it with a yellow paint. A better plan is to varnish the envelope with linseed oil, though it must be admitted that it has the unpleasant property of becoming very sticky in hot weather. Great care must be taken in storing such balloons, as they are very liable to catch fire spontaneously. The methods that were employed in making the old varnishes are unfortunately no longer known. Several other things have also been used for making the coverings airtight; but nothing better is known than linseed oil varnish, or rubber solution. One square foot of "ponghée" silk, as used for French military balloons, with five coats of varnish weighs 1·2 ounces, and one square foot of double thickness of cambric with five coatings of rubber solution weighs about one ounce. At any part of the covering where the wear and tear is likely to be specially great it must be stiffened by an extra layer; this is particularly the case at the parts in the neighbourhood of the valve. The spherical covering is made by sewing together a number of pieces of the material, the breadth of these pieces depending on the width in which the material is delivered. It varies generally from 20 to 55 inches, and about 2 inches must be allowed for the seams. The number of widths of material that will be needed can be found by dividing the known circumference by the width of the stuff. There will be a certain amount of tapering at the top and bottom, and instead of tedious calculations, this is usually

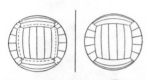

FIG. 109.—Professor Finster-walder's patterns for balloon envelopes.

adjusted by some sort of pattern, the bottom being of course exactly the same as the top. There are many different ways of working to patterns, and Professor Finsterwalder of Munich has proposed several new methods, by which a saving of 30 per cent. of material can be obtained.

He inscribes a cube in the sphere, and produces its surfaces till they intersect the surface of the sphere. In this way, six square pieces are formed with twelve dividing lines, three of which meet at a corner. It is easy to see from the diagram how the pieces are put together. The seams are covered with strips, both on the inside and outside, which are made to adhere with rubber solution.

At the bottom of the envelope the tubular opening, used for inflation, is secured to a wooden ring. It is generally left unclosed, so that, as the balloon rises, the gas can freely escape. A Frenchman, named Mallet, devised an arrangement by which air is prevented from being sucked into the balloon, and used it on one of his expeditions with success. He remained in the air for $36\frac{1}{2}$ hours, and covered a distance of 560 miles. The neck is joined to the ring by ropes; by cutting away these ropes the balloon will fall like a parachute, in case it should lose its gas.

At the top of the balloon is placed the valve, which is either in the form of a disc or of the butterfly type. Strong springs are used to close it after it has been opened for any purpose, and the valve is made tight by pressing its sharp edge against a rubber seating. It was the general custom, years ago, to lute the valve with some kind of cement to make it fit tighter ; but this plan was given up, as it was found that the valve no longer fitted tightly after it had been once opened. The valve is opened by a cord, which passes through the inflation tube to the top of the balloon.

On the covering there is a strip, which begins at a distance of 20 ins. from the valve, and extends half the way down, gradually broadening towards the

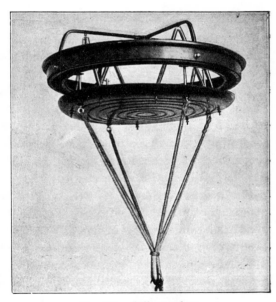

Fig. 110.—Balloon valves.

bottom ; it is covered by a similar strip on the inside, the two being cemented to the envelope, but not sewn. At the moment of reaching the ground, this strip is ripped off by means of a cord, and helps the balloon to empty suddenly. The danger of bumping along the ground is in this way generally avoided.

In Germany, the ripping-cord is always used, because it ensures a safer landing. A clever aeronaut with a little practice and with the use of the ripping-cord can alight with certainty where he chooses, even in a strong wind ; and this is a matter of great importance, particularly in order to avoid damage to growing crops. Gusty winds often make the landing a matter of difficulty ; but in this way it is possible to descend suddenly on any convenient spot that may present itself. As a matter of history, it may be stated that the first man who was called upon to pay damages was Testu-Brissy in 1786. Of course the greater part of the damage was done by the rustics who flocked to see what was going on, as, indeed, always happens ; but Testu-Brissy was expected to make good all the havoc that had been wrought by their ill-timed zeal.

In other countries the ripping-cord is only used in cases of emergency. The French sew the " corde de la misericorde " tightly down, so that it can only be pulled with a very vigoorus tug. The ripping-cord was the invention of the American aeronaut, Wise, in 1844; Godard introduced it into France in 1855. The present form in which it is used in Germany was devised by Major Gross. A safety-catch prevents it from being used unintentionally. It has indeed happened that the wetness of the ropes has caused it to act, but luckily nobody is known to have been killed by such an accident, though a sudden fall from a great height may easily cause a most serious accident. It has also happened that at the moment of reaching the ground the wind has blown the balloon over, so that the opened seam was downwards ; the consequence was that a long series of bumps and jolts followed before the balloon came to rest. This can, however, generally be prevented by the guide-rope. The ripping-panel is placed on that side of the covering to which the guide-rope is attached. The friction caused by the trailing of the rope will cause this side of the balloon to be at the back, and any shock caused by the bumping of the car against the ground will drive it upwards and give the gas a clear passage for escape. The guide-rope was first introduced by Green in 1820, in order to lessen the shock caused by the bumping of the car at the moment of landing.

In order to protect the envelope and to distribute the load equally to all its parts, it is covered with a net which is secured to the valve, and serves also to support the basket.   The ring of the balloon is either made of steel or of several thicknesses of wood ; the ropes for supporting the basket are secured to it, as well as the guide-rope and the holding-ropes.   The ring itself is hung from the network, and the basket is hung by a number of strong ropes from

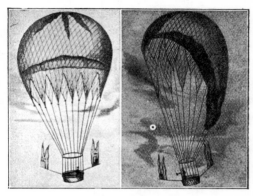

Fig. 111.—The first ripping-panel used in a balloon in 1844.

the ring.   It carries the passengers, together with such instruments and ballast as are necessary.   It is from 2 ft. 6 in. to 4 ft. deep, and the area of floor space is usually about 4 ft. by 5 ft., though this of course depends on the number of passengers it is intended to accommodate.   It is proposed by the International Balloon Association to fix the size of cars, so that they can always be easily carried on any luggage train.

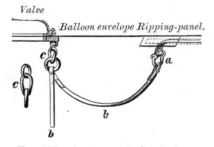

Fig. 112.—Arrangements for ripping-panel.

(From Moedebeck's " Pocketbook.")

The basket is made of rattan and osier work, the whole thing being, as it were, woven together.   The supporting ropes pass through the bottom and are woven in with it.   Buffers are fitted on the outside to take up the shocks.   It is generally padded on the inside so as to prevent damage to the passengers in case of heavy bumping.   Baskets are provided in the place of seats, and are

used to hold the instruments, provisions, etc. Aeronauts who
object to the use of the ripping-panel always take a grappling
iron, which is intended to help the landing operations, but it is
of course practically useless if the ground is rocky or frozen. The
designs for grapnels are very numerous ; all, doubtless, are
made with the intention of improving the grip under unfavourable conditions. The shocks which a balloon
sustains from bumping on a windy day are
only made worse if the grapnel succeeds,
every here and there, in getting a momentary
hold. It throws a very serious strain on all

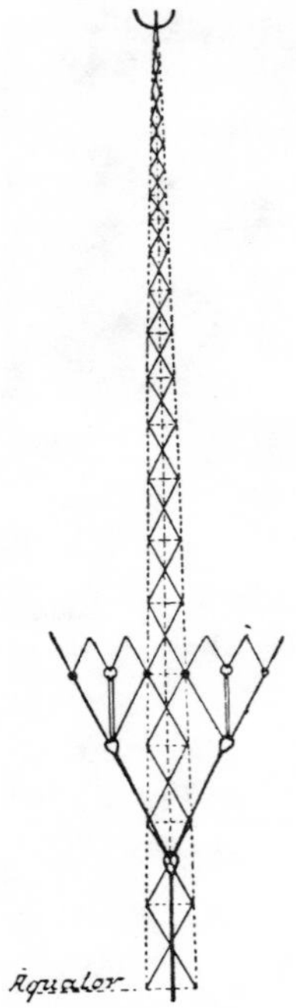

FIG. 113.—Net of a
balloon.

(From Moedebeck's
"Pocketbook.")

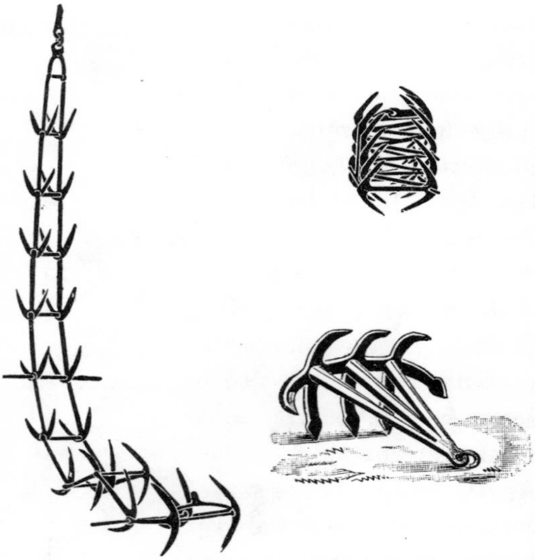

FIG. 114.—Different kinds of grapnel.

(From Moedebeck's "Pocketbook.")

parts of the construction, and would appear to offer no advantages
as compared with the use of the ripping-cord. Ballast is kept
in strong bags of sail-cloth, from 12 to 15 in. high, and 8 to
12 in. in diameter; they are suspended by four ropes from
a hook. A large piece of sail-cloth is used to protect the balloon
after it has been rolled up and is ready for packing; this is tied
on the outside of the balloon during the journey ready for use.

The Captive Balloon.

A captive balloon is very much at the mercy of the wind. If the breeze happens to be strong it will be blown hither and thither, and may indeed be pitched heavily on the ground. With a free balloon there is a feeling of perfect restfulness, and no symptom either of sea-sickness or giddiness. One glides peacefully along, and even the most giddily-inclined person feels no sensation of discomfort. It is entirely different with a captive balloon, with its incessant rolling and vibration; the discomfort is often very great. This naturally interferes with any observations, and the use of a telescope is often quite impossible. The height to which it can ascend is limited, and a captive balloon can scarcely be used in a wind exceeding 26 ft. per second.

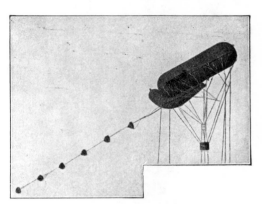

FIG. 115.—The kite-balloon designed by Major von Parseval and Captain von Sigsfeld.

All sorts of attempts have been made to improve this state of things, mainly by special systems of suspending the basket. But nothing has really been effected by these methods. The real improvement has come through the invention of the kite-balloon by Captain von Sigsfeld and Major von Parseval, and this allows the use of a captive balloon in a wind blowing at 66 ft. per second.

The main idea embodied in the kite-balloon consists in using a longish balloon, that sets itself diagonally, like a kite, to the direction of the wind. Archibald Douglas proposed it about 1845, but the balloons that were then constructed were not successful. The kite-balloon is manufactured by the firm of Riedinger in Augsburg; it is now in use in most countries, and has proved

successful even under trying conditions.   It possesses the great
advantage of having no rigid parts in its construction, with the

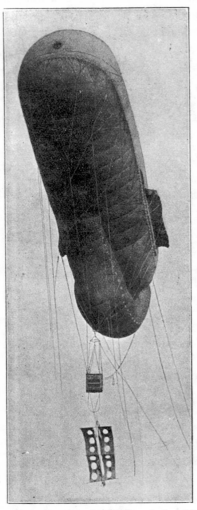

single exception of the valve.
The envelope consists of a
cylindrical portion about 50 ft.
long, with hemispherical ends,
having a radius of 10 ft.   The
shape is preserved by the use
of an air-bag, with a capacity of
5,300 cubic feet; an ingenious
arrangement is used by which
it is automatically filled by the
wind under pressure.   Suppose the balloon to be slightly
inclined to the horizontal, and
that a section is made on a
horizontal   plane   passing
through the middle of the
lower hemispherical end.   The
air-bag is then fastened to the
body of the balloon round the
edge of this sectional plane.
It is therefore joined to both
the hemispherical and cylindrical portions, and forms a
sort of inner envelope, leaving,
however, a space between the
two, into which the air can be
driven by the wind.   In this
state the balloon must be supposed to be fully inflated.   As
soon as it rises, the gas
expands, and the pressure on
the envelope would increase to
the bursting point if the gas

FIG. 115A.—The kite-balloon designed
by Major von Parseval and Major
von Sigsfeld.

were not allowed to escape.   The valve is however opened by
a cord as soon as the air-bag is completely emptied.   The careful

adjustment of this rope is therefore a matter of great importance. As soon as the volume of the balloon begins to contract, air enters through an opening into the air-bag, and the valve closes of its own accord. A non-return valve prevents the air from escaping, and the capacity of the air-bag is about 5,300 cubic feet, when it is completely filled. The air is slightly compressed by the action of the gusts of wind, and this pressure extends to the hydrogen and reacts upon the envelope. This is resisted by an internal pressure equal to that on the outside, and also by the static pressure acting on the top of the balloon, which, according to Parseval's reckonings, amounts to the pressure of a column of water, 0·3 or 0·4 in. high. If there is a sufficiency of gas the envelope must always retain its shape. As soon as the pressure increases owing to the rising of the balloon, the air is pressed out of the air-bag into a " steering-bag " through a connecting valve. The wind therefore automatically fills up any deficiency which may arise.

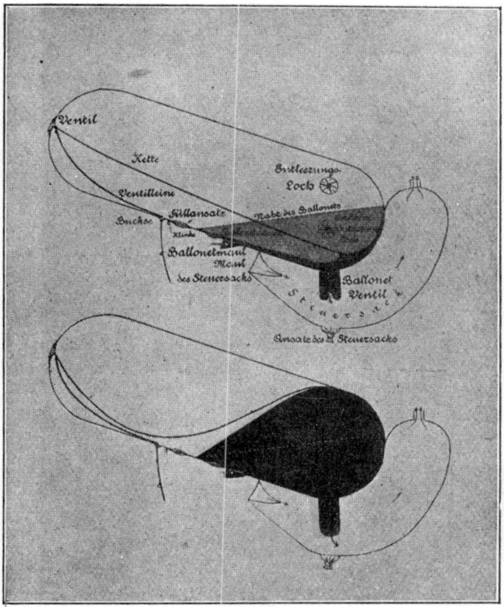

Fig. 116.—Drawing showing the design of the kite-balloon.

Ventil = valve. Kette = belt. Entleerungsloch = hole for emptying the balloon of its contents. Ventilleine = valve-line. Buchse = stuffing box. Füllansatz = inflating neck. Naht des Ballonets = seam of the air-bag. Ballonetmaul = opening into the air-bag. Maul des Steuersacks = opening into the steering-bag. Ballonet Ventil = valve of air-bag. Steuersack = steering-bag. Ansatz des Steuersacks = neck of steering-bag.

The balloon assumes an inclined position at an angle of about 30° or 40° to the horizontal ; this is effected through the method by which the ropes are attached. It is held captive by a rope

which is not attached to the basket, but to the front and back
of the balloon. These ropes are so arranged as to prevent the
long body of the envelope from being bent, and it is very important that the longer axis of the balloon should be kept pointing
in the direction of the wind. This is effected by means of a
steering-bag, which is connected to the lower part of the cylindrical and hemispherical portions of the balloon. The wind is
driven into the steering-bag through one or more non-return
valves, and escapes again through an opening at the back
towards the top. There is therefore a slight excess of pressure

FIG. 117.—Basket suspension.

in the steering-bag, but it must always be less than that in
the air-bag itself, which discharges into it. The result of the
excess of pressure in the steering-bag is that the balloon
always follows the direction of the wind. But in order that
these movements should not take place too suddenly, a kite's
tail is tacked on behind, and secured to the main body of the
balloon by means of a rope on either side. The kite's tail
consists of a number of windbags, which look like inverted
umbrellas, blown up by the wind, and therefore tending to
check any movement. But this arrangement has the draw-
back that the balloon is somewhat dragged down, and a
portion of the kite-effect is lost. This is, however, neutralised

by the use of two sails, which are mounted at the sides of the body, and contribute also to an increase of stability.

The balloon has no actual net. Instead of this there is a strong belt, which passes round the sides at a depth of 10 ins. below the middle line, and parallel to the longer axis. It is fastened securely to the envelope by stitching, and by cementing it to the body with bands coated with rubber solution. Ropes are attached at various points to the girdle, but they might happen in very windy weather to be broken. A ripping-panel is therefore provided at the front, in order to bring it quickly to the ground. Experience shows that a free kite-balloon maintains its position with very little change, if held by a rope attached to the front, though in this case it is generally inclined at a greater angle to the horizontal.

CHAPTER XVII.

INSTRUMENTS.

THE most important instrument is the barometer, which is used for determining the altitude. The balloonist must know the height to which he has risen, and also notice any tendency to rise or fall as soon as possible. There is a certain sluggishness about aneroids, which can be corrected by gentle tapping. The method, which has been described, of throwing out pieces of paper or feathers forms a useful indication of a rise or fall, and may conveniently supplement the use of the barometer.

Fig. 118.—Aneroid barometer.

On an ascent in a free balloon, a barograph is always taken, which records the barometric reading on a roll of paper, and therefore, together with the notebook, forms a concise statement of the facts of the journey. The statoscope has also been described, and is by no means indispensable, but a compass must be taken in any case. For meteorological observations, a wet and dry bulb thermometer, preferably of the Assmann type, should be taken, in order to measure the temperature and the moisture in the atmosphere. Radiation is, however, more important than actual temperature. The gas inside the balloon is warmer than the surrounding atmosphere, except by night, when the temperatures of the two are nearly the same, the gas being sometimes slightly the colder of the two, owing to losses by radiation.

It is very necessary to take good maps of the district. But on a long journey, they are apt to be so numerous that they are now often replaced by maps on a very small scale, which are read by means of a magnifying glass. As this system is possibly a matter of some general interest for other purposes than ballooning, it may be as well to describe it a little more fully. The method is due to an officer of the Bavarian Balloon Corps, named von Weinbach, who communicated his ideas to Dr Vollbehr of Halensee. An instrument, called the microphotoscope, was therefore designed. It consists of two parts, which are quite separate from one another, viz., the eyepiece or magnifier, which is used in daylight, and a lighting device, which is used by night. The magnifier consists of a lens, which is so mounted as to

FIG. 119.—Barograph, or recording barometer.

be capable of moving in slots, either up and down, or to the right and left. Microphotographs, which represent photographic reductions of maps published on a larger scale, are taken on celluloid films, and mounted in position between thin sheets of glass, two inches square. The lighting arrangement contains a small electric glow-lamp and a battery, the lamp being switched on and off as required. This arrangement works well on night journeys, and it is generally possible to determine the locality by noting the lights in the towns and the positions of the railways. The daylight apparatus weighs 4 oz., the lighting apparatus 5 oz., and the complete thing together with the case weighs 13 oz. The price is twenty-five shillings, which may easily be saved in the cost of maps.

It is extremely necessary to see that the whole of the material is maintained in thoroughly sound condition. Everything must

A.   o

be carefully examined before starting. With a free balloon, this
is particularly necessary, seeing that damage may have been done
at landing or by the ripping-cord. It is always emptied after a

FIG. 120.—Balloon basket and its contents.

journey; the gas soon becomes adulterated by diffusion, and it'is
not generally possible to anchor an inflated balloon. Sometimes
a balloon can be loaded with ballast and left in its inflated con-

FIG. 121.—Vollbehr's microphotoscope for reading maps on a reduced
scale, together with illuminating device for night work.

dition during the night, if the weather is very fine ; then on the
next day it is possible to continue the journey with a smaller
number of passengers than before. Things are somewhat
different with a captive balloon, which is often left in the inflated

state for several days, in order to save expense; when at last it
no longer has sufficient lift, it is emptied and refilled. Lébaudy's
motor-balloon worked for several months with one filling of gas.
When it is emptied, the gas is simply passed into the air, and is
useless for any further purpose. In Germany, a balloon is emptied
by means of the ripping-cord; in other countries, a usual method

FIG. 122.—Microphotoscope in case.

is to open the valve, or to raise the mouth of the neck. The
kite-balloon is emptied through a special opening towards the
back at the top. The ripping-panel must of course be very carefully cemented down after use, and this ought to be done not
more than three days and not less than one day before making
a fresh start. If it is left for a longer time, it often sticks so fast

FIG. 123.—Microphotoscope, with magnifying glass for use in daylight.

that it requires the efforts of several persons to pull it apart
again, and in rough weather this may easily cause a great deal
of unpleasant bumping. The opposite happens if the patch is
closed too soon before starting, or if the benzine contained in the
rubber solution is not allowed to evaporate sufficiently before
putting the piece in position on the covering.

The examination of the envelope on the inside is carried out by several persons, after it has been filled with air. The most minute leaks can easily be detected; the light which passes through them draws attention to their existence, even though it is impossible to see any trace of a hole on the outside. All such holes must be patched both on the outside and inside. Rents are first sewn together and then patched, and any kind of injury must be made good by covering with fresh material.

With kite-balloons it is necessary to see to the adjustment of the valve ropes. The balloon must therefore be filled with air, and if the valve does not open properly when the envelope is full, the connecting cord must be shortened. Everything in fact must be carefully overhauled before a start is made. Great care is necessary if accidents are to be avoided, and even though it is impossible to avoid them altogether, it is none the less a fact that the danger in ballooning is no greater than in driving a motor car or sailing a yacht.

CHAPTER XVIII.

PROFESSIONAL aeronauts made their appearance soon after the invention of *Montgolfières*. Blanchard, Robertson, and others soon found that it was possible to make a little money out of the new discoveries, and it can be easily understood that the tricks of the showman's art soon brought the sport into discredit.

A balloon, made out of goldbeater's skin, was sent up on December 27th, 1783, without passengers, from the Lustgarten in Berlin by Professor Achard. In 1789, Blanchard made one of his ascents; but the first properly managed expedition with passengers was made in Berlin on April 13th, 1803, by Garnerin, who was accompanied by his wife and a man named Gärtner. A full description of this journey has lately been published from documents in the possession of one of Gärtner's descendants. It appears that the ascent was made in the presence of the King and Queen of Prussia and an immense concourse of people. The start took place in the garden of the Veterinary School in Berlin, and the balloon eventually came to the ground near Mittenwald in the forest of Wusterhausen.

Nothing further was done with regard to the sport of ballooning in Berlin till 1881, when the German Club for the Promotion of Ballooning was founded by Dr. Angerstein. The search for a dirigible balloon appeared at that time to be as likely to be successful as had been the efforts to discover a perpetual motion. It therefore required no little courage to appear before the public as the founder of a Balloon Club with all its hopes and aspirations. Far-seeing men, like Moltke, looked forward to the future with confidence and prophesied great things for ballooning. On the other hand, a well-known scientific man stated in a lecture about that time that the idea of dirigible ballooning was an

" unfortunate form of lunacy," and the organ of the club was
spoken of as a "curiosity."

The well-known painter, Arnold Böcklin, took an active part
in the practical work of the club,[1] but without any great success.
He made a flying machine in the form of a Hargrave box-
kite, and thought to rise or fall by altering the position of the
sails, trusting to the wind for any forward movement. He
entirely forgot that a kite could only rise if held at the end of a
string. He invited Colonel Buchholtz, who commanded the first
Balloon Corps, to witness an experiment on the Tempelhofer Feld;
the apparatus finally succeeded in rising a foot from the ground,
and was then broken to pieces. Böcklin always defended his
ideas with much vigorous argument, but did not continue his
experiments.

The club made great advances when the meteorologist,
Professor Assmann, was elected president in 1890, and was able
to interest the Kaiser in its proceedings. A large sum of money,
placed at the disposal of the club by the Kaiser, enabled a
series of ascents to be carried out according to Assmann's
plans, the results of which have opened new prospects for
scientific ballooning. These will be discussed in a later
chapter.

In addition to its scientific activity, a great deal was done to
develop ballooning as a sport. A large number of expeditions
were organised by Captain von Sigsfeld and Major von Tschudi,
amounting now to nearly one hundred every year. This contributed to arouse a general interest in the matter. Since the
spring of 1902, the president's chair has been occupied by Professor Busley, who has devoted himself with great energy to the
sport. He contributed largely to the foundation of the German
Balloonists' Federation, which led the way for the long-cherished
French scheme of the " Fédération Aéronautique Internationale."
The Kaiser showed his further interest in the proceedings of the
club by attending a lecture on the French dirigible balloons in
December, 1905, and presented a prize for a long-distance race,

---

[1] See " Twenty-five Years in the History of the Berlin Balloon Club," by H. W. L.
Moedebeck, 1906. Published by K. J. Trübner, Strassburg.

which was won on October 14th, 1905, by Dr. Bröckelmann, in the balloon " Ernst."

Many people fail to see how ballooning can properly be termed a sport, seeing that the airship is entirely at the mercy of the wind, provided, of course, it is not of a dirigible type. They leave out of account the fact that much practice and experience give the aeronaut such control over his surroundings that he is at any rate not so helpless as a mere novice, whose only idea seems to be to make as long a journey as possible. The longest journey made in a balloon was that undertaken by Count de la Vaulx and Count Castillon de Saint Victor, in 1906, with the " Centaur," which had a capacity of only 55,000 cubic feet. They started from Paris and landed at Korostischeff in Russia. The distance, as the crow flies, was 1,200 miles, and the journey lasted $35\frac{3}{4}$ hours. In so far as length of time is concerned, the longest expedition was undertaken by Dr. Wegener of the observatory at Lindenberg, on April 5th, 1905, when he remained in the air for $52\frac{1}{2}$ hours.

Fig. 124.—Professor Busley, president of the Berlin Balloon Club.

Another long expedition was undertaken by Professor Berson and Dr. Elias, who made an ascent for meteorological purposes, and travellel from Berlin to Kieff in Russia, a distance of about 930 miles.

The ascent made by the French aeronaut Godard in 1897 caused a good deal of excitement. He started from Leipsic with seven passengers, in a balloon of a capacity of 100,000 cubic feet, and landed at Wilna. He stated that he had passed above the clouds over a number of large towns in the east of Germany,

and had covered 1,030 miles. A record of this kind is of no
value ; the determining factor is the distance in a straight line
from start to finish, seeing that there is obviously no means of
checking any statement as to distances covered above the clouds.
It is indeed possible to determine one's actual position by astronomical means, even if the balloon is above the clouds and the
earth is out of sight ; but evidence of this kind is apt to be
somewhat inconclusive.

The compass is of no use for mapping out the course of a
balloon above the clouds. If the balloonist is moving at the
same rate as the clouds, it would appear to be absolutely at rest.
It would therefore be impossible to tell in what direction he is
moving or at what rate. He knows whether the north is on the
right or left ; but beyond this, the compass has no information
to give. Let us suppose that the clouds appear to be travelling
towards the east. Then it is either possible that the clouds are
actually moving towards the east and that the balloon is moving
slower, or on the other hand the clouds may be standing still or
moving towards the west, while the balloon is moving much
faster towards the west. The information could therefore only
point decidedly to the fact that the wind is either in the east or
in the west. Such a fact might certainly be useful if there were
any danger of falling into the sea ; and supposing the start had
been made at Berlin, it would be evident that the journey could
be continued without anxiety. The aeronaut is in any case
liable to most sudden surprises. At great heights changes in
the direction of the wind are very frequent. In the northern
hemisphere, the wind usually veers in the direction of the hands
of a clock ; in the southern hemisphere, the reverse is the
case.

Generally speaking, the length of a journey is a matter of
accident ; without the necessary wind, it is impossible for the
greatest dexterity to be of any use. Skill can be shown, if
several balloons ascend at the same moment and it is a question
as to who can remain in the air for the longest time, in which
case it is necessary to be as sparing with the use of ballast as
possible. Handicaps can be arranged by adjusting the amount

of ballast to the size of the balloon, and allowances can also be made for the kind of gas with which the several balloons are filled, though generally the gas would be the same in all cases. Rules have been drawn up by the Fédération Aéronautique Internationale, governing the conditions of competitions, and these have received the approval of all the clubs represented at

Fig. 125.—A bank of clouds.

the conference. The first race for the Gordon-Bennet prize took place on September 30th, 1906, and was won by Lieutenant Lahm, an American competitor. A second competition was held at Berlin on October 14th, and was won by Dr. Bröckelmann.

Theoretically we know that a large balloon loses more gas than a small one; all balloons do not, therefore, require the same amount of ballast, which must be distributed somewhat in proportion to their sizes. A big balloon is not so easily managed as a smaller one; as it descends it gets up a greater speed, and therefore more ballast must be thrown out to neutralise this. It is often said that the main thing which requires skill is to find a level at which there is a stiff breeze. But this a counsel of perfection. If the driver sees from the flight of the clouds, or from the pilot balloon, that the breeze is stronger at a higher level, he can throw out ballast, provided he has a sufficiency, and rise to that level. But the converse is not possible. If he sees from his bits of paper that the breeze is stronger at a lower level, he can open the valve and descend to that level, but, as already explained, it is not generally possible to remain at that

FIG. 126.—Balloon after the ripping-cord has been pulled.

altitude. Under normal conditions, a falling balloon goes right down to the ground. If the fall is checked in any way, the balloon will rise again to the same height as that from which it has fallen, and may even go higher than before. Moreover, experiments of this kind must be paid for in gas and ballast, and therefore tend indirectly to lessen the distance which it is possible to cover.

The fastest journey in a balloon was made from Paris at the time of the siege. The distance from Paris to the Zuyder Zee, amounting to 285 miles, was covered in three hours, at an average speed of ninety-five miles an hour. The greatest speed over a short distance was probably attained by Captain von Sigsfeld and Dr. Linke on their fatal journey from Berlin to Antwerp, when a velocity of 125 miles an hour was recorded.

In competitions over great distances or for great lengths of time, it is very important not to get worn out. At night time it is a good plan to take it in turns, and for one to sleep in the intervals. Warm clothing is an absolute necessity, as the cold may be sufficient to prevent a man from sleeping. Should the provisions run short, that may be an even more serious calamity, and it is generally found that something hot to eat and drink

FIG. 127.—The Hofburg, Vienna.
Photograph by Captain Hinterstoisser

would add to the pleasures of existence. But fires are an impossibility, and enterprising persons have therefore thoughtfully provided the aeronaut with a variety of tinned provisions which can be cooked by adding water to the quicklime with which the tins are surrounded.

Injury to health may result from an ascent to a great height, and therefore competitions of this kind are not organised. But races are started with a view to reaching a definite place, the winner being the man who comes nearest to the mark. Naturally in this case everything depends on the direction of the wind, which must be ascertained before the start by means of a pilot balloon. Motor cars can be set to chase and capture a balloon, and many other forms of competition may be organised, of which examples may be found in Moedebeck's Handbook.   Ballooning is the most exhilarating of all forms of sport ; the impressions of the journey excite the imagination, and there is also a certain charm in knowing so little about the journey's end.   Before the start pilot balloons are sent up, the speed of the wind noted, and every likely contingency carefully weighed ; plans for the evening's arrangements are then made.   But prophecy is a gratuitous form of error, and calculations of this kind are equally waste labour.   Nothing generally happens in the course of the day's march except the unexpected.

It seems to be generally supposed that ballooning must cause a sensation of giddiness, and one is often asked as to the sensations experienced in travelling at a furious speed through the air.   It is, however, a curious fact that persons who suffer from giddiness under ordinary circumstances entirely lose the sensation in the basket of a balloon.   Perhaps this is due to the fact that it is impossible to form any precise estimate of the height ; the basket is so small and the height so great, it seems impossible to compare the two.   Moreover the guide-rope always seems to touch the ground.   The following incident is an illustration of this fact.   A certain man, who suffered from giddiness to such an extent that he was scarcely able to look out of the window of a room on the first floor, was induced, for the purposes of a bet, to undertake a trip in a balloon.   After two hours he was able to get up from his seat in the corner, and cautiously look at the horizon from the middle of the car.   At a later stage he was able to look over the edge of the basket without any feeling of anxiety or giddiness ; but when he reached the ground he was just as bad as before.

In a free balloon there is no sensation of sea-sickness, as the balloon floats gently along ; but with a captive balloon things are very different on a windy day, and sooner or later everybody succumbs.   The first ascent offers curious sensations for the novice.   He seems to see the earth sinking away from him, and when he comes down again, the trees and houses rush to meet him and welcome him back.   The speed can be estimated by

FIG. 128.—Heligoland.

Photograph taken by a member of the Prussian Balloon Corps.

noting the time which it takes to reach places on the map, but an experienced balloonist can generally make a fairly accurate guess. The height affects the apparent speed, and must be taken into account.

In the year 1899 Captain von Sigsfeld made an ascent in the company of the author and Herr von Haxthausen, and the incidents of this journey may be of interest to the reader. The balloon started in clear weather from Berlin, and reached Breslau in two hours, the speed having been about 92 miles an hour. The start had been made under difficulties, and no kind of proper balance was possible, seeing that the balloon was almost thrown to the ground by the wind. Ordinarily, after the passengers have taken their places, the ballast is loaded into the car until the "lift" appears to be reasonable. If the balloon seems inclined to rise too fast when the ropes are somewhat slackened, ballast must be put in the car; on the other hand, if it seems too heavy, it must be correspondingly lightened. During this stage it is important to keep the balloon vertically above the car, as otherwise it is not possible to form any exact estimate of the lift. In a strong wind this balancing is a difficult business, and requires great experience. Sigsfeld, however, gave the order to let go; and we were immediately bumped along the ground by the wind, and did not succeed in rising till we had thrown out two sacks of ballast. The balloon then rose at once to a height of about 2,500 ft. The inflating tube is opened just before the start, and is kept closed till the last moment, as otherwise the wind would drive too much gas out of the envelope. If it should happen that the inflating tube has not been opened, the rule is to empty the balloon, because otherwise it would rise to a great height and burst, and it is seldom safe to trust to letting out the gas by the valve.

The view which met our eyes was magnificent, and the great speed caused a rapid succession of varied landscapes. An express train, going from Berlin to Breslau, seemed to us to be going in the opposite direction, and was soon out of sight. In all we had 12 sacks of ballast, and seeing that the weather was very cloudy, and the balloon had only been inflated with coal gas, it did not look as though the trip was likely to be a long one. But in spite of the strong wind, the balloon sailed quite steadily along, and every now and then a few handfuls of ballast were thrown out in order to keep to a level of 6,000 ft. We wanted to remain where we were because it was colder below with a wind blowing more in the direction of Russia, which we had no intention of visiting. The Austrian frontier was passed between Dab and Chelm, and soon our stock of maps was exhausted. A small hand-atlas was our only resource, and was probably as useful as full-sized maps would have been, so great was the speed. The Tatra range was as clear as could be away towards the S.S.E., and the balloon, flying at full speed over the hills and valleys, soon reached the Carpathian Mountains. Eddies now began to be noticed, and this made travelling less pleasant. Soon we had a remarkable experience, which Sigsfeld duly recorded in the notebook. A slight vertical movement towards the back was noticed in the car. The balloon was soon thrown about in all directions, and finally rotated at a considerable speed. The guide-rope and the four holding-ropes became completely entangled; but at the end of a minute it all passed off. Soon after the guide-rope struck against some trees and made a great noise, which we thought at first was the sound of rifle firing.

The next place we clearly recognised was Neu-Sandec, near the mountains of Galicia. The place was only seen after passing the heights of Chemiecka-ga, and it was therefore impossible to land owing to the great speed. We thought it might be possible to find another track on the other side of the Carpathians, but this idea had to be given up, because the mist and fog made it at times almost impossible to see anything. The valve was therefore opened, and in a side valley, immediately to the south of Bogusza, the ripping cord was pulled at a height of 30 feet. We landed in deep snow after being bumped along the ground for about 20 yards; luckily the hills broke the violence of the wind. Just before landing we noticed two men, who appeared to be following the balloon. We shouted to them to come and help, and also blew our torpedo-boat whistles; but they were nowhere to be seen. At last we found them hidden away behind a stack of wood, trembling from head to foot.

They said that they had never seen a balloon in their lives before, and supposed that it must contain some emissary of the devil; and the unearthly noise made by the guide-rope as it crashed through the trees had only added to their fright. Gradually they took courage when they saw that the balloon had almost disappeared in the snow, and fetched other wood-choppers to come and help. Finally the packing was finished after many misunderstandings, mainly due to our imperfect knowledge of the local dialect, and the balloon was put on a sledge and taken to the village. Here we were informed by the local magistrate that our journey was to end, and that we must consider ourselves under arrest; our movements were indeed so suspicious that we could be nothing better than spies, and his opinion would probably be confirmed by his superior authorities in the course of a few days. We protested loudly and showed him our passports, but this was of no use. The magistrate was unable to read German, and consequently our passports were little better than waste paper. He refused to send a telegram to headquarters, and believing us to be Russian officers, treated us with scant courtesy. Nothing remained but to do as we were told. We put up in a room of the village inn, which was the only available accommodation, and devised a plan by which we were to get the help of one of the villagers who could speak a little German, and send a telegram to our ambassador at Vienna. The man had already done what he could on our behalf, and he was readily induced to act as guide. Under cover of darkness, about 6.30 p.m., we left the house, and went on foot to Kamionkawielka, where was the nearest telegraph office. The snow had begun to melt, and the road crossed a little swollen stream about ten times. Sometimes there was nothing better than a ford, and sometimes the trunk of a tree served as a slippery bridge. It was now pitch dark, and rain was falling heavily. We reached the telegraph office in three hours, and sent a telegram to the magistrate at Grybow, seeing that it was in his province we had made our unlucky descent. It was thought unwise to telegraph to the German Embassy according to our original plan, and we therefore asked the authorities at

Grybow to instruct the magistrate who had arrested us to the effect that he was to let us go and hand over to us all our goods and chattels.

I thereupon began the return journey, and was persuaded by my guide to spend the night at his house, which was in a wood at a short distance from the high road. The kitchen of his house was occupied by a variety of animals, and the other apartment was of the nature of a bed-sitting-room for the entire family, which included children, parents, and grandparents. Amid such surroundings, I was only able to eat a couple of eggs,

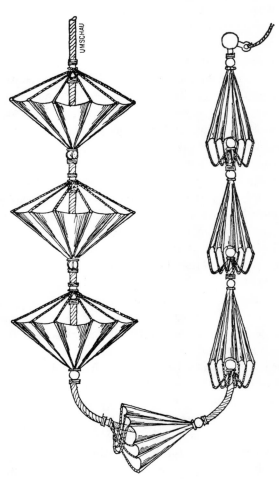

FIG. 129.—Water anchor for balloon.
(From " Die Umschau.")

though in reality I was very hungry. Violent gesticulations followed, and I was ultimately led to understand that this hospitality must be paid for on the spot, though the sum demanded seemed somewhat out of proportion to the benefits received—at least so I thought. A very small room, ordinarily occupied by

A.   P

the head of the family, was assigned to me as a bedroom, and I
was invited to retire. So I laid myself on the bed in full uniform
with my sword at a convenient distance, as I could not help
feeling that the continued whispers of father and son were not
reassuring. The situation was certainly not very encouraging.
I was in a shanty, away from the high road, in the middle of
the Carpathians, among people who looked almost like brigands.
Not a word of their language could I understand. They probably
knew I had some money about me, and my sleepy head was soon
full of all the highwaymen of whom I had ever heard. What
added to my suspicions was the fact that every now and then
the father came to the curtain, which served as the door, and
peeped in to see whether I was asleep. Naturally enough I
suspected him of the most sinister designs, and clutched at my
sword as soon as I heard his footsteps. Luckily this state of
tension came to an end about 12.30 a.m., when there was a
knock at the front door, and an Austrian policeman demanded
to know whether I was there. The authorities at Grybow had
sent the man in answer to my telegram with instructions to do
what was wanted, and accordingly he was on his way at the dead
of night. He reassured me as to the character of my hosts, and
said that their account of the matter was they supposed *I* was
going to kill *them*, otherwise why did I take my sword to bed
with me. Now I began to understand the stealthy visits of the
father, who had only been anxious all the time to see that I was
not meditating a descent upon his unprotected family. The
gendarme left about 1 a.m., and I was soon asleep.

   The next day I went to Grybow, where general indignation
was expressed at the proceedings of the magistrate at Bogusza.
This worthy was not a little surprised at the turn events had
taken, and did his best to make amends by providing a sledge
with six oxen to carry the balloon to Grybow, where Sigsfeld and
Haxthausen arrived in the course of the afternoon after a very
toilsome journey. All's well that ends well. We were received
in the most friendly manner at Grybow, but notwithstanding
this, we should recommend the balloonist to steer clear of the
backwoods in the Carpathian Mountains. Still, it must be

admitted that this sort of accident is very uncommon in Austria; in Russia difficulties sometimes arise. It is not uncommon in Russia to receive the most hospitable welcome on landing, but to be obliged to submit to a most wearisome cross-examination before being allowed to depart. Still, it is part of a balloonist's business to learn to extricate himself from tight places of one kind and another, and if he should have the misfortune to be involved in any such adventure, he can console himself with the reflection that variety is the spice of life.

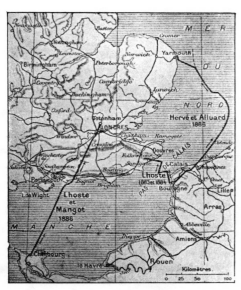

Much enjoyment is to be derived from a journey over a large expanse of water. There is undoubtedly some danger attached to it, for descents into water are always attended with risk. The most usual trip of this kind has been across the English Channel, and oddly enough, the start has generally been made from the

Fig. 130.—Balloon expeditions across the English Channel.

French coast. The direction of the wind is not so important in going from Dover to Calais as it is if the journey is made in the opposite direction. In the one case, the wind may veer through nearly 90 degrees on either side before the balloon would be carried out to sea; whereas in going from Calais, a deviation of 45 degrees would be sufficient to prevent a landing.

An Englishman, named Green, proposed in 1837 to fasten a number of buckets to the guide rope, and drag them through the water. He thought this would help him to guide the balloon, but he would naturally only be helped by such local currents as existed. A Frenchman, named l'Hoste, experimented with similar dragging devices. He made several trips, of which the

Fig. 131.—Count de la Vaulx' balloon over the Mediterranean.

most remarkable were those from Cherbourg to London and from Calais to Yarmouth. But on November 13th, 1887, l'Hoste and his companion, named Mangot, were drowned. One of his

Fig. 132.—Basket of Count de la Vaulx' balloon, showing the deviators.

countrymen, named Hervé, continued these experiments, and made many successful expeditions. He used floating timbers in conjunction with sails, and succeeded in producing a deviation of about 70 degrees from the direction of the wind. Such

" deviators " consist of a frame into which a number of straight
or bent pieces of wood are fitted, one behind the other, somewhat
after the fashion of a ladder.   From the ends of this contrivance,
ropes are taken to the balloon, by means of which the position
of the rungs can be altered so as to present a variable angle to
the course of the balloon.   If the rungs are placed parallel to
the direction of flight, the balloon is subjected to a slight braking

FIG. 133.—Count de la Vaulx' deviator in action.

action, but the direction of its course is unaffected.   If the
rungs are placed obliquely, the resistance, due to the water, is
increased, and the balloon's course is deflected to that side on
which the rope has been shortened.

Count de la Vaulx has a balloon specially arranged for such
water expeditions.   He has an air-bag, which is not a necessity
in the case of a free balloon ; but it helps to preserve the shape
of the envelope, seeing that from some points of view his balloon
may be considered as being of the captive type.   Many failures

have resulted, but a man of his energy is not easily beaten. The car of his balloon also contains a small motor for driving a propeller. His plans have been well laid, and he thinks there is no danger in making a descent on the water. His water-anchor produces such a braking action that in case of need the accompanying steamship could easily overtake him. Others have talked about crossing the Atlantic ; but schemes of this kind are too much in the air to be worth serious discussion. Several attempts have been made to cross the sea from Germany, but these have mostly been in the neighbourhood of Kiel or Jutland, where there are a number of islands convenient for a descent.

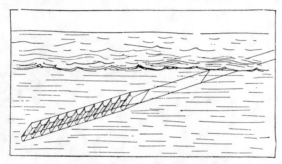

Fig. 134.—Deviator offering the maximum resistance.
(From " Die Umschau.")

But such trips have no real value, and the risk of coming into the water is too great to justify them in most cases, though an exception may certainly be made if there is some distinct scientific object in view. Two soldiers belonging to the Prussian Balloon Corps were nearly drowned on March 24th, 1906. They had been for some time above the cloud level, and on descending found they were over the Baltic. All instruments were thrown away, the basket was cut adrift, and they even threw away some of their clothing. Finally the balloon drifted over the land near Karlskrona ; if the course had been a little more to the east, they would undoubtedly have been drowned.

A change in the direction of the wind may bring serious consequences, and the dangers of a journey across the sea may be well illustrated by an account of a journey which the author made with the meteorologist Berson of Berlin, on January 10th, 1901. The start was made at Berlin, and the descent took place at Markaryd in Sweden. There were many lucky circumstances in connection with the journey across the sea. In the first instance it was intended to make a high ascent, and the basket was furnished with instruments for this purpose. But the sky was cloudless, and it seemed likely to be possible to remain at a moderate altitude for some time without any great loss of ballast. The idea of crossing the sea was then considered, and the original plan was given up. The first consideration was to be able to

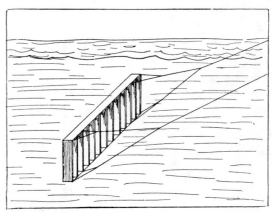

FIG. 135.—Deviator offering the minimum resistance.
(From "Die Umschau.")

reach the coast with a sufficiency of ballast, but other things had also to be taken into account. Generally speaking, the balloons which start from Berlin have lost too much ballast by the time they reach the coast to make it possible to continue the journey. A fortunate circumstance in connection with our journey was the fact that the wind was blowing towards the north, and at a low level it was indeed blowing towards the north-west. The usual wind is from the south-west over the northern hemisphere, and this carries a balloon from Berlin too far towards the east to make it possible to cross the sea. We were also able to judge, from the time at which we arrived at the coast of the Baltic, that we should be able to cross the Baltic in daylight, supposing that the wind did not drop. As a matter of fact, we did not actually reach Trelleborg till after dusk, though under the circumstances we were, I think, justified in undertaking the journey. Both of us might fairly be considered to have had experience in the work, and we agreed that the crossing might safely be undertaken ; so that had any accident resulted, neither would have had to reproach himself with having alone undertaken the responsibility. It generally happens that on a balloon there is one experienced aeronaut, and the rest of the passengers are without any special experience. It is therefore impossible to submit any proposal to the

UMSCHAU

FIG. 136.—Map showing the course of the balloon from Berlin to Markaryd.

vote, even though the passengers have already made several trips and will in time become experienced men. The man who leads the expedition has to bear all the responsibility in case of accident, and should it appear that he has not given the word of command with sufficient emphasis in an emergency, he is likely to lay himself open to the severest censure.

The expedition was intended to be devoted to meteorological purposes, and the basket, which was very small and uncomfortable, was fitted out with the requisite instruments. We had warm clothing, and a stock of provisions, and set sail accordingly at 8.17 a.m. The temperature at Berlin was 21° F., and elsewhere it was colder still. The balloon passed from Berlin over the targets at Tegel at a height of 500 to 600 ft., where a second balloon with recording instruments was sent up from the Aeronautical Observatory. We soon found that at levels below 2,500 ft. we were being driven very slightly towards the west, at levels between 2,500 and 4,500 ft. the course was due north, and at still higher levels there was a slight tendency towards the east. The temperature, too, rose so much that we were glad to do without our furs. At a level of 3,000 ft. the temperature was 27° higher than on the ground. Generally the air gets colder at higher levels; it is usual to expect a decrease of $\frac{1}{4}$° or $\frac{1}{2}$° in a rise of 100 ft., and therefore in the present case we might have expected to find the thermometer nearly down to zero. As a matter of fact the thermometer did not sink to the freezing point till we

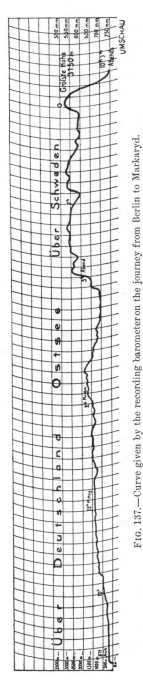

Fig. 137.—Curve given by the recording barometer on the journey from Berlin to Markaryd.

(Über Deutschland = over Germany.   Ostsee = Baltic Sea.   Über Schweden = over Sweden.   Grösste Höhe = greatest altitude.   3,150 m. = 10,350 feet.)

reached an altitude of 8,000 ft., and at 10,000 ft. we reached again the temperature of the ground level. We were unable to read the lowest temperature, because there was no light, and we had not provided ourselves with an electric lamp. The sky was cloudless, except for a small amount of cirrus which seemed to be at a great height. A thin mist covered the ground, and the balloon floated above it without throwing out any ballast. Herr Berson had studied the state of the weather on the evening before the start, and it was seen that there was a steady south-easterly wind over all the parts between Berlin and the north-west. It therefore seemed likely that it might be possible to cross the Baltic, and we consequently took maps of Denmark and the south of Sweden. He told me his plan after we had been under weigh for an hour and had reached the Finow Canal. The various possibilities were discussed, and the fact that the wind was more westerly at a lower level was much in our favour. It seemed certain that in any case we could reach Denmark, as our speed was about 25 miles an hour. Our only fear was that we might have a long journey over the sea slightly towards the east of Denmark ; but there seemed to be no reasonable probability of the wind shifting to the east and carrying us therefore right out into the open sea, which would expose us to a most serious risk. We did not make up our minds all at once ; it was at a later stage, when we reached Neustrelitz, that we definitely resolved after further careful deliberation to cross the Baltic. The view from the balloon was splendid ; we heard a peculiar, dull sound as we crossed small lakes with their thin covering of ice, caused, as we supposed, by the cracking of the ice. Every now and then we heard shouts of the beaters at a shoot; but otherwise nothing broke the stillness of the air. In fact it seemed to me as if this journey was much quieter than usual ; we seldom heard the wheels of a cart or the shouts of the schoolboys ; ordinarily the balloon is greeted with shouts at every village it passes. The pigeons, as usual, were terribly frightened ; no doubt they think that a balloon is some gigantic bird of prey, and fancy there is safety in numbers.

The recording balloon was at a great height above our own, and

was partly hidden in consequence. Suddenly there was a great
jolt, and a peculiar noise drew our attention to the fact that one
of our sacks of ballast on the outside of the car had tumbled off,
and that we had suddenly been shot up a few hundred feet, which
was the last thing that we had intended to do. This point was
duly noted on the curve which recorded our height by a sudden
upward bob between 10 a.m. and 11 a.m. We passed Neustrelitz
and Demmin on our left, and Neubrandenburg on our right. At
1.15 we reached the coast at Stralsund, and passed Rügen. We
could see a number of fishers with their nets on the ice, trying
to catch fish out of the holes. At Stralsund the water was also
frozen ; we could clearly see the channel for the ferry boat between
Stralsund and Rügen. At two o'clock Rügen was left in the rear,
and we were over the open sea. The Baltic was free from ice,
and fairly calm ; but we could see the foam of the waves, which
glistened brightly. There were multitudes of gulls, who were
much perturbed at our appearance and flew anxiously hither and
thither. We fixed our precise position on the map, and it seemed
that we had come slightly to the east, but not sufficiently to
cause any anxiety.

The view over Rügen and the chalk cliffs of Stubbenkammer
and Arkona was splendid ; the atmosphere was perfectly clear.
On the horizon we could see the coasts of Sweden and Denmark,
looking almost like a thin mist ; east and west there was nothing
but the open sea. About 3.15 the balloon was in the middle of
the Baltic ; right in the distance we could just see Rügen and
Sweden. The setting of the sun at 4 p.m. was a truly
magnificent spectacle. At a height of 5,250 ft., in a perfectly
clear atmosphere, the effect was superb. The blaze of colour
was dimly reflected in the east by streaks of a bluish-green. I
have seen sunsets over France at heights of 10,000 ft., with the
Alps, the Juras, and the Vosges mountains in the distance ; but
this was quite as fine. The sunsets seen by the mountaineer or
sailor are doubtless magnificent ; but I hardly think the spectacle
can be finer than that spread out before the gaze of the balloonist. The impression was increased by the absolute stillness
which prevailed ; no sound of any kind was to be heard. As

soon as the sun went down, it was necessary to throw out some ballast owing to the decrease of the temperature. The highest temperature registered by the black-bulb thermometer was 79° F., the balloon being at that time over the Baltic. Now it could be put away, as there was no more work for it to do. Even with the compass we could not tell in what direction we were moving; the guide-rope was trailing through the water, but it was useless for telling the direction of the motion. We noticed the direction in which the sand seemed to fall when we threw out the ballast. At a great height we concluded that we were being driven towards the east very slightly; at lower levels the tendency was towards the west. It therefore seemed clear that if the conditions remained unaltered we should be driven slightly towards the east. But this had to be prevented at all costs, and we therefore kept as high as possible in order to get a whiff of the easterly breeze. Soon land came in sight. During the three hours we had been over the water we only saw two steamers. One of them directed its course towards us at first, as we thought; but soon it went on its way, as it seemed we had no need of help. It is useless for the aeronaut to reckon on help from a steamboat under such circumstances. It is not every steamboat that can come far out of its course on the off-chance that help is needed; besides which, the difference of speeds may be so great that help, if it does arrive, would be too late.

We reached the Swedish coast about 5 o'clock, and passed over Trelleborg at a height of 2,000 ft. The question then arose as to whether to land, or to continue during the night. Although it was well past sunset, there was sufficient light in consequence of the snow to see our way to the ground, and to land quite easily. It is always a little awkward to land in a strange country after dark; moreover, we wanted to do more meteorological work. It was thought there was still sufficient ballast to take us up to a much greater height, even allowing for necessary losses, and the balance of the arguments seemed to be in favour of deferring the descent. We therefore proposed to continue for another sixteen hours during the night in spite of the cold. We were able to see a good distance ahead, and if we should reach the sea either on the east or the west, there would be plenty of time to descend before we should be in any serious danger.

We were now quite low down, and going almost direct for Malmö, which would probably be left on the right-hand side. But this did not suit our plans, as a drift towards the west might

FIG. 138.—Stockholm seen from an altitude of 3,000 feet.
(Photograph by Oskar Haldin.)

bring us over the sea long before the fifteen hours were over. We therefore threw out a lot of ballast and rose higher than ever, getting into a southerly breeze. Malmö was therefore passed on the left, and the university town of Lund on the right. After this the map was of no further use, as it was quite dark and we had no lamp. The whole outlook was like a transformation scene. Floods of light rose up from Trelleborg, Malmö, Copenhagen, Landskrona, Lund, Elsinore, and Helsingborg, while the little towns beneath our feet sparkled with many lights. We were now at a height of more than 10,000 ft. and consequently all these places were within sight. The glistening effect of the snow was heightened by the blaze which poured from the lighthouses along the coasts of Sweden and Denmark. The sight was as wonderful as that of the sunset had been, though of a totally different nature. We supposed the light in Malmö to be from arc lamps;

FIG. 139.—Mischabelhorn, seen from the east, showing also the Fee and Hohbalen glaciers.

(Photograph by Spelterini.)

its brightness was very marked. We found later on visiting the town that there was no electric light in the streets, but only Welsbach burners; yet the effect produced in the distance was really brilliant. The Pole-star was our guiding light; the compass was useless in the dark. We also guided ourselves to some extent by the lights below, and as soon as we saw that the course was not due north, more ballast was thrown out, and at once we got again into the southerly breeze. There seemed now to be no tendency to drift towards the east.

Sometimes there was a slight mist on the ground, but this obstructed the outlook very little. Soon we were struck by the fact that the earth seemed to be covered with dark patches. Herr Berson thought there were clouds beneath us, through which, here and there, we could see the shining snow. I had better eyes than he had, and thought I could see lights in these dark patches. My theory was that the dark spots were villages where the snow had melted, but we soon found this was not so. Gradually everything disappeared beneath us, and it was evident that the clouds had closed up, covering the earth from our sight. What was to be done? The blaze from the lighthouse in the Bay of Halmstadt had been too close to be pleasant. We were moving rather to the west than to the east. It was just possible to see the pointer on the aneroid, but even supposing we kept at the same level we might quite easily get into a current and be carried to the west. The only prudent thing to do was to come down at once, and this we did. We found out later from the weather-chart, published that evening, that in the middle of Sweden and south-east of Norway a north-east wind was blowing at 8 p.m., while in Copenhagen, the Kattegat, and Jutland it was from the south or south-east. If we had continued, we should have been carried across the Kattegat and Skagerrack into the North Sea, and sooner or later the balloon would have been at the mercy of the waves.

The valve was opened and the balloon descended through the thick clouds. We could see nothing, but the little jerks showed us that the guide-rope was touching the ground. In a few seconds we saw the ground, and soon learnt that we were descending into a forest which enclosed a number of small lakes. At once more ballast was thrown out, and we skimmed along over the tops of the trees. Soon we crossed a big lake, and saw a place that seemed suitable for a descent. The valve was then opened, both of us gave a tug at the ripping cord, and after a few bumps we found ourselves on the ground. We had come down in deep snow on the side of a wood, about 14 miles from the railway station at Markaryd, in the province of Smaaland. We packed up our instruments, and began to look out for

a cottage; but this is not always an easy task in the dead of
night in a foreign country. In a quarter of an hour, we found
a farm, and succeeded in rousing the inmates. A much more
difficult job was to induce them to open their front door. Here
were two men, talking some sort of double Dutch, who suddenly
appeared at a farmyard, miles off the high road in the middle of
the night, and demanded admittance. Berson can talk six
languages, but unfortunately Swedish was not among them.
Our situation was far from pleasant. Berson begged in the
most humble way for shelter, while I contented myself with
walking up and down, as I was unused to negotiations of this
kind, and unable to add anything to his convincing arguments.
We thought at least they might ultimately admit one of us. At
the end of three-quarters of an hour the farmer, who turned
out to be a very pleasant fellow, opened the door. We showed
him some pictures of a balloon we luckily had with us, and they
then began to understand the situation. We were then received
with truly Swedish hospitality, and provided with supper. They
even proposed to let us have their beds; but this we naturally
declined with many thanks. After supper we set out to search
for the balloon, and were guided by the son and daughters of the
family, who brought a lantern with them. It was soon found
and rolled up as well as was possible under the circumstances;
the instruments and maps were more carefully packed. We
then wended our way back to the farmhouse. The yard contained hens, pigs, cows, and sheep; an empty corner was found,
which was well packed with straw, and served as a couch for our
tired limbs. We covered ourselves with great-coats, and tried to
sleep. But the temperature was 10° Fahr., and as the place was
only an outhouse with the boards roughly nailed together, and
the wind whistling through the cracks and crevices, we were not
sorry when the daylight came. We got up and were glad to
warm ourselves before the fire, while they fetched some labourers
from the next farm, which was a couple of miles off, to come
and help us pack up our balloon. It was finally done, and we
managed to make ourselves understood through talking English
to one of the labourers, who had lived in America for some time.

We then parted from our host on the best of terms, and set out on a sledge for the railway at Markaryd. Such an extraordinary cavalcade had never before been seen in those parts, or probably anywhere else for that matter. At the front was the basket ; at the back was the rolled-up envelope, bound round with the ropes, and standing up on edge, on the top of which we seated ourselves, one behind the other, and acted as drivers. We only regretted there was no camera to take a picture of the group. The rustics looked at us with open eyes, and probably thought my uniform looked a little strange amid its surroundings. They greeted us in friendly fashion, but realising that we were foreigners, they asked no questions. Our horse managed the hills remarkably well; we switchbacked up and down, and the whole thing was done automatically without the driver's interference. Every now and then it looked as though we should be landed in the snow, but the heavy balloon steadied it at the critical moment. Soon we reached a sort of high road, very hilly still, but better than before ; and after a drive of three hours, we landed safely at Markaryd at 5 p.m. We first went to the telegraph office to allay the anxiety of our friends, and after a long conversation, carried on for the most part in dumb show, we discovered that this was only a telephone office, and no telegrams were taken in. But our troubles were near their end, for we found a stationmaster who was able to talk German. We handed him our messages, and he sent them by telephone to Hessleholm, whence they were forwarded by telegraph to Berlin. We paid off the driver, and packed the balloon on the train, being glad of an opportunity of getting something hot to eat and drink at the little railway hotel.

Our messages evoked an unexpected response in the shape of telephonic enquiries from the Swedish newspapers at Malmö, Stockholm, Wexio, and other towns, which reached us long before our telegrams reached Berlin. Our balloon had been noticed as it came across the Baltic. Accordingly we gave particulars to the stationmaster, and he relieved us of any further bother.

We reached Malmö next day, and I called on the officer

A.   Q commanding the regiment of hussars, which was stationed there. We were received in a most hospitable manner, and invited to join their mess, after which we were driven round Malmö and the neighbourhood before making our departure for Copenhagen on the way to Berlin. Our journey had been thoroughly interesting with its ups and downs, and we felt, even from the scientific point of view, to have collected facts of some importance.

A few figures will give some impression of our general results. The total distance travelled across the water was 77 miles, of which 50 miles was over the open sea. Our mean speed was 31½ ft. per second over the whole journey; in Germany it was 41 ft. per second; over the Baltic 33 ft. per second; and in Sweden 25 ft. per second. The temperature at the moment of starting was 22° F.; at a height of 2,200 ft. it was 40° F.; at 3,200 ft. it was 44° F.; and at 8,000 ft. it was at the freezing point. As for the recording balloon it started at 8.3 a.m., and landed at 10 a.m. in Lychen, in the Uckermark, 44 miles due north of Tegel, after a journey at the average speed of 42 ft. per second. The greatest height was 23,150 ft., where the temperature was 22° below zero. Its instruments showed also a temperature of 40° F. at a height of 4,800 ft., and the freezing point was reached at a level of 8,300 ft.

A balloon expedition through the mountains is also a delight, and exposed to similar risks. Captain Spelterini is well known for his many journeys over the Alps. During the exhibition at Milan a prize was offered to the man who should succeed in crossing the Alps after starting from Milan. It was won by an Italian aeronaut named Usuelli, who succeeded in crossing over Mont Blanc. This can only be done in suitable weather, and it is very important to find out the direction of the currents at the higher levels by means of a pilot balloon before making a start. Anyhow it is necessary to rise to such a height as to be outside the range of the lower breezes, and to mount to altitudes of more than 20,000 ft. straight away. Steel cylinders containing oxygen must therefore form part of the outfit, which means a serious addition to the deadweight. There must be at least two, if not three, passengers; consequently this would require a balloon of 70,000 cubic feet capacity, which must be filled with hydrogen.

The first attempt was made by Spelterini on October 3rd, 1898. Professor Heim and Dr. Maurer went with him in a balloon of a capacity of 115,000 cubic feet, named the "Vega." He stated from Sitten, and in 5¾ hours he reached Rivière, in the

FIG. 140.—The Lake of Lucerne.

(Photograph by Spelterini.)

department of the Haute-Marne, having covered a distance of 140 miles. His idea had been to reach the Bodensee after crossing the Finsteraarhorn and the Urner and Glarner Alps. On August 1st, 1900, Spelterini started from the Rigifirst and crossed over Tödi and Glärnisch. In 1903 he made an expedition from Zermatt and crossed the Dom in the Mischabel Chain, then turned towards the south-east over Lake Maggiore, and then after several turns to the Chinti, above Bignasco, where the descent was made. The most interesting expedition was in

1904, over the Jungfrau, the Breithorn, the Blümli-Alp, and the Wildstrudel. The photographs which were taken on these occasions give a good impression of the pleasure which can be derived from journeyings in the Alps.

It is difficult to describe the joy of this kind of ballooning to those who have not experienced it. In November, 1904, the author joined Captain Spelterini and Freiherr von Hewald in a trip from Zurich over the Lake of Lucerne, past the Rigi and Pilatus. We then went towards the south-west, and at heights of 13,000 ft. we passed over some of the bigger ranges. The weather was perfectly clear, and the mountains seemed so close as to be within a stone's throw. We passed the Jungfrau, the Eiger, the Mönch, but the most beautiful thing we saw was the Great Aletsch Glacier, glistening in the sun. For three hours we experienced such delights as had never fallen to human lot before. There was always something fresh, some new feature in the panorama, and all spread out for us to enjoy in perfect stillness. We turned later to the north, and came to the ground on the north-west side of the Lake of Neuchatel. The course was curious, inasmuch as it seldom happens that one passes along the Alps. Spelterini had himself never before had such luck. The turn to the right was an essential feature of the scheme, for our balloon had only a capacity of 55,000 cubic feet, and was filled with coal gas, and any attempt to cross the higher ranges was therefore impossible. Moreover, a landing effected at a great height is a very awkward affair, and is likely to cost a great deal of money. It need hardly be said that it is also about as dangerous as anything connected with ballooning can well be. But it is as well not to talk too much about "danger." The most erroneous notions exist about the risks attaching to the sport, largely because the newspapers easily convert trifling incidents into alarming accidents. The death of a jockey is dismissed in a few lines ; but the slightest accident to a balloonist seems to afford unlimited scope to the inventive and descriptive faculties. Professor Busley, President of the Berlin Balloon Club, read a paper on the supposed risks of ballooning with reference to the question of insurance. He showed that ballooning is not much more dangerous than any other sport, and that such accidents as occur are mostly due to the defective material used by the balloonists employed at country shows. He made a careful examination into the records of accidents which have happened to members of clubs affiliated to the German Association of Balloonists, and also to the Prussian and Bavarian Balloon Corps, and found that 36 accidents had happened as compared with a total number of 2,061 ascents. The injured amounted to 0·47 per cent. of the number of passengers, the total number

FIG. 141.—Balloon and balloonists on their way home.

of whom was 7,570. But an improvement is even noticeable among professional aeronauts, and they are now beginning to know that confidence cannot be placed in an old patched balloon. Still they are not in a very enviable position; their profession is a difficult one, and the profits are scanty. They cannot afford to keep a number of assistants, and have to trust to the intelligence of such local helpers as they can scrape together. It takes several hours to inflate the balloon, and he is obliged to be present during the whole time because nobody else knows anything about it, and any delay at the last moment might expose him to the wrath of the mob. An amateur generally mounts into the basket after all the work of inflation has been done by experienced balloonists, whereas the professional has already done a hard day's work before the start is made. Consequently in a tight place he is at a great disadvantage. Professionals, too, have to make the ascent, whatever may be the state of the weather. In summer a thunderstorm often comes unexpectedly, and in the early morning, when the inflation begins, there may be no sign of the likelihood of anything of the sort. The professional has no great balance at the bank, and can ill afford to lose the money which is represented by the gas in the balloon. Besides which he would lose all the money of the crowd of sightseers if the show were abandoned. Therefore he is hardly in the position of a free agent, and makes an ascent under hazardous conditions. Still the authorities ought to be in a position to prevent an ascent when the conditions are unfavourable. It often happens that persons without any sufficient technical experience take upon themselves to announce balloon trips, and find unsuspecting passengers who may be exposed to the greatest risks. If the professional chooses to run the chance of breaking his own bones, that is his affair; but some means ought to be found of preventing him from involving others in his fate.

A typical instance took place in the Rhine Province in 1905. An engineer, named Vollmer, had been on three short trips with a professional balloonist, and then started from Remscheid with an unsuspecting passenger. The weather was perfectly clear, and in spite of this they fell into the North Sea and were drowned. They attempted to descend too late, as was evident from the messages sent by carrier pigeon, wherein they stated that the sea first came in sight when they were at a height of 10,000 ft. This was clearly a case in which the ascent should have been forbidden. But we must not go to extremes, or we may find the engineer hoist with his own petard. Thus it was clearly an excess of zeal which prompted the Chief of the Berlin police to prohibit all ascents in the year 1884 before the 15th of August, on the ground that otherwise much damage might be done to the crops by the descent of the balloon. Generally speaking, since the introduction of the ripping-cord in Germany, the number of accidents has greatly decreased; even in a stiff wind the dangers of being dragged and bumped along the ground are much smaller if the envelope is suddenly emptied of its gas.

A landing normally takes place somewhat as follows.[1] As soon as it is determined to make the descent a suitable spot is selected, partly by consulting the map, and partly by taking account of the general lie of the land. When the place has been chosen, a rough calculation must be made as to the height at which it is best to open the valve. Experience shows that the fall takes

FIG. 142.—Landing in a tree.

place at the rate of 8 or 10 ft. per second; therefore, if the horizontal velocity is known, as also the distance of the point of descent, it is easy to fix the level at which the valve must be opened. The rate of falling is about 6 miles an hour, and let us suppose that the balloon is travelling at a speed of 12 miles an hour, the distance of the spot selected for landing being one mile, i.e., 5,280 ft. The height at which the valve must be opened will be $\frac{6}{12} \times 5{,}280$, i.e., 2,640 ft. Shortly before the landing place is reached the balloon must be brought to rest by means of the guide-rope, ballast being thrown out if necessary.

[1] See Dr. Richard Emden's article on the "Theory of Landing," in the *Illustrierte Aeronautische Mitteilungen* for March, 1906.

This is a very simple matter if there are no telegraph wires or
other obstacles. But this seldom happens; there are usually
trees or something of the kind in the way, and then it is necessary to proceed cautiously, for fear of getting entangled. Ballast
must be thrown out in order to avoid these obstacles and rise

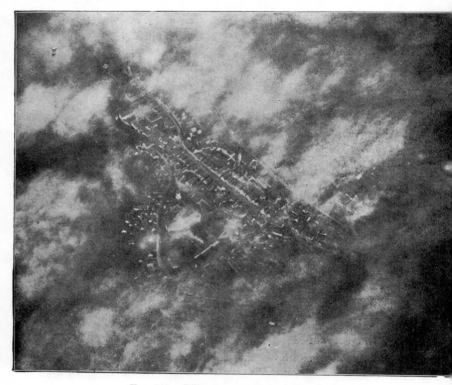

Fig. 143.—Dillingen, seen through the clouds.
(Photograph by A. Riedinger, of Augsburg.)

above them; but care must be taken that the balloon does not
rise too much, otherwise there is a danger of its rising to the
height from which it has fallen. After leaping over the obstacle,
the valve must be pulled at once and the balloon brought to the
ground. Such manœuvres can be very tedious; sometimes it is
necessary to jump over houses and villages, which must on no
account be touched by the guide-rope if there is still sufficient

ballast to be able to rise above them.   The importance of reserving a certain amount of ballast for the end of the journey will now be evident.   A journey cannot be continued till all the ballast is thrown away, leaving none for the purpose of landing ; otherwise a guide-rope, rattling along the tops of houses, may be a source of great danger to the inhabitants of a village, and quite apart from this, the lives of the passengers themselves may be exposed to serious risks.   One cannot too strongly insist on the necessity for this precaution ; in fact, the recklessness of the man who neglects it is almost criminal.

As soon as the balloon has been brought by means of the guide-rope to a suitable spot for landing, the valve is opened, and the basket comes with a heavy bump to the ground.   The reaction causes the balloon to make a jump, and as it comes down again the ripping-cord is pulled as quickly as possible. The envelope empties itself almost at once, but a very strong wind may occasionally cause the basket to be dragged for some little distance along the ground.   It is, of course, possible to pull the ripping-cord before the balloon touches the ground at all, but this must rest in the discretion of the man in charge.

The following description of a journey undertaken by the author may help to illustrate the dangers of the descent. I was in charge of all the arrangements, and had as my companions Dr. Stollberg and Lieutenant George.   We started from Strassburg in a balloon with a capacity of 70,000 cubic feet, and the following is an account of the expedition, written by Dr. Stollberg.

" The balloon seemed to be tugging almost viciously at its moorings, when the order was given to let go.   At 9.8 a.m. we started off, with a fairly strong north-west wind behind us. At once we threw out ballast, but still remained close to the telegraph wires, and it was only after we had lost $4\frac{1}{2}$ sacks of ballast that we managed to get clear away.   We passed away from the ramparts, and were soon far above the housetops, even the Cathedral itself seemed far beneath us.   In three minutes we passed over the railway station, and rose rapidly through a thick grey fog.   In another three minutes we had

passed through the clouds with all their damp and cold and were
now face to face with the sun in all its glory. Towards the east
was the hump of the Hornisgrinde, and some of the peaks of the
Kniebis showed through the mist; on the west, parts of the
Vosges could be faintly seen, looking like dark streaks against
the horizon. Towards the south was a heavy bank of clouds,
which looked almost like the snowy Alps; and right below us on
the fog was the mysterious shadow of the balloon. But there
was no feeling of loneliness, although at 9.23 a.m. the reading of
the barometer was 25·5 in., and of the thermometer 46° F. We
could clearly hear the rolling of the trains, and the drums and
bugles at the barracks. All of a sudden the fog disappeared,
and directly beneath us we saw the railway station. At
9.37 a.m. the barometer reading was 23·8 in., corresponding
to an altitude of 6,550 ft.; the temperature was only 40° F.,
yet the heat from the rays of the sun bothered us not a little.
The Cathedral looked no bigger than a footstool, with its cross
at a depth of 5,500 ft. below us. But it seemed so hot that I
was glad to take off some of my winter clothes, and would have
taken off my boots as well, if it hadn't been a little awkward.
The others experienced the same sensation, and if we had stayed
there long we should have been as brown as berries.

   " However, I had no time to think about these things, and set
myself down on a sack of ballast to write postcards to my friends.
In case anybody should be interested in my method, I may as well
describe it. I order them at the bookseller's, and each card is
provided with a kind of pigtail, consisting of two yards of
coloured paper, or better still, of a length of bright
red ribbon. On the front I write the address and the word
" Balloon," and the thing is done. I then throw it over the edge,
and it amuses me to see the card with its long red tail go tum-
bling slowly and gracefully down to the ground. On this occasion
I threw out only two cards, and they both reached their destination in due course. At 9.43 a.m. the barometric pressure was
24·6, the altitude being 5,250 ft. above the sea. We had therefore fallen about 1,300 ft. in six minutes, but we were still higher
than at 9.23. The Hornisgrinde was our landmark, and seemed

to be in the same direction as before; we heard the same sounds from below, and concluded that we were still hovering over the town.   The balloonist is generally described as rushing furiously through the air; but this was hardly the case with us; there seemed to be something very circumspect about our movements. As there was to be nothing to occupy the mind, our thoughts gravitated in the direction of caring for the body, and an interval

FIG. 144.—Building a pontoon over the Spree.

was therefore devoted to refreshment.   Suddenly our leader said very decidedly that we must land.   We looked at the barometer— it was just before 10 o'clock—and saw that we were already descending very rapidly.   I couldn't understand it; nobody had touched the valve rope.   Still, the pointer on the aneroid was turning round almost as fast as a seconds' hand.   Each little division on the aneroid meant a fall of 36 ft.   We held out a feather at the end of a fishing-rod, but it floated over our heads, and our scraps of paper disappeared at once.   It was quite

evident that we were going at a breakneck speed to the
ground.

"We threw out some of our precious ballast, but this did no
good.   We came down faster than the sand, and now there were
only five sacks of ballast left, each weighing 66 lbs.   Unfortu-
tunately there came a cloud between us and the sun ; the
temperature of the gas in the balloon went down quickly, and
this further helped us on our downward journey.   There would

Fig. 145.—Bridge over the Iller, near Kempten.

(Photograph by A. Riedinger, Augsburg.)

have been no danger if we had had a little wind to carry us out
into the open, but as it was, we could hear from the sounds
below that we were close to the town and probably directly above
it.   Soon we saw the barracks below us, and came, all at once,
into the strong breeze in which we had started.   I thought we
should have landed in front of my own house.   But we passed
over the centre of the town, and soon our guide-rope began to
rattle along the tops of the houses.   "Hold tight," said our
leader ; we felt a bump, and found that the rope had knocked a
ricketty chimney into the street.   Soon after this the rope
managed to coil round the telephone wires, and the only thing to

do was to cut it off. The strain on the rope was tremendous ; why it didn't break is a mystery. I thought Lieutenant George was a little nearer the rope than I was, so I suggested to him that he should lean over the edge and pull it in. We both got hold of it after a while, and I brought my trusty knife to bear on it. It was lucky I had it with me ; but then I had all my wits about me when I started, although I must admit I felt a little bustled just now. I had succeeded in cutting half-way through it, when there came an overpowering wrench, and it vanished over the side of the basket. The jolt was something to remember, and we should certainly have been shot out if we hadn't held on like grim death.

"At this critical moment our only policy seemed to be to get rid of the rope at any cost. Our chief got on the edge of the basket —not a position I should choose at the best of times—and after a while succeeded in cutting through the rope at the point I had started on. The rope fell down on the roofs of the houses, and one end tumbled in the river to the great astonishment of a boatman who was close by. We bumped up against one or two houses without doing much damage beyond the fact that we knocked off a bit of an old chimney, and swept away a few square feet of roof. All our ballast was gone, even our maps, our empty ballast bags, and the case for holding our instruments. Finally we seemed to reach a clear space, and being near enough to the ground, we all gave a mighty tug at the ripping cord. We came down on the left bank of the river, but the balloon fell unfortunately with the ripping panel downwards, and so the gas to some extent was prevented from escaping. We were dragged a short distance along the grass, and ran into a gun-carriage, which brought us finally to rest. We pulled the valve open, in order to empty the balloon completely, and many willing helpers were soon on the spot."

This account of the journey is sufficient to show that a well-constructed basket is capable of withstanding tremendous shocks. It is generally possible to escape from the most hazardous positions, and it requires an extraordinary combination of mishaps to bring about such a tragic episode as the death of Sigsfeld at Antwerp.

CHAPTER XIX.

SCIENTIFIC BALLOONING.

THE examination of atmospheric phenomena with the help of balloons or kites has added considerably to our knowledge of the subject. Meteorology has naturally attracted most attention, but astronomical work has also been done in the observation of eclipses, shooting stars, etc. The balloon has also been used on Polar expeditions, but meteorology was undoubtedly the first branch of scientific knowledge to which the balloon was usefully applied.

A Frenchman, named Périer, discovered in 1647 that the barometer stood at a lower level at the top of the Puy de Dôme than in the vallies. In 1780 Bénédict de Saussure made preparations for a scientific journey to Mont Blanc, which was carried out in 1787.[1] In the meantime the inventions of the brothers Montgolfier had become generally known, and the results of Charles's expeditions had reached scientific circles. On his first trip on December 1st, 1783, in the " Charlière," he had taken barometric readings, the minimum being 20 in., which corresponded to an altitude of 11,360 ft. His thermometer also showed a reading of 16° F.

Saussure recognised at once the importance of the new methods, and travelled to Lyons in order to obtain information. He was there received on January 15th, 1784, by Joseph Montgolfier and Pilâtre de Rozier, who were making arrangements for a proposed ascent. He took great interest in the theory of ballooning, and suggested that it might be possible to find favouring breezes at different heights, and therefore to move in any desired direction. On September 19th of the same year, the effect of

---

[1] The most comprehensive work on the subject of meteorological ballooning is a book entitled " Wissenschaftliche Luftfahrten," by Assmann and Berson, published in 1899 by F. Vieweg & Son, Brunswick.

the heat of the sun's rays on the temperature of the hydrogen in the balloon was carefully noticed by the brothers Robert. Lavoisier, who discovered the method of generating hydrogen by passing steam over red-hot iron, published in 1784 a comprehensive programme for scientific balloon ascents. The first electrical observations were made on June 18th, 1786, by Testu Brissy, who ascended into thunderclouds, and said that he drew remarkable discharges from the clouds by means of an iron rod, carried in the car. A pilot balloon was sent up by the Abbé Bertholon and Saussure, who repeated the observations Franklin had made with his kites, proving the existence of atmospheric electricity.

The first ascent, made solely for scientific purposes, was undertaken by the American, Dr. Jeffries, of Boston, whose adventurous journey across the Channel has already been mentioned. He started on November 30th, 1784, with Blanchard from London, and came down in $1\frac{1}{4}$ hours near the Thames at Dartford. The attempt to make use of wing-like oars failed utterly, but his meteorological observations were of interest. A height of 9,000 ft. was reached, and the temperature fell to 29° F., whereas in London it was 51°. He took with him a Toricelli barometer, a pocket thermometer, a hydrometer, an electrometer, and a compass. Besides these things, Cavendish, the discoverer of hydrogen, suggested he should take small bottles filled with water, in which he should collect samples of the atmosphere at different heights. His results may be tabulated as follows:—

Time.	Temperature Fahrenheit.	Barometer in inches.	Hydro-meter.	Altitude in feet above sea level.	Rate of ascent in feet per second.	Rate of change of temperature per 100 feet.	Remarks.
2.20	51	30·0	0	262	—	—	—
2.45	40	27·0	—	2,880	1·64	−0·42	cloudy
3.3	35	25·0	3	4,850	1·83	−0·254	cloudy

The direction of motion above the clouds was determined by throwing out a number of cards. The description of the preparations that were made for the journey shows that it was done on strictly scientific lines with the greatest care, and the results are interesting, though no account was taken of the direct effect of radiation from the sun, and consequently the temperature values are only correct so long as the sky was covered with cloud.

Jeffries made a second expedition on January 7th, 1785, which

FIG. 146.—Dr. Jeffries with the barometer used on his ascents.

has already been described in some detail. It may be noted that on this occasion the first trigonometrical observations of the height of a balloon were made from the French coast, and the altitude was found to be 4,800 ft. No barometric readings appear to have been taken on the ground level, so that it is not possible to deduce much from his readings.

Hellman, the meteorologist of Berlin, has clearly shown that

Jeffries was the first to attempt meteorological observations from a balloon, though for many years it was supposed that a man named Robertson was the first scientific balloonist. He made an ascent on July 18th, 1803, in the old French military balloon " Intrépide," which had already done duty at the battle of Fleurus. The start was made at Hamburg with another man, named Lhoest. Robertson was clearly shown to be an impostor, but he gave the following description of his journey in one of the Hamburg papers : " We continued to ascend as long as we were able to withstand the atmospheric influences. The cold was like that of the depth of winter ; a kind of coma came over us, with buzzing in the ears and swelling of the veins. I made some experiments with the galvanic battery, and noted carefully the flight of the birds, as long as it was possible to do so. My companion complained that his head was swelling, and I found my own head swollen to such an

FIG. 147.—Apparatus for generating hydrogen.

extent that I could not put on my hat, and my eyes were bloodshot. We therefore descended. But I noticed the terrified aspect of the peasants, and as I had forgotten an important experiment, I made up my mind to make another ascent. We continued on our way till two o'clock in the afternoon, when we came to the ground near Wichtenbeck without any injury to ourselves or the balloon. The peasants evidently thought we had come from the infernal regions." The results of Robertson's observations have been lost ; but he was either hopelessly incompetent or an impostor, or, very possibly, both. He said he reached an altitude of 24,300 ft., that his experiments with frictional electricity were a failure, that a galvanic battery only gave five-sixths of its normal current, and that the atmospheric electricity was positive, as examined by his gold-leaf electroscope. Neither did the air contain as much oxygen at great heights as it did on the ground level. Laplace induced the Académie des Sciences to investigate the truth of these assertions ; and consequently Gay-Lussac and Biot undertook an ascent for that purpose, with the result that the statements made by Robertson were found to be incorrect. They rose to a height of 10,000 ft., and found that the experiments with frictional electricity worked perfectly ; the battery continued to give the same current, and the atmospheric charge was alternately positive and negative. Gay-Lussac undertook a further ascent alone, and reached an altitude of 23,000 ft. He found that the percentage of oxygen in the atmosphere was constant, and independent of the altitude. It was further proved that Robertson had only reached a height of 21,400 ft. His descriptions of the effect of the reduced pressure on the human organism were found to be much exaggerated, but none the less it is still commonly believed that at great heights it is not unusual for blood to flow from the eyes and ears. This point will be dealt with later.

These expeditions aroused much interest in scientific circles, but till 1850 no further work of the kind was done in France. In Germany, on the other hand, ascents were made by Professor Jungins from Berlin between the years 1805 and 1810 ; he occasionally reached an altitude of 21,000 ft., but nothing noteworthy was done in the way of observations. In the years 1838 and 1839, the professional aeronaut Green, and the astronomer Spencer-Rush made ascents in England, but their results appear to be absolutely worthless. Assmann considers that the temperatures are too high by at least 36° F., and their altitudes are probably 3,000 ft. too high, so that instead of having reached a height of 29,000 ft. they got no further than 26,000 ft. Interesting observations were made in America by Wise, who has been already mentioned as the inventor of the ripping panel. He sent up two balloons in Philadelphia on a calm day. They remained close to one another for some length of time ; but one eventually rose to a height of 200 ft. above the other, and they were then separated. This was owing to the fact that the one was carried away by an easterly breeze while the other was still being driven in a southerly direction.

Some ascents were made in France in 1850 by Barral and Bixio, who recorded the very unexpected temperature of 39° F., at an altitude of 23,000 ft., whereas Gay-Lussac at the same height had found a temperature of 10° F. Assmann, how-ever, thinks that all the figures are probably correct. There is nothing which tends to depress the reading, because it is impossible to show a reading lower than the temperature of the atmosphere. On the other hand, the radiation from the sun or from any other hot body might tend to raise the reading, and therefore to show a figure higher than the actual temperature of the air. Arago defended the results of Barral and Bixio, because he well understood that the direct effect of the radiation of the sun must be excluded. Glaisher and Welsh tried to find the true temperature by the use of aspirators. Glaisher's results were the most important that were in existence till 1887, though Assmann showed that there was still considerable doubt as to the correctness of the temperatures. French balloonists also undertook scientific ascents about this time, but they did nothing to improve on Glaisher's results. Among them may be men-tioned Camille Flammarion, the popular astronomical writer; Wilfrid de Fonvielle, the brothers Tissandier, Sivel and Crocé-Spinelli (who lost their lives at the work), Moret, Duté-Poitevin, Hermite, Besançon, and many others. It is impossible to do more than mention their names, though the importance of their work, in some cases at any rate, was undoubted. A member of Parliament named Powell made an ascent for meteorological purposes, with Captain Templer and Captain Gardner; but he was unfortunately drowned through falling into the sea, while the officers barely escaped with their lives.[1]

Glaisher made twenty-eight ascents for scientific purposes, and was the first to adopt really accurate methods. His plans were carried out with the greatest care, and included a wide range of

[1] See Wilfrid de Fonvielle, "Les Grandes Ascensions Maritimes." Paris. Auguste Ghio. 1882.

observations, which were made at short intervals throughout the
journey. His results are embodied in the reports of the British
Association, and included observations from the following points:—

(1) Determination of the temperature of the atmosphere, and
of the amount of moisture contained in it at different heights,
particularly at the higher levels. Determination of the dew-

FIG. 148.—Glaisher and Coxwell in the basket.

point by means of Daniell's wet bulb thermometer, Regnault's
condensation hygrometer, and of the psychrometer both in its
ordinary form and with the addition of an aspirator. In the
case of the latter, large quantities of air were to be passed
through the vessels containing the thermometers at different
levels, more especially the higher levels ; special attention to
be directed to the highest levels which are suitable for human
habitation, with special reference to the mountains and plateaux

of India.   At these heights the readings of the psychrometer to
be carefully compared with those of Daniell's and Regnault's
hygrometers.

(2) Comparison of the readings of an aneroid with a mercury
barometer up to heights of 5 miles.

(3) Determination   of   the   electrical   properties   of   the
atmosphere.

(4) Determination of the properties of the oxygen in the
atmosphere by means of ozone paper.

(5) Determination of the period of oscillation of a magnet at
the ground level and at different altitudes.

(6) Collection of samples of air at different levels.

(7) Notes on the height and
constitution of the clouds, their
density and depth.

(8) Determination   of   the
velocity and direction of the
breezes, in so far as this is
possible.

(9) Acoustical observations.

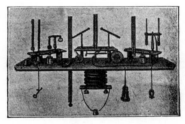

FIG. 149.—Glaisher's instruments.

(10) Any   general   atmo-
spheric observations, not included under the foregoing heads.

Anybody who has ever made a meteorological ascent will well
understand the amount of work involved by the numerous observations, and the careful method which would be necessary to cover
so vast a range.   It has been shown that on a journey made on
July 21st, 1863, Glaisher must have made in a space of 60 seconds
seven readings of the aneroid, accurate to the hundredth of an inch,
and 12 readings of the thermometer, accurate to the tenth of a
degree.   On June 26th, 1863, he carried out the following observations in 1 hour 26 minutes, viz.: 107 readings of the mercury
barometer, a similar number of the thermometer attached to the
barometer, 63 readings of the aneroid, 94 of the dry, 86 of the wet
bulb thermometer, 62 of the gridiron, 13 of the dry and 12 of the
wet bulb thermometer fitted with aspirator, besides several observations with the hydrometer, and noting the time on 165 different
occasions.   Each observation must therefore have taken on an

average 9·6 seconds, including such necessary attention as was given to the adjusting of the various instruments and apparatus.[1] At first these instruments were mounted on a bench placed in the middle of the basket, with its ends projecting over the edge ; but in the later expeditions this was altered and the bench was placed on the edge of the basket, so as to prevent, as far as possible, any effect of radiation from the observers themselves.

It has been already stated that the influence of the radiation of the sun on the temperature readings was well known. Gay-Lussac and Biot first noticed it owing to the burning sensation produced on the skin; they tried to protect the thermometer from the effects of the sun by enclosing it in a pocket handker-chief, an arrangement which was wholly insufficient. Arago proposed to determine the temperature by means of a thermo-meter suspended by a string, which would be dashed about by the air, and consequently continually brought into contact with fresh volumes of air. In this way an approximately correct reading could be obtained. Welsh used an aspirator in connection with his thermometer, not with a view to neutralising the effect of the sun's radiation but in order to be able to detect any variation of the temperature as soon as possible. His work was done close to the sea, and it was therefore impossible to undertake any very lengthy expedition. Assmann has, however, shown that even this type of instrument does not give reliable results, though Welsh's work was unknown to him when he devised his well-known aspirator-psychrometer, which forms an indispensable item in the outfit of the scientific balloonist.

This instrument contains two thermometers, having their mercury bulbs protected by highly polished metal tubes, about half an inch in diameter. These tubes are open at the top, and communicate at the bottom with a central metallic tube, about one inch in diameter and 8 inches long. At the top of the instru-ment there is placed a clockwork apparatus, driven by a spring, which serves to put two metal discs in rotation. The rotation of these discs sucks the air through the central tube, and con-sequently past the thermometer bulbs, at a speed of 8 or 10 ft. per

---

[1] See Assmann's " Wissenschaftliche Luftfahrten," vol. i., page 56.

second. The rays of the sun are reflected by the polished metal surrounding the bulbs of the thermometers, which are therefore protected from external influences and register the temperature of the air as it is sucked past them. In this way the true

FIG. 150.—Basket fitted with instruments according to the method proposed by Assmann.

temperature of the atmosphere can be found, supposing that the thermometers are kept at a sufficient distance from the observers, etc., to be free from any of the effects of radiation that may be due to the contents of the basket. The instrument is preferably mounted on [some kind of support which keeps it at a suitable distance from the basket on the outside. It is then quickly

drawn up to the edge of the basket for the purpose of taking
a reading; or, if very great accuracy is needed, it may be read
through a telescope. The working of this instrument has been
tested by long exposure to the rays of the sun on the top of the
Säntis, and its readings were found to be very accurate.

Professor Assmann proposed to Professors Berson and Süring
that they should make an ascent in a balloon, and compare the
readings obtained by Glaisher's methods with those obtained by

FIG. 151.—Assmann's aspi-
rator-psychrometer.

means of the aspirator-psychrometer. It
was found that the readings given by the
latter were considerably lower than
Glaisher's figures, the difference amounting on an average to 27° F. It therefore
seemed likely that Glaisher's results
were to some extent vitiated by his
defective apparatus. Assmann examined
Glaisher's work very carefully, and determined that the best way of doing this
would be to make some fresh ascents.
In the years 1884 and 1885 some ascents
had been made by a man named Jeserich,
who had principally confined his attention to taking samples of the air for
chemical analysis, though he also made
some electrical and meteorological observations. After this the officers of the
Prussian Balloon Corps made scientific
observations. This was due in the first instance to Captain
Buchholz, who entered into communication with the Meteorological
Institute, and arranged that Lieutenants von Tschudi, von Hagen,
and Moedebeck should undertake meteorological observations. At
a later date, work was done by Major Gross, who pointed out the
effect produced by the radiation from the sun on a thermometer,
and recommended the use of the Assmann instrument. This was
first done by Assmann and Sigsfeld on the occasion of an ascent
in a captive balloon at Berlin in May, 1887, and Moedebeck was the
first to use it in a free balloon on June 23rd of that year. Soon

afterwards Sigsfeld made a large balloon, named the " Herder,"
and went up in it on June 23rd, 1888, in company with Kremser
of the Meteorological Institute.   Assmann's instrument was used
on this occasion, but still the results were not wholly satisfactory,
and it was necessary to have recourse to the subscription list.

FIG. 152.—Professor Assmann and Professor Berson.

Help was speedily forthcoming from various quarters, and the
" Herder " was soon followed by the " M. W." and the " Meteor."
In the latter Assmann made five successful ascents in company
with Gross, Killisch, Berson, and others.   Assmann was indefatigable in the matter of raising money ; he clearly saw that general
conclusions could only be drawn from a long series of observations taken under all sorts of different conditions.   The Kaiser
placed the sum of £2,500 at his disposal, and money was also

obtained from other quarters. The balloon "Humboldt" was then built, and started its career under an evil omen. At the first descent Assmann broke his leg; on the second journey the balloon settled down on a lightning conductor; on the third something went wrong with the valve at a height of 10,000 ft., and Gross and Berson sustained rather serious bruises from the bumping of the basket on the ground; and finally, on the sixth journey the whole thing exploded when it came to earth through the gas in the balloon coming in contact with an electric spark.

It seemed very doubtful whether the work could be continued, until the Kaiser again subscribed £1,600. The "Phœnix" was then built, and in it Berson reached the greatest height on record, viz., 30,000 ft. Twenty-two journeys were made in this balloon altogether, and the results obtained were of great importance. Others were also pressed into the service. Mr. Patrick Y. Alexander lent his balloon, the "Majestic," which had a capacity of 106,000 cubic feet and was made of varnished silk. The Balloon Corps did its part, and took meteorological observers on many of its trips. Forty-six ascents were made with the funds that had been raised. The results were so encouraging that the Kaiser placed a further sum of £1,000 at the disposal of Professor Assmann, and also showed his interest in the work by attending some of the ascents in company with the Kaiserin and his sons.

On working out the results, Assmann noticed that Glaisher's results showed that the temperature in England at certain heights was greater than that in Germany, and that this difference increased with the height. At a height of 8,200 ft. the difference appeared to be 2·5° F., whereas in one case at 26,000 ft. it appeared to be no less than 37·2° F. Consequently it must either be warmer over England than on the Continent, or on the other hand, there might be something wrong about the figures. Welsh had found lower temperatures in England, and in any case there was some doubt about Glaisher's figures. On September 5th, 1862, he had made an ascent, and became unconscious at a height of 26,000 ft. He stated, however, that he had actually reached an altitude of 37,000 ft., and this figure was calculated

in the following way.   At an altitude of 29,000 ft. he was rising
at the rate of 16 ft. per second, and in thirteen minutes, when
he regained consciousness, he found that the balloon was falling
at the rate of 38 ft. per second.   Therefore he calculated that he
must have risen to a height of 37,000 ft., while his minimum
thermometer registered 12·1° F.   Coxwell, who was also
in the balloon, succeeded in gripping the valve-rope with his
teeth and let out some of the gas.   He said that the pointer on

Fig. 153.—The Kaiser attending the ascent of a recording balloon on the
Tempelhofer Feld, near Berlin.

the aneroid coincided in position with a string fastened across
the basket, and that this was found to denote a reading of 7 in.,
corresponding to an altitude of 37,000 ft.   It has been pointed out
by Assmann that observations made under conditions bordering
on unconsciousness are very liable to error.   It is known that a
balloon falls with a maximum speed of 16 ft. per second.[1]   But
Glaisher's figures point to a fall at the rate of 130 ft. per second,

[1] During the summer of 1902 a descent was made by the author in company
with Professor Miethe ; the readings of the barometer certainly showed a maximum
speed of more than 33 ft. per second.   But a thunderstorm was raging at the time,
and the strong downward wind increased the speed of falling.

and if it had actually fallen at anything like that rate it would doubtless have been torn to pieces. The apparent errors in Glaisher's results are doubtless due to the effects of solar radiation.

It was evident that a number of important problems could not be solved by ascents from a single spot, and that it would be necessary to organise ascents from many places, and, if possible, to establish observatories for the purpose. It was further

FIG. 154.—Major Moedebeck.

FIG. 155.—Captain von Sigsfeld.

desirable to make simultaneous ascents from a number of places with a view to mapping out the state of the atmosphere after the manner adopted in the meteorological reports published from day to day. This has given rise to an international organisation for the purpose of making such ascents, which mostly take place on the first Thursday in every month. Gaston Tissandier started the idea, and on July 14th, 1893, simultaneous ascents were made from Berlin and Stockholm. On August 4th, 1894, ascents were made from Berlin, Göteborg, and St. Petersburg. Later tests on these lines were undertaken by an international organisation consisting of Rotch, the director of the Blue Hill Observatory in America; Besançon, de Fonvielle, Hermite, and Teisserenc de Bort in France; Assmann, Erk, Hergesell, Moedebeck and the Balloon Corps in Germany; Mr. Patrick Y. Alexander in England; Colonel von Kowanko, Colonel Pormortzeff, and General Rykatscheff in Russia, and Andrée in Sweden.

A conference for meteorological purposes met at Paris in September, 1896, and an international commission for scientific ballooning was then inaugurated, under the presidency of Dr. Hergesell, the director of the Meteorological Institute for Alsace and Lorraine. Most civilised countries are now represented at the conferences which take place every two years, and meetings have been held in Strassburg, Paris, Berlin, St. Peterburg, and Milan. It is perhaps difficult for an outsider to understand the many-sided activity of the balloonist in this field of research, and to form an idea of the problems that are awaiting solution. It may therefore

FIG. 156.—Captain Gross.

be as well to quote a portion of the speech made by Dr. Hergesell when he opened the conference at Berlin in his capacity of president. " Our first task consists not in carrying out the largest possible number of simultaneous ascents, either with or without observers in the car, but in organising the basis of co-operation by the employment of accurate instruments, which are constructed on similar principles. The outlines of such arrangements as are possible to secure the use of similar instruments were discussed at our first conference at Strassburg. Since that time, such balloons as carry observers have been fitted with the aspirator-psychrometer devised by Assmann and Sigsfeld; and balloons without observers have carried the recording instruments due to the indefatigable industry of Teisserenc de Bort. The recording balloon has become a most useful auxiliary, and has brought us most surprising results out of the icy regions at a height of twelve miles above our heads. Berson and Süring rose to heights of six miles, and in so far as their records go they confirm the results obtained.

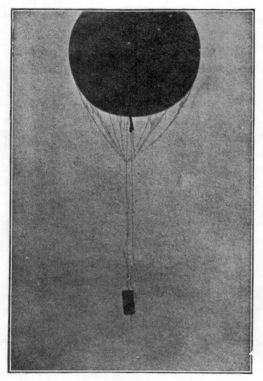

Since the month of November, 1900, simultaneous ascents are made on the first Thursday in the month at Paris, Strassburg, Munich, Berlin, Vienna, St. Petersburg, and Moscow; and on May 5th, 1902, the 213th recording balloon was sent up.

"The seed thus sown has borne good fruit. It had generally been believed that Glaisher's results were correct, and that at fairly low levels the temperature remained constant

FIG. 157.—A recording balloon with instruments.

throughout the year. But this has been shown to be altogether wrong. There is eternal change even at great heights, and the temperature varies just as much at levels of 30,000 ft. as at 1,200 ft. Moreover, at the same heights above Paris and St. Petersburg there may be differences of temperature amounting to 60° or 70° F. Our observations have also proved that the variation of temperature is not continuous, but that the atmosphere is composed of layers, as it were, which often show considerable differences of temperature. This layer-formation is one of the most important subjects at present under investigation.

" The future has still much work to do. At present, systematic observations are made in few parts of the earth, and such portions of our own continent as Italy, Spain and Norway are unrepresented at our conference. We are proposing to cover the ocean by means of balloons sent up from steamers, and our work must also be extended to the tropics. In this province the assistance of England is very important, seeing that India offers great scope for these observations. Our aim must be to explore the great unknown above our heads, and to discover from it the secret of the weather chart."

Since this speech was made, some of its hopes have been fulfilled; Italy, Spain, and Sweden have joined the conference, and much work has been done by sea as well as by land.

We must now describe methods by which meteorological instruments can be sent on a journey in the air. The oldest method is the kite. In 1749 Wilson used it to send up thermometers for the measurement of temperatures; in 1883 Professor Douglas

FIG. 158.—A wickerwork basket with instruments for a recording balloon.

Archibald used it for finding the velocity of the wind; and since 1894 the American observer Rotch has used it largely for the work of his observatory. It was due to the success of Rotch's work that the kite has since been used almost everywhere for the purpose of atmospheric observation. Teisserenc de Bort has followed Rotch's example; he has made excellent arrangements for sending up kites and balloons at Trappes near Paris, and this has been done at his own expense and with little help from outside. Professor Hergesell tried to induce the provincial authorities to provide him with funds; but there happened to be no

available surplus in the exchequer.   Still kite ascents have been
regularly made for these purposes in Strassburg since 1896.
Professor Assmann succeeded in erecting an observatory on a
large scale, and started on this work as soon as the sum of
£2,000 had been voted for the purpose.   The building began
on April 1st, 1899, and on October 1st of the same year it was
possible to make the first ascents with kites and balloons.   A
site was chosen at Tegel in the north of Berlin, because the
Balloon Corps was stationed there, and their help was thought
likely to be useful, seeing that the preparation of the gas and

the inflation of the balloon would
be a difficult matter for the limited
staff of the observatory.   Moreover, the Balloon Corps might, on
the other hand, derive considerable advantages from association
with scientific work.   The observatory contained a carpenter's shop
for making kites, a balloon shed,
a house from which the winches
were worked, with a tower 90 ft.
high, and also the necessary working and living rooms.   Assmann
saw that kites would not be
sufficient for the carrying out of

FIG. 159.—Dr. Hergesell.

his plans; he intended to take observations at great heights
every morning for several hours, and therefore ordered a kite-
balloon, which was to be used when the velocity of the wind was
less than 18 or 20 ft. per second, a speed insufficient for the flying
of kites.   Ordinarily either kites or the kite-balloon are used;
but on "international" days free balloons are sent up, either
with or without observers.   The latter are used in a special
manner that has been gradually evolved as the result of
experience.

The use of balloons without observers but carrying recording
instruments was the idea of Hermite and Besançon, and the
details were carefully elaborated by Teisserenc de Bort in his

"Observatoire de la Météorologie dynamique." Balloons are used, made of the lightest silk, cambric or paper, varnished with rubber solution or linseed oil; their capacities vary from 1,000 to 17,500 cubic feet. The weight of the instruments is very small, and therefore the size of the balloon depends generally on the height to which it is proposed to ascend. The net is of

Fig. 160.—Ascent of a balloon, fitted with a parachute, at Lindenberg.

very light construction; it has merely to resist the internal pressure and carry the basket containing the instruments. Assmann has designed an arrangement whereby an alarum clock opens the valve after a certain time, and therefore causes the balloon to descend after it has reached a certain height. In order to prevent the effects of solar radiation, the balloon must be prevented from hovering in one position, so that the thermometers are continually brought into contact with fresh

A.   S

volumes of air, in a manner similar to that adopted in the
aspirator-psychrometer.   If the balloon is made to rise quickly
and then to fall at once, the thermometers give correct values ;
but if it is allowed to drift gently along, exposed to the rays of
the sun, the readings will be too high.   Attempts have been
made to shield the instruments by placing them in a wicker
basket, covered with highly polished silver or nickel paper, but

FIG. 161.—Ascent of a box-kite containing meteorological instruments
(Photograph by the Berliner Illustrationsgesellschaft.)

this is not sufficient.   Kites have been sent up in the early
morning before sunrise, and figures, obtained in this way, have
been compared with those recorded in bright sunlight.   But the
daylight ascents are much the more important, as the effect of
the sun on the atmosphere must on no account be neglected.
Assmann has also invented a system by which rubber balloons
with diameters of one or two yards are sent up, gradually
expanding as they rise, till they finally burst ; a linen cap acts
as a parachute, and the case with the instruments falls gently to
the ground.   Such balloons will remain in the air from one to

three hours, and give good results.   They are now employed in most observatories.

It is of course important that the balloons and instruments should be returned to the observatory as soon as possible.   This matter was thoroughly discussed at the conference at St. Petersburg, and it was suggested that bells should be mounted on the balloon, so as to attract attention.   Hitherto the loss has amounted to something in the neighbourhood of 4 per cent. If the balloons fall into water the instruments are naturally lost, unless Hergesell's plan is adopted of attaching floats and

FIG. 162.—Winch house at Assmann's aeronautical observatory.

drawing attention to the spot by means of a second pilot balloon.   If they fall into a wood they are generally found, sooner or later.

There is a general impression that ascents with kites are much cheaper than those with balloons, but this is not the case.   Anyone who has done practical work with kites will know that they are cheaper in the first instance, but the cost of maintenance is greater.   A kite is often smashed to pieces by the wind, and the instruments are either destroyed or rendered more or less useless. Even if great care is taken, the wire holding the kite may be broken, and several miles are either lost or unfit for further use. Consequently the cost of maintenance is so great that kites are not less expensive for this form of work than balloons. The ascent of a kite is often a matter of some difficulty, and it is only by the exercise of the greatest care that accidents of one kind or another can be avoided. It is therefore a wonderful feat on the part of Assmann to have succeeded every day for the last four years in making an ascent either with kite or balloon. The ascents are made with the help of an electrically-driven winch, and there are means of telling the pull on the wire. The winch is used to pull the kite down, and also sometimes to help it to start. Suppose the wind to be very light. A considerable length of wire, amounting perhaps to 500 or 1,000 yards, is laid along the ground; the kite is held in the air, and the winch is started at full speed. In this way, the necessary air-resistance is created, and it gradually rises to an altitude where the breeze is blowing more strongly. The breakage of a long wire may be very dangerous in the neighbourhood of towns. It may fall across telegraph or telephone wires, and still more serious accidents have arisen from its coming in contact with the overhead tramway conductor. At Tegel it often happened that the kite got carried away by an overhead breeze, blowing in a different direction from the ground breeze, and its wire became entangled with the ropes holding the military captive balloon. Mishaps of various kinds induced Assmann to move his observatory from Tegel to Lindenberg, which is at a distance of 40 miles to the south-east of Berlin. The winch-house is here arranged at the top of a small hill, and is capable of being rotated so that it can follow the flight of the kite in any direction. Naturally enough, the experience of the four years at Tegel was very valuable, and consequent improvements in the arrangements at Lindenberg were therefore made. Assmann has two assistants in the scientific department, and two others who render technical assistance. The whole of the staff, including helpers of one kind and another, consists of 18 persons, and together with their wives and families they constitute a little colony of 50 persons. On October 1st, 1906, Assmann had accomplished the feat of making ascents on 1,379 consecutive days; but with the means at his disposal it is impossible to make ascents both by

day and by night without intermission. In the neighbourhood
of Lindenberg is a small lake, called the Scharmützelsee, about 7
miles long; and this seems likely to be useful for kite ascents

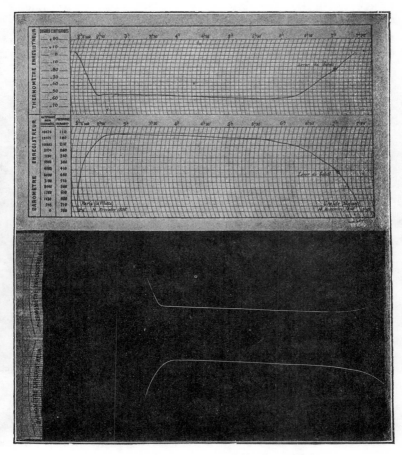

FIG. 163.—Curves taken by recording instruments.

In the lower half the curves are marked by a pointer on a piece of paper that has been coated with
soot. These curves are shown clearly in the upper half of the illustration.

It is intended to use a motor-boat for the purpose of starting the
flight. The Kaiser has taken great interest in scientific ballooning, and was present at the inauguration of the new observatory,
together with the Prince of Monaco and other well-known
meteorologists.

The greatest height reached by a balloon with recording instruments was 85,000 ft.; and this took place at Strassburg on August 3rd, 1905. The highest ascent with a kite was made from Lindenberg on November 25th, 1905, when an altitude of 21,100 ft. was reached. The height which a balloon will reach under these conditions depends of course entirely on the quality of the materials. It is possible that some little time will

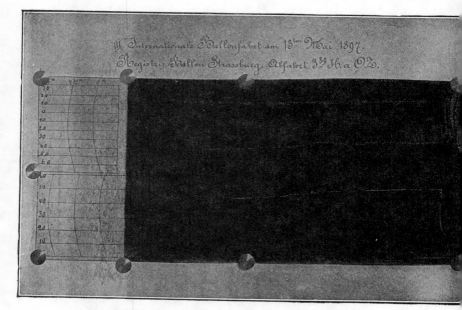

FIG. 164.—Curves given by recording instruments.

elapse before ascents will be made over the surface of the Scharmützelsee, and it will therefore be well to consider what has already been done by way of carrying out observations above the surface of lakes and seas.

The greater part of the earth's surface is covered with water, and the exploration of the atmosphere that lies over the sea is an absolute necessity if any progress is to be made towards the discovery of general laws. Rotch first pointed this out, and sent up balloons with recording instruments over the sea. In the spring of 1900, Professor Hergesell sent up a kite by means of a motor-boat over the Bodensee, and soon the number of observers increased. Rotch and Teisserenc de Bort crossed the Atlantic, Berson and Elias went to the North Cape, and Hergesell made an expedition with the Prince of Monaco in the Mediterranean and Atlantic. Hergesell has lately started an observatory for the purpose of studying the air over the Bodensee, and a motor-boat has been constructed for starting the kites.

The results of the observations of Hergesell and the Prince of Monaco are very interesting, as are also those of Rotch and Teisserenc de Bort. It is here only possible to give a general outline of their results.[1] With kites Hergesell reached altitudes of 20,000 ft., and with balloons of 47,000 ft.; and he concludes that above the Atlantic, which he crossed in the yacht *Princess Alice*, belonging to the Prince of Monaco, there are three atmospheric layers. The lowest of these has adiabatic temperature gradients, with a decrease of 1° F. per rise of 180 ft., and contains much moisture. The middle layer is very dry, and shows no decrease of temperature, but rather, on the other hand, a slight increase. The uppermost layer has a very decided temperature gradient in a downward direction, and contains little moisture. This last layer reaches to a height of 30,000 ft., at which level Teisserenc de Bort and Assmann have found that the air tends to become warmer over the mainland.

An interesting investigation related to the question of the trade winds. In consequence of the revolution of the earth on its axis, the trade wind blows from the north-east in the northern hemisphere, while in the southern half it appears as a south-east wind. Between the two comes the belt of calm. Seeing that the trade winds blow from the poles, it seems reasonable to suppose that at higher levels we should find winds blowing in the opposite direction towards the poles. But it now seems that this view is likely to be incorrect, though it is said that the smoke from the volcano Pic de Teyde on Teneriffe blows from the south-east after it has reached a certain height. Hergesell examined the zone lying between 26° and 38° northern latitude

[1] Fuller particulars are to be found in the "Annals of the Astronomical Observatory of Harvard College," vol. 43, part 3, which contains the results of Rotch's expeditions; also in "Beiträge zur Physik der freien Atmosphäre," 1904 and 1905; and in the *Meteorologische Zeitschrift*, November. 1905.

and between 10° and 42° longitude west of Greenwich up to levels of 47,000 ft., and found that the wind mostly blew from the north ; only on one day at a height of 6,000 ft. it appeared to blow from the south. Teisserenc de Bort and Rotch did their work slightly to the north of the Canaries, near the Azores ; they found, like Hergesell, winds blowing from the north-east and east at the lower levels, and at greater heights it blew from the west and south-west. This work promises interesting results, but it does not appear to be quite so simple as was supposed.

FIG. 165.—A. Laurence Rotch.

It may be interesting to describe the sensations of the human body at these high levels. An account of a journey undertaken by Count Zambeccari at Bologna, in 1803, is still in existence. He made an ascent with two friends in a *Charlière*, which was to be heated with a big spirit lamp. The balloon had so much lift that Zambeccari and one of his companions soon became unconscious, while the other, who had not done so much hard work on the preparations before starting, was quite unaffected, and succeeded in waking them as they were on the point of falling into the sea. Before they had succeeded in throwing out any of the ballast they found themselves in the water, and then proceeded to throw overboard everything on which they could lay hands, including instruments, clothing, lamps, propellers, ropes, etc. The balloon at once rose to a great height, reaching a higher level than that from which it had previously fallen. Breathing became very difficult ; one became seasick, another had bleeding at the nose, and in consequence of the severe cold all their wet clothes were covered with ice. The balloon soon descended again, and once more fell into the sea, the aeronauts being rescued as they were on the point of drowning. Several of Zambeccari's fingers were so frostbitten that they had to be cut off.

Glaisher and Coxwell made a remarkable ascent in September, 1862. The balloon had so much lift that at the end of 18 minutes it was 10,500 ft. high, having risen at the rate of 10 ft. per second. At this height the temperature was at the freezing point. At 16,000 ft. Coxwell began to lapse into a comatose state, whereas Glaisher was unaffected. They soon

FIG. 166.—Kite ascents on the Prince of Monaco's yacht in the Mediterranean.

reached an altitude of 29,000 ft., where the thermometer registered 2° F. The sensations they experienced have been well described by Glaisher in the following words:—

" Up to this moment I had been able to take my observations without being inconvenienced by any breathing troubles, whereas Coxwell had often lapsed into unconsciousness. But I soon found that I was no longer able to see the mercury column of the wet-bulb thermometer, and after a while the same thing happened with the hands on the clock and the fine marks of division on the instruments. I therefore asked Coxwell to help me, as I could no longer see to do the work. But the balloon had been in a constant state of rotation, so that the

ropes connected to the valve had become entangled ; Coxwell
therefore climbed up from the basket and managed to free them.
I made another reading, and noticed that the barometer reading
was 9·71 in., which denoted a height of 29,000 ft.   I placed my
right arm on the bench ; and when I tried to move it again, I
found that it hung from my side in a paralysed state.   I then
tried to use the other arm, but it was also helpless.   I roused
myself as far as I could, and tried to lean over to read the
barometer ; but I found that I had lost the use of my limbs,
and my head fell on my left shoulder.   I made another attempt

FIG. 167.—Recording balloons on the ss. *Planet*.

to regain the use of my limbs, but it was impossible to move my
arms.   I was indeed able for a moment to raise my head, but
it sank again on my shoulder.   I fell with my back against the
side of the basket, and my head rested on the edge.   My arms
and legs seemed to have lost all their strength, but my spine
and neck seemed capable of some movement with a very great
effort.   But this did not last long, and I was soon entirely
incapable of making any movement whatever.   I saw Coxwell
sitting in the ring, and tried to talk to him, but did not succeed.
Then everything suddenly appeared dark ; the nerves of my
eyes refused to work, but I had by no means lost consciousness.
I was in fact just as clear in the head as I am at the moment
of writing this.   But it was perfectly evident that death was

staring me in the face unless we descended at once.   Suddenly
I lost consciousness.   I cannot say what the effect of all this
was on my hearing, seeing that there were no sounds to be heard ;
we were at a height of 36,000 ft., where it would be impossible
for any sounds to reach us from the earth.

   " At 1.54 I had made my last observation, and assuming that
two or three minutes had elapsed in the interval, it would now
be 1.57.   Suddenly I heard Coxwell pronounce the two words
' temperature ' and ' observation ' ; this was a sign that I
had recovered consciousness, and was able to hear.   But I could

FIG. 168.—The American meteorologist, Rotch, making some
kite ascents on the Atlantic.

neither see him nor speak to him, nor could I make any movement.   Again I heard Coxwell say to me, ' Try to do it.'   I
saw the instruments very indistinctly, but all at once everything
became quite clear.   I said that I had been unconscious, and
Coxwell said he had nearly been so, too.   He showed me his
hands, which had been quite paralysed and looked black.   He
said that while he had been sitting on the ring he had been
overcome by the cold, and had slid down on his elbows into the
basket, as he was unable to use his hands.   When he saw that
I was unconscious, he seized the valve-rope with his teeth,
thereby opening the valve.   I resumed my observations at
2.7 p.m.''

Glaisher's report contains no further reference to his bodily sensations on this journey, and after landing he suffered no further discomfort.   He estimated the maximum height at 36,000 ft., but, as already stated, Assmann considers that it did not exceed 29,500 ft.   In any case, the journey was a very remarkable performance ; no human being has penetrated to such heights either before or since without taking a supply of oxygen.   Glaisher's account gives us a good idea of the condition of the human organism under such circumstances. This led the way to experiments with animals in order to find how they behaved in a more rarefied atmosphere, and how their condition improved if they were supplied with pure oxygen. Paul Bert carried out some experiments with small birds, which were placed on the receiver of an air-pump.   He showed that all the symptoms disappeared as soon as the animal was supplied with oxygen, and therefore constructed a large airtight chamber in order to continue his experiments with human beings.   These observations gave the same result.   It was found that the quick breathing with rapid pulse, the buzzing in the ears, the fainting fits and mental exhaustion, ceased at once as soon as oxygen was supplied.

In March, 1874, two Frenchmen, named Sivel and Crocé-Spinelli, made an ascent in order to try the effects of breathing oxygen at great heights.   They then found that whereas in the vacuum chamber they could very well stand a pressure as low as 13 in. of mercury, the same pressure in a balloon caused very great discomfort.   They ascribed this to the temperature, which was very low, the thermometer reading only 11° F.   The inhaling of oxygen produced under these conditions very great relief.   They continued their experiments, but unfortunately with fatal results.   On April 15th, 1875, Gaston Tissandier, Sivel and Crocé-Spinelli made an ascent with the intention of reaching still greater heights than Glaisher had done.   They therefore took with them small balloons, which contained a mixture of oxygen and air.   These balloons were fitted with tubes, through which the gas might be inhaled as occasion required.   Sivel was the first to be attacked by a fainting fit,

which, however, quickly passed off.   Tissandier meanwhile
continued meteorological and physiological observations without
interruption.   His pulse made 110 beats in the minute at a
height of 13,000 ft., while it made 80 under normal conditions;
at 17,500 ft. Sivel's pulse was beating at the rate of 150 per
minute, and Crocé's at 120, and the rate of breathing increased
in much the same proportion.   At 23,000 ft. their strength

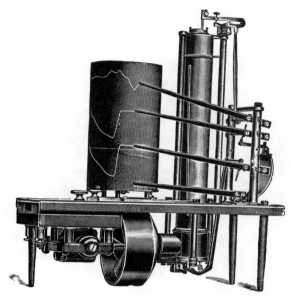

FIG. 169.—Baro-thermo-hygrograph, designed for balloons with observers
by Dr. Hergesell, and made by Bosch, of Strassburg.

(From " Die Umschau.")

began to fail, and they fell into the usual listless condition.
Their hands became stiff from the severe cold, and they were
attacked by giddiness and fainting fits.   Sivel and Crocé sat
motionless on the bottom of the basket, but Tissandier was able
to see from the barometer that they had reached a height of
26,000 ft., and then also became unconscious.   After some time
he was aroused by Crocé, who suggested that some ballast should
be thrown out, as the balloon was falling rapidly.   But Crocé
had to do it himself, as Tissandier again lost consciousness.

After a while Tissandier recovered his senses, but he was unable
to arouse his companions, who had been suffocated in the meantime.   He managed to land after being dragged heavily along
the ground for some distance.   Sivel and Croce had been
suffocated at a height of .27,000 ft., owing to the fact that they
no longer had the power of inhaling the oxygen.

In Germany, expeditions to great heights have been made by
Herr Berson, Dr. Süring, and Captain Gross.   A few particulars
may be of interest.   The first ascent of any importance was
made in the "Humboldt" on March 14th, 1893.   The valve

FIG. 170.—Baro-thermo-hygrograph, designed for kites by Dr. Hergesell,
and made by Bosch, of Strassburg.

(From "Die Umschau.")

opened unintentionally at a height of 10,000 ft., while on the
descent, and the balloon fell to the ground in 10 minutes.
Gross and Berson had proposed to rise to the greatest height
possible, without the use of oxygen.   Pulse and breathing began
to be hurried at a height of 16,000 ft.   Even the slightest exertion was found to be an effort, and to be accompanied by very
decided beats of the heart.   At a height of 20,000 ft. they were
unable any longer to do their work, and the lifting of the heavy
sacks of ballast became an impossibility.   The stomach is unable
to take food under these conditions, but a sip of wine or brandy
acts as a restorative, though this effect soon dies away.   In spite
of their rapid fall the balloonists sustained no serious injuries.
Captain Gross was slightly injured in the ribs ; otherwise they

only suffered from bruises, and, after resting a few days, were able to return to Berlin.

The ascent of December 4th, 1894, ought also to be mentioned, because Berson then reached an altitude of 30,000 ft. The balloon "Phœnix" was used on this occasion. It had a capacity of 92,000 cubic feet, and was filled with hydrogen at Strassburg. Berson made the ascent alone, and took with him a cylinder containing 35 cubic feet of oxygen. In order to reduce the work to a minimum, the sacks of ballast were suspended outside the car, and it was therefore only neces-sary to cut the string round the mouth of the sack in order to empty the bag. Berson had learnt a good deal from his previous trips, and accordingly had a long night's rest before starting. He was conse-quently able to reach an altitude of 23,000 ft. without the use of oxygen and without any serious inconveni-ence. At a height of 26,000 ft. he noticed that his heart was beating rather strongly when he happened accidentally to drop the tube con-nected to the cylinder of oxygen. With a great effort he rose still higher,

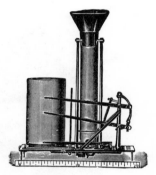

Fig. 171.—Baro-thermo-hygro-graph, designed for recording balloons by Dr. Hergesell, and made by Bosch, of Strassburg.

(From " Die Umschau.")

to 30,000 ft., when all the ballast was exhausted and the thermo-meter showed a reading of − 54° F. He was obliged to descend, though he was still in a physical condition to hold out longer, even at a greater height. On another occasion Berson and Dr. Süring succeeded in reaching a level of 35,500 ft., which is probably the greatest height at which existence is possible. A balloon with a capacity of 300,000 cubic feet was used, and in the middle of July, 1901, a trial trip was made, Berson and Süring being accompanied by Dr. von Schroetter of Vienna. The balloon was filled three-quarters full with coal gas, and rose to a height of 25,000 ft., during which time Dr. von Schroetter carried out physiological observations. The training which the observers underwent was curious. Bert had placed himself in a vacuum chamber, where the pressure had been reduced to 9·75 in. of mercury in 85 minutes. A man named Mosso had withstood a pressure of 7·5 in., which corresponded to a height of 38,200 ft. Berson, Süring, and Schroetter went into the vacuum chamber, and the pressure was lowered in 15 minutes to 8·85 in. The pump did not admit of a more perfect vacuum. At this pressure,

FIG. 172.—Professor Süring, of the Prussian Meteorological Institute.

rabbits were killed in 1½ hours, but pigeons managed to survive, though they tumbled about helplessly on the ground. Schroetter made careful observations on the pulse, rate of breathing, etc., and reports as follows: "We were now surrounded by an atmosphere at a pressure of 11·8 in. While the mercury was sinking, we noticed a feeling of lethargy, against which we struggled by breathing as hard as we could. But this did not help much. Our faces became very pale with a somewhat livid colour; our heads were drowsy, our legs trembled, our hands lost all power, and gradually we lapsed into a state bordering on unconsciousness. We breathed a little oxygen out of the receivers, and felt at once refreshed. All the distressing symptoms disappeared, and we seemed once more to be in full possession of bodily and mental faculties. The pressure gradually sank still further; but as we continued to breathe oxygen, I was able to continue my observations on the pulse, reflex actions, dynamometer, etc. The pressure fell below 10·25 in., which corresponds to a height of 28,000 ft. ; the observations were then concluded, and it was possible, even at this pressure, to smoke a cigarette." Schroetter is satisfied that the balloonist is liable to be attacked by all the symptoms of mountain sickness. A sleepy, lethargic state is induced, and the simplest thing requires a great effort. To stand up or to bend the body becomes a very exhausting operation. The muscles do not remain under control ; both sight and hearing are affected, and the mere effort of thinking is wearisome.

Fig. 173.—The balloon, " Prussia," belonging to the Aeronautical Observatory, an having a capacity of 300,000 cubic feet, is being filled with gas.

As an instance of the way in which the bodily and mental processes are affected, two specimens of Schroetter's writing are here reproduced ; the one was done under normal conditions, and the other under a pressure of 9·45 in. The trembling of the hand is very noticeable, and the difficulty of focussing the mind is shown by the fact that the word *nich* is repeated, whereas *nicht* should have been written once. If the patient sits perfectly still, the loss of power takes place more slowly ; but if the smallest effort is made, such, for instance, as standing up or lifting the lightest thing, it is certain to be accompanied by staggering or trembling. Shortness of breath and beating of

A.   T the heart are accompanied by severe headache; the pressure of the blood decreases, while the rate of the pulse increases.

On the trial trip, when the balloon rose to a height of 24,500 ft., and the thermometer fell to −8° F., all Schroetter's conclusions were verified, and in particular it was found that the inhaling of oxygen was sufficient to ward off most of the troublesome symptoms. The three observers were perfectly well, and able to undertake the most complicated measurements as well as to

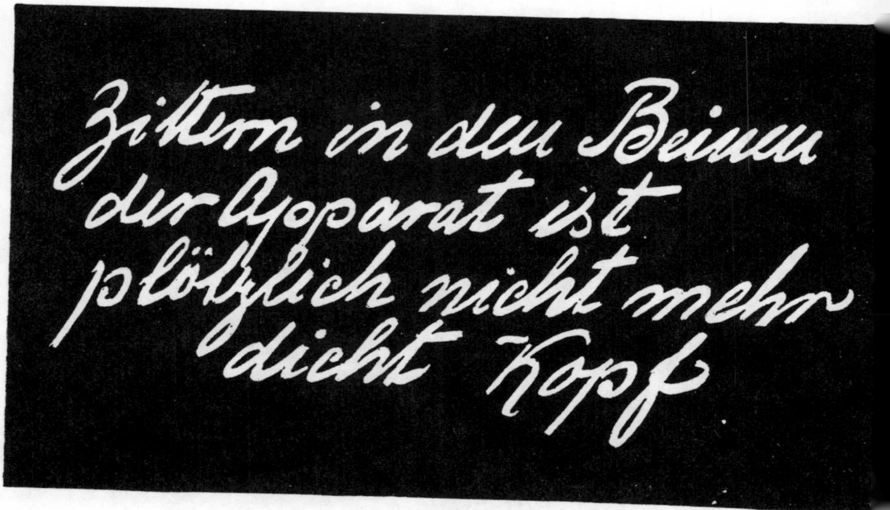

FIG. 174.—Herr von Schroetter's ordinary handwriting.
(Photograph from Zuntz' " Höhenklima und Bergwanderungen.")

enjoy the view from the car. Schroetter considers that Sivel and Crocé undoubtedly met their death through neglecting to take a sufficient supply of oxygen, and possibly also through waiting too long before beginning to inhale it. Bert showed that one-third of a cubic foot of air mixed with oxygen, and containing 70 per cent. of oxygen, is required per minute up to a height of 23,000 ft., but for heights above this pure oxygen is necessary. Therefore Crocé-Spinelli and Sivel ought to have taken 46 cubic feet of air mixed with oxygen, and 64 cubic feet of pure oxygen, and it is certain that their stock was nothing like this.

All preparations had been carefully made when Berson and Süring started on their record-breaking journey on July 31st, 1901. They rose to a height of 35,400 ft., and calculated beforehand from theoretical considerations that human life was impossible at a height of 36,100 ft. Süring's description of the ascent is as follows:—" At 10.50 a.m. the balloon ' Prussia ' began to ascend. It had a capacity of 190,000 cubic feet, and had been filled with hydrogen. It carried about 3½ tons of sand and iron filings as ballast, and rose very gently in the air under a slight

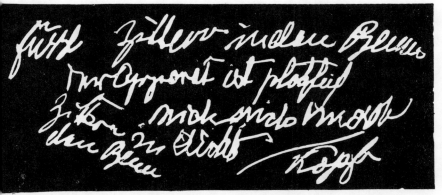

FIG. 175.—Herr von Schroetter's handwriting under an atmospheric pressure of 9·45 inches of mercury.

(Photograph from Zuntz' " Höhenklima und Bergwanderungen.")

north-west wind, the sky being partially covered with cirrus and cumulus. The balloon was rather more than half full and rose quickly but steadily; in 40 minutes it had reached a height of 16,000 ft., and at this stage it had assumed a spherical shape. We had with us four cylinders of compressed oxygen, each holding 35 cubic feet. Soon we began to turn to the right, and our course was directed somewhat towards the south of Potsdam. Before the start the temperature had been 74° F.; it had now sunk to 19° F. We began to inhale oxygen at a height between 16,000 and 20,000 ft., but rather as a precaution and with a view to saving our strength than from any actual necessity. The balloon seemed to be rising steadily, and we threw out large quantities of ballast continually, in amounts varying from 130 lb. to 330 lb. Then when a position of equilibrium was reached, a complete series of observations would be taken after which more ballast would be thrown out.

"Besides the ordinary readings on the barometer, we took note occasionally of the readings given by two black-bulb thermometers, one of which was specially protected from downward radiation and the other from upward radiation. After three hours

FIG. 176.—The balloon, "Prussia," half full of gas.

we had risen to a height of 26,000 ft., and in four hours we reached an altitude of 29,500 ft., and soon after we eclipsed the record, which till then had stood at 30,000 ft. This height had been reached on December 4th, 1894. The pressure was now less than 10 in., and the temperature was −25° F. Our sleepiness increased, which was not remarkable, seeing that we had had only four or five hours' sleep the night before. But it got no further than nodding, and we roused one another from time to time. Each little effort seemed to require more will power. We had sufficient energy to carry out the readings and note them in the book, and we could also throw out the ballast; but as for looking about us and determining the direction of our course, that was quite beyond us. After drifting along to the south-west, we thought that we came into a calm region, and that soon a breeze began to blow us back towards Berlin. After which there began again a slow drift towards the south-west, and at a very great height there was a strong west wind, which carried us rapidly towards the east.

Fig. 177.—The balloon, " Prussia," getting ready for an ascent.

" The last observation was made at 3.18 p.m. at a height of 33,500 ft., when the barometer read 8·27 in., and the thermometer stood at −40° F. These figures were clearly written down in our notebook. We soon fell at intervals into a state of unconsciousness; Berson pulled the valve-rope several times, when he saw me dozing off. While pulling the rope, i.e., about 5 minutes after the last recorded reading, he looked at the baro-meter, which registered exactly 8 in., corresponding to a height of 34,500 ft. At 33,500 ft. we had thrown out 400 lbs. of ballast, and our recording barometer shows that we were still ascending when Berson took his last reading. We probably rose another 1,000 ft., and certainly reached an altitude of 35,500 ft., or possibly 36,000 ft. But at this moment the effect of the valve-rope began to be felt, and we began the downward journey. No doubt we passed from a state of unconsciousness into a heavy sleep, and we awoke in three quarters of an hour to find the balloon still sinking. It was then at a height of 18,000 or 19,000 ft. We were still overcome by a feeling of great exhaustion, which was specially noticeable when we tried to move hands or feet; and though we had regained consciousness completely, it was still impossible to do anything or to move anything or anywhere. Later we pulled ourselves together to such an extent that we had control over the balloon, but it was still quite impossible to resume our readings."

The fact that the observers lost consciousness was due, according to Schroetter, to the method of breathing; it is quite likely that they did not, as a matter of fact, inhale a sufficient amount. Sivel and his companions inhaled oxygen out of balloons; at a later date compressed gas in steel cylinders was used, the cylinders being fitted with a rubber tube which ended in a mouthpiece of glass. There is a certain element of danger about this plan, inasmuch as it is possible for the mouthpiece to drop out of the mouth. Attempts have been made to use liquid air or liquid oxygen, but so far without any great success. Schroetter believes that accidents would be impossible if a mask were used.

The methods used for exploring the atmosphere by means of recording instruments are being daily improved. It will, therefore, be no great loss if the use of balloons with observers is abandoned, especially seeing that such ascents are much more expensive and laborious. It may, however, be remarked that these high ascents have not permanently injured the health of any of the observers, and that the ill effects pass off almost at once, as soon as the ground is reached. Still it must be admitted that Tissandier has become deaf as the result of his memorable ascent. Quite lately, too, the tympanum of a man's ear was cracked at a height of 10,000 ft., though he had previously made over 100 ascents, and had often reached heights of 23,000 ft. In any case it is to be hoped that there will be no further attempts to break the record in this department.

On meteorological expeditions observations on atmospheric electricity ought not to be neglected. There is much to be done in this field ; as a matter of fact, we know even nowadays little more than was known in the days of Franklin and his immediate successors. The potential gradients ought to be investigated, as also the conductivity of the atmosphere. The term "potential" is used to denote the difference in physical state of two bodies carrying electrical charges. A body at high potential can only discharge by being placed in electrical contact with a body at lower potential, and potential gradients are measured by the fall over a given distance. The principal workers in this department are the Frenchman Le Cadet, together with Professor Börnstein,

FIG. 178.—Viktor Silberer, president of the Aero Club, of Vienna.

Dr. Linke, Dr. Ebert, Dr. Gerdien, Professor Boltzmann, Dr. Erner, Dr. Tuma, Dr. Schlein, etc.

Lately meteorological observations have been made in Vienna at the instigation of Viktor Silberer. He has fitted out several such expeditions at his own cost, some of which have been carried out by members of the Aero Club, such as Dr. Schlein and Dr. Valentin. Viktor Silberer has frequently had to apply to the Austrian parliament for funds and has not always met with a very ready response. Still it must be admitted that under rather disadvantageous conditions the Austrians have done good work.

Meteorology has derived considerable benefit from balloon ascents and the astronomers have also done the same. The balloon is specially useful when it is a matter of observing some rare phenomenon which may be hidden by a cloudy sky. The first ascents of this kind were made by Spencer-Rush in 1843, and Welsh also did work under similar conditions for the Kew Observatory. On November 16th, 1867, Wilfrid de Fonvielle made an ascent in one of Giffard's balloons for the purpose of observing falling stars. It has been already stated that the astronomer Janssen left Paris in a balloon on December 2nd,

Fig. 179.—The shadow of the balloon is seen on the clouds, together with a halo.

1870, in order to go to Africa for the observation of a solar eclipse, and this perhaps is some explanation of the interest which he has since taken in ballooning. Wilfrid de Fonvielle and Madame Klumpke made further ascents for the purpose of observing falling stars. In November, 1899, by international arrangement, several simultaneous ascents were made to observe the Leonids as they crossed the path of the earth's orbit. In France Madame Klumpke and Count de la Vaulx made ascents, in Strassburg the author in company with Dr. Tetens and Dr. Bauwerker did the same, while England was also represented. On the evening of November 15th, the sky at Strassburg was entirely covered with cloud; consequently no observations could be made in the ordinary way. But from the balloon ten falling stars were seen, five of which were in Leo, and consequently belonged to the group called the Leonids. There was, however, a slight miscalculation in the matter. It subsequently appeared that owing to disturbances caused by Jupiter, the maximum took place a day sooner than had been predicted, and the whole thing was on a much smaller scale than had been expected. In France and England ascents are made every year in order to observe the falling stars, and this was also done in Germany in 1900. In Germany astronomers are apt to look askance at balloon observations, though Janssen and others are of a different opinion.

At the conference at St. Petersburg the commander of the Spanish Balloon Corps, Don Pedro Vives y Viches, stated that he intended to organise a number of ascents for observing the total eclipse of the sun which would be visible at Burgos on

FIG. 180.—The shadow of the balloon is cast on the clouds, and the car is seen surrounded by a rainbow.

August 30th, 1905, and that he was prepared to offer a seat in the car to a member of the conference. Accordingly three balloons made the ascent at Burgos on the eventful day. Vives y Viches was on board one of them, and with him were a Spanish physicist and Professor Berson. Several meteorological questions were to be considered. In the first place it was to be ascertained whether there was a decrease of temperature during or after totality. Berson stated that any fall in temperature would be very unlikely, seeing that at a height of several thousand feet no effect is produced on the thermometer by the setting of the sun. It was further to be discovered whether the wind veered round through almost an entire circle ; the Americans Helm-Clayton and Rotch asserted that this was the case, and they had already made observations of five total eclipses.

The breadth of the zone over which the eclipse was total was only 112 miles, and it was necessary to prevent the balloon from being carried out of this zone before the event happened. The ascent was therefore deferred till the latest possible moment, and the balloon only just succeeded in rising above the bank of heavy cumulus with which the sky was covered before the eclipse took place. It only lasted $3\frac{3}{4}$ minutes, and the astronomers on the ground level had a rare piece of good fortune when they saw the clouds clear away just at the moment of the eclipse. As for the balloon, it was only at the last minute that it succeeded in surmounting the clouds at a height of 12,500 ft. This was due to a curious accident. A large frame, 6 ft. square, had been covered with linen, and was intended for observing some of the peculiar effects of the eclipse. It had unintentionally been allowed to slip down during the ascent, and it was impossible to pull it up again. It consequently remained below the car in such a position that it caught most of the ballast that was thrown out. The situation looked serious until one of the occupants of the car noticed that they were over a mountainous district far from human habitation, and suggested that it might be possible with a bit of a swing to throw whole sacks of ballast, filled just as they were, without doing any damage. This was done, and they managed to ascend in time to see the eclipse.

The results of the meteorological observations were that no decrease of temperature was noticed during or after the eclipse, and that no conclusions could be drawn as to the direction of the wind because the earth was hidden by clouds. Berson gave a description of the scene before the Berlin Balloon Club. The sky assumed a hue of many colours, and the flames shot out from the corona produced a marvellous effect, with the brightness of beaten silver. The size of these flames seemed rather smaller than when seen from the earth. The speed with which the shadow of the moon was chased over earth and clouds was tremendous; this apparition was difficult to describe in words, and looked like the flight of some huge bird, shadowed against the clouds. The darkness was so intense that an electric lamp had to be used to read the instruments. When it is remembered that at any given spot the duration of a total eclipse is only 8 minutes, and that they are so rare as only to occur once in 200 years at the same place, it seems a wise precaution to prepare balloons for the event, in case of a cloudy day.

The compass is a very necessary instrument in a balloon, and is particularly useful on a cloudy day, when intermittent glimpses of the earth are obtained through gaps in the clouds. It has also been proposed to use the declination and inclination for determining the exact position of a balloon above the clouds, but at present nothing is known of the application of such a method. Various optical phenomena can be observed from a balloon, such, for instance, as the aureole. An enormous shadow is cast by the balloon on the brightly lighted clouds, and the car appears to be in the middle of a rainbow. Sunrise and sunset either over the water or in the mountains are wonderful sights, and anyone who has once seen them is not likely to forget it.

Balloons have also been used on Polar expeditions. The main difficulty appears to be to make suitable arrangements for a journey that may be much longer than is expected, and also to be able to meet dangers caused by unexpected descents on the ice. The unhappy results of Andrée's expedition will help to point the moral. More plans have lately been suggested for reaching the poles by means of balloons. Wellman and Count de la Vaulx propose to fit out an expedition for this purpose, and it can hardly be doubted that success will sooner or later attend the efforts of some of those who propose to float over the North Pole.

CHAPTER XX.

It was on August 10th, 1839, that Arago made known to the Académie des Sciences the discoveries that had been made by a painter named Daguerre and a cavalry officer named Niepce. With the aid of light they were able to make pictures of any object, and with their discovery the modern art of photography had its birth. Arago suggested that the making of plans and maps would be much simplified, and a Frenchman, named Andraud, in 1855 drew attention to the value of the bird's eye view as a piece of documentary evidence. But Andraud can hardly be said to have been the inventor of balloon photography, any more than Jules Verne with all his adventurous tales can be called the inventor of the dirigible airship. A man, named Nadar, in 1858 was the first actually to take photographs from a balloon, but in those days the method of operating was very cumbrous. The original process consisted in the preparation of the photograph on a copper plate, that is to say, one finished product corresponded to one exposure; from this, the next stage consisted in the idea of the "negative," from which any number of "positives" could be printed. Still even so, wet plates had to be used, and it was necessary to expose and develop them immediately after they had been prepared. Naturally a process of this kind did not readily lend itself to balloon work.

According to the wet process the glass plate was covered with iodised collodion, and then dipped in a bath of silver solution. If such plates are used, they must be exposed and developed before they become dry, otherwise the silver iodide crystallises out and no picture is obtained. Nadar made his first attempt in a captive balloon, in the car of which he had fitted up a sort of dark room, consisting of a round tent made of an orange-coloured material and lined with black. The ascent was a very costly affair, but was unsuccessful owing to an accidental leakage of coal gas from the balloon, which spoilt the plates. The reason of this was that the car was too close to the inflating tube of the balloon, a defect in the design which was common enough in those days. On a later occasion he succeeded in taking his photograph on freshly prepared plates and then descended immediately for the purpose of developing them. This plan worked well and was always adopted afterwards. During the war between Italy and Austria, he was invited by the Italian Minister of War to take some balloon photographs of the enemy's position at Solferino, but these attempts turned out failures.

Two or three years later we find the art adopted in England and America. King and Black took photographs of Boston from a balloon, and Negretti, who had already done work in Italy with the encouragement of the king, now turned his attention to London, where he took photographs from a balloon. No details are known as to the results of these experiments.

During the American Civil War, balloon photography was used for scouting purposes. An amateur balloonist, named Lowe, went up in a captive balloon at Richmond, and took photographs of the fortifications in the neighbourhood, going as far as Manchester on the west, and Chikakominy on the east. These exposures, when developed, showed the disposition of cavalry and artillery, together with all the earthworks. The several photographs were divided by lines into a number of spaces, which were indicated by letters A1—A64, B1—B64, etc. General Mac-Clellan kept one copy and Lowe kept the other, an arrangement being made by which Lowe was to communicate the movements of the enemy's troops to headquarters by means of the lettering on the maps. The system is still used, if the circumstances are suitable, as for example in the case of a siege. For the observer in a balloon, a photograph is much more convenient than a map for finding a given place; the effect of perspective produces distortions not shown on a map, and buildings, forests, fields, etc., are much more easily recognised on a photograph. On June 1st, 1862, Lowe signalled from a height of 1100 ft., that the disposition of the enemy's forces showed they were intending to make a sortie. General MacClellan was therefore able to make arrangements accordingly, and in the course of the same day much more useful information of a similar kind was sent to headquarters from the balloon.

Some years later Nadar's son continued the work, and made a series of photographs of Paris in this way in 1868, which may still be seen in the Musée Nationale. During the Franco-Prussian War Colonel Laussedat suggested that photographs of the German positions should be taken from a captive balloon, but the attempts were unsuccessful. A photographer, named Dagron, made use of a dark room, similar to that originally used by Nadar, and with the help of one of Giffard's balloons, succeeded in taking some photographs of Paris of a size 11 by 8½ in., which were fairly successful. Triboulet first used dry plates on an ascent undertaken for meteorological purposes. He was an architect by profession, and being much interested in meteorology, made an ascent on a very wet day with the intention of photographing some of the rain-clouds. His well-meant efforts deserved a better fate. The balloon was driven down by the heavy rain, and he barely avoided a collision with one of the towers of Notre Dame, only to fall a minute or two later into the Seine. He was soon rescued from the water, but fell a prey to the authorities of the octroi, who had seen his balloon float in from the suburbs. They subjected him to a lengthy cross-examination, and finally insisted on examining his belongings in order to see whether he had anything liable to duty concealed about his balloon. His double-backs naturally caused suspicion, being then something of a novelty, and the plates were therefore ruined by exposure to the light.

Excellent results were obtained by Desmaret in a free balloon in 1880. He made his exposures at a rather greater height than had been usual up to that time, and certainly worked in a very skilful and scientific fashion. He used a lens of 11½ in. focal length, and his pictures, which were taken on plates 8 by 10 in., showed every detail clearly, even at great distances. He was able to take an area of 10,000 square feet on one plate, reducing it in the proportion of 1 to 4,000. Most of his exposures were made through an aperture in the floor of the car, and the shutter was worked electrically. He determined the exact height at which the photographs were taken by means of two barometers, and endeavoured to find the effect produced by the movement of the balloon, noting, as far as possible, the speed at the moment of exposure. Dry plates at that time were sufficiently sensitive to allow of exposures of a twentieth of a second, and he consequently got some very sharp pictures. The speed of the balloon was about 20 ft. per second, and it therefore travelled over a distance of 1 ft. during the exposure, a distance which was insufficient to cause any perceptible lack of sharpness in the detail. He also took some good photographs of the clouds, and enlargements of his results may be seen in the Conservatoire des Arts et Metiers.

From this time onward, photographic work was continually done both in France and England. Shadbold took some photographs of London, and Woodbury in 1881 proposed an arrangement by which captive balloons could be made to do the work without an observer. The plan was complicated but ingenious. The apparatus included a rotating prism, which supported the plates, the rotation being effected electrically by pressing a button at the ground level. The shutter was similarly worked. But it was found impossible in this way to obtain a photograph of any particular spot, and naturally enough there was generally found to be some part of the mechanism which obstinately refused to work. Triboulet therefore proposed to mount a basket of wickerwork beneath the balloon on gimbals, and to arrange seven cameras so that their shutters could be simultaneously worked from below by the electrical method. Six of these cameras were pointed through openings in the sides of the basket, and one was directed downwards through a hole in the floor. In this way it was supposed that a fairly complete panorama would be able to be made, and contrivances of this kind have since been often suggested for military purposes. In the eighties, balloon photography was solely employed for military purposes in England and Germany; and in this connection, the names of Elsdale and Templer may be mentioned, as well as those of Tschudi, Hagen, and Sigsfeld.   In Austria, the first attempts at photographic work were made by Viktor Silberer, who interested himself in this as in every other aspect of ballooning.   He usually made his exposure directly after the start and while the balloon was still rising.   During this time the horizontal motion is usually small, and the vertical movement does not largely affect the sharpness of the negative. Consequently it is an advantage to take the photograph during the time of ascent, assuming that the conditions are otherwise favourable.

An amusing tale is told as to a dispute between Silberer and the man who had provided him with his photographic apparatus.

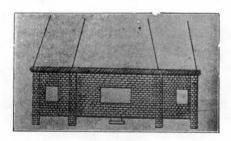

FIG. 181.—Triboulet's panoramic apparatus.
(From " La Photographie en Ballon," by Tissandier.

The latter declared that he was entitled to describe himself as having assisted in taking the photographs, though in point of fact he had never been in a balloon in his life.   He accordingly printed some of the negatives, and added words to the effect that he had helped Silberer to make the exposures.   In fact he stated that it was an act of courtesy on his part to allow Silberer's name to appear on the photographs at all.   He naturally found experts, both legal and technical, to help him in a court of law, and they endeavoured to persuade the jury that the photographer was perfectly correct in his attitude.   Silberer pointed out that it was unreasonable to allow one man to undertake a polar expedition at his own cost and make all the exposures, while another man quietly developed them at home and claimed all the credit. The jury eventually agreed that this view was sound, and Silberer, who had been accused of slandering his opponent, by calling him a common thief and a downright swindler, was acquitted.

Balloon photography has received much assistance from the

modern improvements in the art of constructing lenses, which
are now made of great focal lengths. In 1885 Tissandier and
Ducom employed one having a focal length of 22 in., and this
probably represents the furthest limit likely to be reached by
the amateur.

Cailletet has devised an arrangement for registering the
heights reached in a balloon which does not carry observers. A
camera is carried which has two lenses, both of which project

FIG. 182.—The first photograph taken from a balloon in Austria. It represents
the Reichsbrücke in Vienna, and was taken by Viktor Silberer in 1885.

their images on the same plate. One of these lenses is focussed
on an aneroid barometer, and the other takes the view of the
landscape in the usual way. By means of a piece of clockwork
exposures are made at certain intervals, and fresh films are
automatically rolled into position. The film therefore records
the reading of the barometer as well as the view of the landscape.
Cailletet had a method of checking the readings of the barometer
by comparing the known distances between two places, as
measured on the ordnance map, with their apparent distance
as measured on the photograph. The focal length of the lens

A.   U being known, it was possible in this way to calculate the height of the balloon. He also devised an apparatus with nine lenses

FIG. 183.—The Reichsbrücke in Vienna.

(Photograph by Herbert Silberer, from his book entitled "Four Thousand Kilometres in a Balloon.")

for taking panoramic views for naval purposes, which was brought into use at Lagoubran. The exposures were made electrically, and the results were successful in showing the details of all the forts over a radius of 4 miles. However, it is doubtful whether the result of further experiments on these lines has been altogether encouraging, from the military point of view. Photographs which are taken more or less at random from captive balloons carrying no passengers are liable to more than the average number of accidents, and these are already sufficiently numerous, even in the case of manned balloons. The handling of a camera in the confined space of a balloon is a very awkward matter, requiring much practice. The main difficulty lies in the violent movements of the basket. It is true that photographs can be taken of a bullet as it is fired at a target, and this only requires an exposure of one hundred-thousandth of a second. But during that time the camera must be held perfectly still, and this is not always as easy as it sounds on a balloon. We may consider the effect of the various movements of the basket on the photographer. These may be of four kinds, viz., (1) horizontal; (2) vertical; (3) rotatory; or (4) oscillatory. In the case of a captive balloon the horizontal motion is very slight, and may be almost neglected; but this is by no means the case with a free balloon sailing along in a strong wind. Looking at the problem generally, let us suppose a line to be drawn from the camera to the object it is desired to photograph. Then the motion of the balloon may take place in the direction of this line, either towards or away from the object; or it may be inclined obliquely to this line, the motion being either backwards or forwards; or finally it may be at right angles to this line, either to the right or to the left. Let us consider the last case, as the camera then suffers the greatest displacement with regard to the object.

Let us suppose that it is intended to take a photograph of an object at a distance of 6 miles with a lens whose focal length is 3 ft. The object will therefore appear on the plate reduced on a scale of 1 to 10,560, and the movement of the balloon, in so far as it is directed along the optical axis, $i.e.$, along the line joining the lens to the middle of the object, will produce no noticeable effect on the sharpness of the image. But consider a

point in the landscape, included in the " object," which is at a
distance from the camera of 6 miles and also at a distance of
half a mile from the optical axis. The image of this point will
be at a distance of 3 in. from the centre line of the plate. If
the balloon is moving at the rate of 30 ft. per second in a
direction at right angles to the optical axis, and if the length
of exposure is one-hundredth of a second, then the balloon will
move in this time over a distance of 0·3 ft. The image of the
point under consideration will then be displaced on the plate by
an amount equal to 0·00034 in. Generally speaking, it is fair
to assume that a displacement of 0·004 of an inch does not affect
the sharpness of an image, and in the given case the displacement is obviously insufficient to produce any effect whatever on
the picture. Of course, it is immaterial whether the object
moves or whether the balloon moves, so long as the movement
is insufficient to produce a noticeable displacement on the plate.
If the state of the light is known, or, in other words, the length
of exposure is fixed, it is possible by simple calculations of this
kind to find the most suitable height or distance from which to
photograph a given object.

Dr. Stolze has given a table by which the length of maximum
exposure can be seen at a glance, provided the speed with which
an object moves is known, and also the distance of the said
object from the lens. The table is drawn up on the assumption
that the want of definition is not to exceed a displacement of
0·004 of an inch on the plate.

Ratio of distance of object to the focal length of lens.	Speed of the object in feet per second.			
	3	6	15	30
100	0·01	—	—	—
500	0·05	0·02	—	—
1,000	0·1	0·05	0·01	0·01

The vertical movements of a free balloon need hardly be
considered, seeing that the photographer does not begin to
make exposures, as a general rule, until a position of equilibrium

is reached at the desired height. But it is very much the reverse with captive balloons.

Rotatory movements usually only happen with a free balloon at the start ; at a later stage they are of such rare occurrence that they may be almost neglected. Here again the case with kites and captive balloons is very different. Let us suppose that there is a comparatively slight rotatory movement, amounting to an angular displacement of 5 degrees 43 minutes a second. The tangent of this angle is 0·1, and if the distance of the object is 10 miles, the optical axis will be displaced through one mile in one second at the point where it meets the object. If the exposure lasts one-hundredth of a second, the optical axis will be displaced in this time through more than 50 ft., with the result that the negative will be hopelessly blurred. It is therefore necessary to find the extreme limit of rotatory motion which will allow of a sharp image, and this will probably be an angle whose tangent is about 0·001. The only way in which this angle can practically be found is to note carefully the rotations of the basket, and to make the exposure at the moment when the rotation in one direction has ceased and is about to give way to one in the opposite direction. At this moment the basket is at rest, in so far as rotation is concerned, and the exposure must be made forthwith. If the conditions are very carefully examined, it may possibly be found that a fiftieth part of the duration of a rotatory movement is available for a sharp image. Suppose the time of such a complete period of rotation is 10 seconds, there would, on this supposition, be only one fifth of a second in which to make the exposure, and it is hardly necessary to say that the taking of photographs under these conditions is a matter requiring much experience.

Horizontal movements of the balloon exert less effect upon the sharpness of the image, the greater the distance of the object from the lens ; with rotatory movements the reverse is the case, and the nearer the object, the sharper will be the image. Oscillatory swings, like those of a pendulum, mostly occur at the start, particularly if the envelope is not vertically above the basket; but they disappear very soon. In the kite-balloon they

are seldom met with, but with captive balloons they are of frequent occurrence.   It is obvious that these oscillations may produce very serious consequences on the negative.   Dr. Stolze says
that the basket performs an oscillation in 4 seconds, if it is at a
distance of 50 ft. from the top of the balloon.   Consequently in
a tenth of a second it will perform one-fortieth of an oscillation.

FIG. 184.—Eastern Railway Station, in Budapesth.

(Photograph by Lieutenant Kral.)

Let us suppose that a complete oscillation extends over an angle
of two degrees, and that the time of exposure is to be one-tenth
of a second.   Then the basket in this time will oscillate through
an angle of three minutes, and this will cause an entire blurring
of the image if the object is at a distance of 5 or 6 miles.
Oscillations of this kind are always larger in the case of small
balloons, and it is not possible to neutralise their effect by
decreasing the time of exposure.   Dr. Stolze has made use of the
principle of the gyroscope in this connection.   He arranges two

discs on axes at right angles to one another, and these are capable
of being rotated by means of strings. The discs are joined by
means of a ball and socket joint to the camera, which hangs
below them, and in this way the combination is practically
uninfluenced by the oscillation of the balloon. Spherical
captive balloons are now more or less out of date, and these
gyrostatic complications may very well keep them company.

It is therefore evident that many factors enter into the calculations of the length of exposure and that the right moment
must be carefully chosen. The speed of the balloon is a most
important factor, but as every photographer knows, the actinic
value of the light is more important. Some compromise is
therefore often necessary. But in so far as the value of the
light is concerned, the balloonist has certain advantages, and his
exposures are generally much shorter than those which are necessary at the ground level. Let us suppose that with a given
aperture and a fairly good light, an exposure of one-eightieth of
a second is needed, and in bright sunlight one-hundredth of a
second; then it is generally found that these can be reduced by
about one-half if the exposure is made from a balloon, and that
one hundred-and-fiftieth of a second will generally be ample.

The peculiarities of the light at great heights can be illustrated by a simple experiment, due to Miethe. Take a piece
of white paper, and hold it over the edge of the basket in a
vertical position on the side where it is not exposed to the direct
light of the sun. Then look directly over the upper edge of the
paper at the earth beneath, and it will at once appear as if the
piece of white paper were the darkest object in the field of sight.

The course of the rays through the air before they reach the
balloonist's camera is very complicated. The ordinary photographer generally confines his attention to those objects which
directly reflect the light from the sun or sky, and such rays pass
through a fairly homogeneous atmosphere direct to the camera.
But with the balloonist things are very different. The rays of
the sun first penetrate through the dense atmosphere till they
reach the illuminated object; thence they pass back again
through the atmosphere till they strike the lens at a much

higher level, and are refracted and to some extent absorbed on the way. It is fair to suppose that the movement of the breezes at different levels produces very little effect on the path of the rays, because such movements are extremely small during the moment of exposure. The main effect is due to refraction, and this depends on differences of temperature and atmospheric pressure. If the density of the atmosphere were everywhere the same, the refractive index would be constant, and no distortion of the image would arise; but obviously enough, this is not the case. If the rays have to pass through a number of atmospheric layers, none of which are homogeneous, the refractive effect is likely to be great. It is well known that in the height of summer the air near the ground is in a state of motion owing to the great heat, and the middle of the day is therefore avoided for photographic purposes. Sigsfeld pointed out that if such air currents existed near the lens, they produced very harmful effects; if, on the other hand, they were near the object to be photographed, they were quite harmless. In that case, the balloon has a decided advantage, because the air in the neighbourhood of the lens is always cool, when compared with that which is found close to the ground. The effects of absorption are of course undesirable. The air contains multitudes of solid particles, which not only reflect but also absorb light. These particles may be so numerous as to amount to a mist or fog, and exist for the most part in the layers of the atmosphere close to the ground. In photographing an object on the ground level, the rays have to pass through a layer of these particles which is equal in thickness to the distance of the object from the lens; such a layer is measured in a horizontal direction. But with a balloon the layer has to be measured in a more or less vertical direction, and as it is at the most only a few hundred feet deep, the balloonist is more favourably placed for photographing distant objects. But in the neighbourhood of large towns, the atmospheric conditions are generally bad. Nearly every day there is a thick mist over Berlin, and the balloon does not rise above it till it has reached an altitude of nearly 1,000 ft. The wind carries a mist of this kind along with it, and one often has to travel 60 miles from Berlin before the last trace has disappeared. An instance of the way in which the path of the rays is affected is given by the results of the observations on the total eclipse of 1905. Professor Berson and a number of other observers stated that the sun's corona looked much smaller when seen from the balloon than when seen from the earth ; and, consequently, Jannsen and other French astronomers are inclined to attach considerable importance to observations of such phenomena from balloons.

The same care must be taken to study the variations of the quality of the light when the photographs are made from a balloon as is the case with everyday photography. The actinic value of the light is a very variable quantity ; it depends on the season of the year, on the time of day, and a multitude of other circumstances. It is greatest in midsummer, and sixteen times as great in June as in December. Moreover, the light in the morning is better than in the afternoon. A thin layer of cloud will absorb 40 per cent. of the sun's light, and if the sky is overcast the absorption may amount to 80 per cent. Direct sunlight is from eight to fourteen times as effective as diffused light from a blue sky, and white clouds, directly illuminated by the sun, add greatly to the value of the light. In the photography of mountains, the contrast between light and shade are apt to be rendered harsh owing to the clearness of the atmosphere, and this must be taken into account.

Boulade has drawn up some figures which may help as a guide towards estimating the time of exposure, and take into account a number of variables.

Co-efficients for—			Aperture.		
Time of year.	Height of the Sun.	Condition of the Sky.	$\frac{F}{32}$	$\frac{F}{16}$	$\frac{F}{8}$
June, July, August = 1·0 April, May = 1·5 March, September = 2·0 February. October = 3·0 January, November = 4·0 December = 5·0	Zenith = 1 50° = 2 65° W. = 6 65° E. = 3	blue = 1 slightly cloudy = 1·5 half covered = 2 overcast = 3 heavy clouds = 6	16	4	1

Colour values must also be considered. The eye sees no such differences between light and shade in a balloon as are noticed on the earth. The shadows seem to be so strongly lighted that in the distance they almost entirely disappear. The ordinary photograph takes no account of colour as such; the various colours are only distinguished from one another by patches of greater or less intensity. Light and shade are reproduced, but

FIG. 185.—Clouds over the Alps.
(Photograph by Spelterini.)

a monochromatic reproduction of a colour effect grades one colour into the next by a more or less abrupt change from light to dark. Nobody can say exactly how dark a certain patch ought to be in order to give effect to the colour of an object, and this depends on the fact that the effect of a colour on the eye is by no means the same thing as the chemical effect of the colour on the sensitive emulsion.

If we consider the Sun's spectrum those colours appear to us to be the brightest which are nearest the red end of the scale.

Red and yellow seem bright; green, blue and violet seem much duller. But on a photographic plate the reverse is the case. The blue and violet rays have the greatest actinic effect, the red ones have the least. Consequently the print shows blue as white and red as black; at least, it has this tendency, and the transformation actually takes place in extreme cases. Thus the chemical effect of the various rays of the spectrum on the photo-

FIG. 186.—Photograph of a village, taken in daylight by the Vega Company, of Geneva. It should be compared with the similar photograph taken by the light of a projector on the next page.

graphic plate is altogether different from the physiological impression produced on the eye. Even if the colouring of the landscape does not appear to correspond to any particular colour of the spectrum, but to be made up of a number of components, each with its own peculiar physiological effect, the photographic reproduction will show a totally different grading. The bright yellow will still appear darker than it ought to be, and the dark blue will produce somewhat of the effect of white.

This effect is exaggerated in balloon photography. The blue

rays are more largely absorbed by the air than the others, and therefore all bright objects appear redder and consequently darker on the plate. An effect of absorption and reflection is that all the bright colours are, as it were, displaced towards the red end of the spectrum and the darker colours appear bluer. It is therefore necessary to supplement the effect of the brighter light, which is partially deflected or absorbed by the aqueous vapour and atmospheric dust, by using yellow filters. On the other hand, the chemical effect of the blue rays must be

FIG. 187.—Photograph of a village, taken at night, by means of an electric projector, by the Vega Company of Geneva.

restrained in order that they may appear darker on the plate. Yellow filters can therefore be used in a good light, because the time of exposure in a balloon can generally be reduced. Probably the best filters are made by inserting a sheet of coloured gelatine between two sheets of glass with optically true surfaces, or a sheet of gelatine can even be used alone. The filters should be used with suitable plates, which are so prepared as to have a tendency to emphasise the red values. For instance, plates can be obtained which give a brighter value to yellow than to blue, but any given plate has a tendency to emphasise some particular colour. In any case, such plates give a better result than the ordinary kind. The Perxanto plates, prepared according to

Miethe's method, give good results, and have the advantage that they allow of a shorter exposure than is required with filters, and this is a great advantage in dull weather. Such days occur so frequently that photography is really only practicable on about one third of the days in the year. If it is necessary to choose between filters and a good brand of isochromatic plates, the latter are much to be preferred.

An interesting application of the use of projectors in balloon photography has lately been made by the Vega Company, of Geneva. A given place is photographed from the balloon by daylight, and then at night a further photograph is taken by the light of an electric projector. The plates are then developed and compared. It is suggested that in this way it might be possible to discover the places where earthworks are being constructed by an enemy at night, and the method would seem to be capable of useful application.

CHAPTER XXI.

THE CAMERA.

THE main points about a camera for balloon work are simplicity and rigidity. It is perhaps not easy for a man who has never been in a balloon to understand the conditions under which exposures have to be made. He may be a capable amateur photographer without having any idea of the most suitable apparatus needed for an expedition of this kind. He would probably suggest a Kodak, or some other form of hand camera, with which he had already done much good work on his holidays. Cameras of this kind are, however, altogether useless in a balloon, because the focal length of their lenses is too short. The object will be possibly at a distance of some miles, and with short focal lenses it is impossible to get any result at this range. Generally speaking, balloon photographs show little detail, and, of course, a great amount is unnecessary. But with lenses of very short focal length, the size of the image is so small that it would be almost impossible to see anything. A further objection to these cameras lies in the general complication of their mechanism, which would probably cease to work altogether after it had been exposed for a short time to the fine sand, which is always floating about a balloon from the ballast sacks, and it need hardly be said that the idea of repairing a camera in a balloon is almost out of the question.

The fact that the focal length of the lens must be at least 8 in. makes it necessary to use an apparatus of some considerable size. The limited space which is available must also be taken into account, and this excludes the use of very long cameras. Probably the greatest focal length of lens which can be usefully employed by the amateur is about 24 in. The best thing is a simple wood camera, solid in construction and easily handled; it must be sufficiently rigid to be able to withstand the inevitable jolts of a landing. It must not take up too much room in the car, and the best plan is to mount it on the side of the basket in a leather case. The lens must be carefully protected by a soft covering of felt, or something of that sort, and it is then less likely to be damaged on coming to the ground. Cameras with bellows are not to be recommended; they are hardly strong enough, the bellows may be injured and cease to be light-tight, and one can never be certain that some jolt has not bent the framework holding the double-back slightly out of the perpendicular. Still one of the smaller folding cameras with a lens of focal length between 8 and 12 in. may well be used if the struts holding the lens front are of thoroughly solid construction. But if a lens of focal length greater than 12 in. is employed, the struts must be more solidly constructed than usual, and a better plan is to use a camera made throughout of wood in the most rigid possible manner.

The use of tripods in balloons is quite out of the question. The best plan is to move the camera into any desired position by hand, which can always be done. Possibly an exception would have to be made in the case of cameras having lenses of very great focal length, e.g., over 24 in. long, or in the case of dirigible balloons where the vibration of the machinery would make photography a difficult matter. It used to be the fashion to point the camera through a hole in the floor of the car in order to direct the lens towards the ground beneath. But this is not actually necessary, and the attempt to point the lens vertically downwards is likely to be unsuccessful. If the optical axis is more or less inclined to the vertical, it makes no great difference; it is easy enough to make allowance for anything of this kind later on. Besides which, it will only be in the rarest cases that the balloon floats immediately over the spot which it is wished to photograph. Another objection is to be found in the fact that this arrangement is very cumbersome from the point of view of those who have to do with the navigating of the balloon; it is not always easy to throw out ballast or let down the guide-rope if a camera is on the floor almost beneath one's feet. And from the point of view of the photographer himself, the arrangement has little to commend itself; he has to bend down over his camera in a very awkward position, and probably ends by making his exposure at random without knowing exactly in what direction the lens is pointing at the moment. If it is actually necessary that the plate should be horizontal at the moment of exposure, the best plan is to mount a level on the camera ; the floor of the car is very unlikely to be sufficiently steady, if only for the very simple reason that it contains a

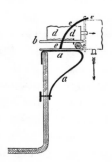

FIG. 188.—Ducom's photographic apparatus.

(From Pizzighelli's " Handbook for Photography," 1891.)

FIG. 189.—Hagen's method of mounting the camera.

constantly shifting load. This plan has therefore been abandoned.

Various arrangements have been suggested by which the camera is mounted on the outside of the basket, and in this way it is generally possible to make the exposure at a convenient moment. The distance at which it must be mounted from the edge depends on the angle of the lens; no part of the basket must come within the field of view. But this arrangement has the disadvantage that it is only possible to photograph the landscape on the one side of the balloon, and it may happen that this is not precisely what is wanted, either owing to the position of the sun or for some other reason. It is largely a matter of pros and cons, and if the ideal is unattainable, one must be none the less content. The camera must in any case be so arranged as to be movable about horizontal and vertical axes, and this allows a certain reasonable latitude.

In 1885 Jacques Ducom designed an arrangement by which a camera, taking half-plates, was supported on the outside of the basket. It was movable about a horizontal axis, and could therefore be inclined at any angle to the vertical, but no allowance was made for any other motion. Lieutenant von Hagen, of the Prussian Balloon Corps, devised a similar method by which the camera was screwed to a bench, which was supported on an angle-iron fitted to the side of the basket. The bench was capable of being tilted about its outer edge, and there was a scale for reading the inclination to the vertical. It was also capable of motion about a vertical axis. Hagen thought it would be necessary to focus for each exposure, and this added to the complication of his apparatus. He therefore had a focussing screen of quarter-plate size, which was placed above the main carrier, and was used with the same lens. The camera was intended to be used with whole plates, and the lens was first placed in front of the focussing screen, its position being very carefully adjusted. After this had been done it was unscrewed, placed in position below for the plate, and the exposure made. Evidently this must all be done very quickly if the balloon is moving fast, and it is desired to take a photograph of a given spot. In a captive balloon, the method would be altogether impracticable.

There is a further objection to the use of cameras with bellows. The frame for carrying the plates is hinged to the bottom board, and if the camera is pointed vertically downwards there is a tendency for the upper end of this framework to fall downwards. The lower part of the plate will therefore be further from the lens than the upper portion, and consequently the image will not be sharp over the whole of the plate. Hagen met this by having two scales, running the whole length of the camera, the one being attached to the base and the other connecting the frameworks of the front and back at the top; when the adjustment was finally made, and the clamps

A.

X

were fixed, the readings on the two scales were the same. In folding cameras with struts, this is unnecessary, seeing that there is no tendency for the plate to fall towards the lens. Hagen suc-

FIG. 190.—Photograph of the Exhibition Buildings, near the Lehrter Railway Station, in Berlin ; taken by Lieutenant von Hagen.

(From the *Zeitschrift für Luftschiffahrt und Physik der Atmosphäre*.)

ceeded in getting some excellent results with his apparatus, and these were exhibited in 1886.

It has been proposed to support the camera on gimbals in order to make it independent of the vibrations of the balloon.

But this has not proved a success, and the necessary movements which are required to make an exposure always communicate a certain amount of vibration. If the apparatus is very heavy, it may be suspended from the ring, but even in that case it is necessary to have some fixed support on the edge of the basket at the moment of making the exposure. But cameras of this size are very seldom employed, except possibly for photographing the sun's corona during an eclipse. A little contrivance, mentioned by Pizzighelli in his "Handbook for Photography" of 1891, may be useful in judging a suitable moment for making the exposure. A vertical pointer is fixed to a board, and throws its shadow on a scale upon the edge of the board. The movement of the shadow will give some idea of the motion of the balloon. But it is very easy to over-estimate the value of such a device.

It is well to know the inclination of the camera to the horizontal at the moment of making an exposure; but with Hagen's apparatus it is only possible to find the inclination of the camera to the iron baseboard. This is of little use unless the inclination of the iron support to the horizontal is also known. The better plan would be to have a level fixed to the camera, and a scale by which the inclination of the level to the optical axis could be determined. But great accuracy would hardly be possible, even if a second observer were available for adjusting the level at the moment of exposure. In 1890 the Prussian Balloon Corps adopted a method by which the camera was mounted at the end of a rifle in a thoroughly substantial but rather primitive manner. On the right hand side of the apparatus a quadrant scale was fixed, by means of which the inclination to the vertical could be read by noting the position of a plummet with regard to the scale. At the moment of making the exposure the cock of the rifle was depressed, and fell against a lever which released the spring working the shutter, and at the same time locked the plummet in the position in which it happened to be at the moment. In this way it was possible to determine the inclination to the vertical with accuracy after the exposure had been made.

Baron von Bassus described a similar construction in 1900,

x 2

and as he was working quite independently of the Prussian
Balloon Corps, he probably knew nothing of their methods.
The camera was mounted at the end of a rifle, and by means of
a quadrant scale it was possible to determine the inclination of
the optical axis to the barrel of the gun when the camera was
fixed in position at any suitable angle.   A small spirit level is
mounted on the barrel of the gun, and its image is reflected from
a mirror into the eye.   As soon as it is seen that the bubble is
in its central position on the level, the trigger is pulled and the
shutter is released.   At the moment of exposure, the barrel of
the gun is therefore horizontal, and the inclination of the camera
to the vertical can be read off the scale, being in fact the inclination of the camera to the barrel.   This construction has the

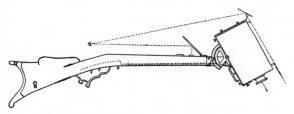

FIG. 191.—Baron von Bassus' rifle apparatus.
(From the *Illustrierte Aeronautische Mitteilungen.*)

advantage of requiring only one network to interpret the results
of the various photographs taken with one setting of the camera,
but, on the other hand, it labours under the disadvantage that it
is impossible to focus the lens on any given object, as it is more
or less a matter of chance what may happen to be in the field of
view.   Still there may be cases in which it is necessary to make
an exposure directed towards some particular object.   To some
extent this may be done by mounting a second mirror on the end
of the camera at such an angle that the field of view is reflected
into the eye; but it will seldom happen that any very certain
aim can be taken in this way.

Vautier-Dufour and the astronomer Schaer of Geneva have
designed a novel type of apparatus, intended for use with a long
focus lens.   This camera is constructed in two halves, placed one
above the other.   The lens is in the upper half, and the light,

passing through the lens, is reflected by a mirror at the back of the upper half to another mirror at the front of the lower half; it then passes from the lower mirror to the plate at the back of the lower half of the apparatus. The length of this camera is, therefore, only one-third of the focal length of the lens. Thus with a lens of focal length 48 in., the camera would measure 16 in.

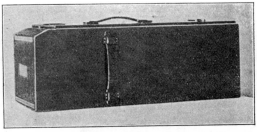

FIG. 192.—Vautier-Dufour apparatus, packed in its case.

from back to front, and with a compact apparatus of this kind, one has all the advantages of the bigger lens.

It is needless to say that the camera must be packed in a solid leather case, well padded on the inside.

PLATE-HOLDERS.

In order to be able to carry as much ballast as possible, the weight of everything else carried in the car must be reduced to a minimum. Films are therefore to be preferred to glass plates. The weight of a film-holder carrying a spool for six exposures

FIG. 193.—Vautier-Dufour apparatus, ready for use.

of quarter-plate size is only one-eighth of that of three double-backs holding six glass plates of the same size. But films are not altogether satisfactory; they vary a great deal, and after being kept for some time their sensitiveness falls off. The manufacturers do their best to prevent disappointment by printing the date before which the films should be exposed. But this does not altogether meet the case. Films are liable to be injured by damp and heat. Great as are their advantages as regards weight the photographer will do well to use glass plates instead, unless of course the photographs are to be used for military purposes and intended to be sent by carrier pigeons. Flat films can only be recommended in the smaller sizes in spite of their many good points. The only thing therefore is to use glass

plates if good results are to be produced. If a large number of exposures are to be made, a saving in weight may result from the use of a magazine camera holding several plates. With cameras of the newest type it is possible to make about twelve exposures in half a minute, and from this it is evident that the changing of the plates is simply and quickly done. But their use can hardly be recommended, even if a type of magazine is used in which the changing of

FIG. 194.—Aiguille Verte, taken with the Vautier-Dufour apparatus by the Vega Company, of Geneva.

the plates is effected by simply turning them over in succession, and so preventing one plate from rubbing against the next. There is indeed a serious objection to their use, which lies in the fact that the changing of plates causes a great deal of dust to settle on the sensitive surface of the gelatine, and produces a partial blurring of the image. There is no means of removing this dust before making the exposure. Further, the plates are very liable to be broken by being dashed against one another if the landing should be accompanied by any violent bumping. So that we finally come to the conclusion that nothing is better than the old double-back. The flexible shutters, used in some double-backs are not to be recommended for balloon work; the linen backing is very liable to contain dust, which cannot easily be removed, and as the shutter is unrolled the dust may settle on the sensitive surface. The best plan is to use double-backs with vulcanite shutters. They are easily cleaned, and if they are rubbed with a piece of washleather they become charged with electricity, and remove any dust that may be on the surface of the plate when they are pulled out. Another advantage lies in the fact that they can be pulled entirely out of the double-back. If a spring closes the slit in the double - back, the light is completely excluded.

FIG. 195.—Aiguille Verte, taken with an ordinary lens by the Vega Company, of Geneva.

Beginners are apt to pay insufficient attention to the dust which collects on the plate and lens, and interferes with the sharpness of the image. It may become a serious matter in a balloon; fine particles of sand from the ballast sacks float all over the basket, and have a habit of penetrating everywhere, even through the tightest joints.

PLATES.

Usually everyone settles for himself the plates to be used, and has his own likes and dislikes. Novelties seldom find favour; they are regarded at first with suspicion, and only after many trials do they cease to be novelties, and become trusted friends.

But in balloon work, certain plates must be used if good results
are to be obtained, though doubtless there is a certain latitude
allowable.

Films are light and convenient, but the reasons for preferring
glass plates have already been explained. Films are seldom
quite flat, and it is therefore impossible to get a perfectly sharp
negative in consequence. The bigger the film the more uneven
its surface is likely to be; even the most modern devices do not
entirely remedy the defect. For the smaller sizes of negative
up to quarter-plate size, flat films in special carriers may be
used. They are packed in black paper, and are placed in a
special carrier against a glass plate, the paper being then pulled

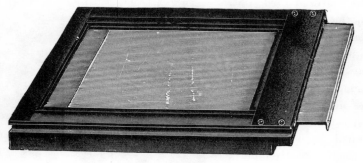

Fig. 196.—Film holder.

off. After the exposure has been made a shutter is pulled out,
and the film is shot forward under the action of a spring into
a storage space, where they remain till they are to be developed.
The storage space is sufficient for thirty films. The whole
apparatus is very light and convenient. But in the larger sizes,
it is not possible to get a perfectly flat surface, and plates must
therefore be used.

For the prevention of halation, plates have a red coating on the
back of the film. The effect due to halation is the result of reflection from the glass, and is very marked in negatives showing strong
contrasts; but it seldom occurs in balloon work. The plate-
holders must be well dusted before the plates are put in them,
and the plates themselves must also be carefully dusted, otherwise poor negatives may result. Sometimes " solarisation " takes

place, *i.e.*, the negative becomes a positive, and all sense of contrast is lost.

The Shutter.

A good shutter should comply with the following conditions. It should be perfectly certain in its action, under all circumstances, even after long use. It should be capable of giving exposures of different lengths, and it should distribute the light equally over all portions of the plate. The most rudimentary form of shutter is the well known leather cap, padded with velvet, which fits over the lens. But it is only suitable for time exposures, and consequently of little use in a balloon. Shutters which work automatically are the only ones worth consideration. They can either be placed in front of the lens, or between the lens and the plate, and a great variety of both kinds can be had. The simplest kind consists of an up and down motion of something of the nature of a flap, usually controlled by the pressing of a rubber bulb. Some sort of framework is necessary for holding it in front of the lens, but it may be said at once that this type is unsuitable for a balloon.

The Iris shutters, by Voigtländer and Zeiss, are better; the blades composing the shutter are quickly opened and closed by pneumatic pressure. But here again it is necessary to say that this is unsuitable; nothing of the nature of a rubber tube can be used in a balloon, unless the photographer is prepared to go through endless trouble. The tube is easily caught in one of the many ropes of the balloon, and a sudden turn or wrench pulls it off; minor troubles arise when the camera happens to be standing on the tube, thus preventing the passage of the compressed air, or it may happen that somebody accidentally fires it off by touching the rubber bulb unintentionally. In any case, one hand is needed for pressing the bulb, and in a balloon both hands are necessarily occupied in holding the camera. Miethe's experience also tends to prove that these shutters work very irregularly at low temperatures, and this is of course a further disadvantage from the balloonist's point of view. The so-called falling shutters give a poor efficiency.

The only one that can be recommended is the curtain shutter, the best known of which is probably the Thornton-Pickard. A long blind is mounted on rollers and has an adjustable slit in the middle, the rollers being placed both at the top and bottom. Before the exposure, the greater part of the blind together with the slit is wound round the top roller, the remainder being tightly stretched by the action of the bottom roller and covering the lens. A small lever is then pressed with the finger, and this releases a catch, allowing a sping to come into action and roll the blind quickly on the bottom roller. The slit therefore passes in front of the lens, and at the end of the operation the blind again forms a light-tight covering. As the slit passes the lens the plate is exposed to the light, and each part receives its image in succession. This arrangement works well, unless it should happen that some object in the field of view is in very rapid motion, in which case there would be some distortion of the image. But the time of exposure is very short, and it is only in very rare cases that it is necessary to take the motion of any object into account, and this never happens in balloon work. This shutter has an advantage which results from the successive exposures of the different parts of the plate. Suppose the camera to be slightly shaken during the exposure, it will be found that portions of the image are quite sharp while others show various stages of distortion. This results from the fact that the shake, such as it is, does not spread itself over the whole time of exposure. During some fraction of the time the camera is really at rest, and the image at such a moment will be sharp ; it is during the actual time of shaking that the corresponding portion of the image will appear in the negative to be blurred. The manipulation of a camera provided with this shutter is very convenient, seeing that it can be worked by pressing a single finger.

An accidental exposure is only possible if somebody unintentionally touches the controlling lever, but in the latest models this is prevented by the provision of a safety catch, which can be lifted by a finger when it is desired to release it. A great advantage lies in the possibility of varying the length of the exposure by increasing or decreasing the width of the slit. The shortest exposure is about one thousandth of a second. The shutter is wound up by hand, and the spring does not come into action till the pawl is raised from the ratchet wheel by pressing the lever. The strength of the spring can be varied by winding it up to a greater or less extent, and a scale reading from 1 to 10 is provided for the purpose: after use the spring should be left unwound in order to prevent it from losing its strength. The following advice may be given to the beginner. Adjust the slit to a certain breadth, say, one inch, and trust to varying the strength of the spring for regulation of the length of the exposure. In this way a little practice will soon show what strength of spring is required for a given exposure in a given light. But it becomes a difficult matter if both the breadth of slit and the strength of the spring are adjusted. The length of exposure can also be varied by suitable use of the stops. Arrangements allowing an adjustment of the slit from the outside are unnecessary in a balloon. A considerable experience of such contrivances tends to prove that they complicate the mechanism without producing any notable improvement.

One objection to all shutters worked by a spring is that the latter gradually loses its power, and the times of exposure have a tendency to increase if no allowance is made. But one gradually notices a thing of this kind; the slit seems to pass across the lens more slowly than before, and the necessary correction can be made. The working of the spring should be examined before undertaking an expedition.

Various contrivances have been designed for determining exactly the length of exposure given by the shutter. The best and simplest consists in an apparatus, devised by Dr. Hesekiel, by which a hand, painted white, is made to revolve over a black background by means of adjustable weights, which drive clockwork. This is photographed by the camera, and the angle through which the hand has turned will be shown by a patch on the negative. By measuring the angular width of this patch it is possible to calculate the length of exposure which has been given. The face over which the hand revolves is divided into one hundred parts, and if the hand makes a

complete revolution in a second, each division will correspond
to 0·01 of a second.   In 1886 Nadar used for this purpose an
apparatus designed by Professor Marey and constructed by
Richard, of Paris, which was taken on his balloon ascents.

The Thornton-Pickard shutter works very well, and as it is protected by being mounted inside the camera is seldom likely to get
out of order.   It also serves as a means of keeping dust out of the
camera, and prevents any fine particles from settling on the lens or
plate.   Moreover it keeps out the moisture, and this is of importance, as it might otherwise condense on the surface of the lens.

The Lens.

The lens is undoubtedly the most important part of the
camera; but the choice of the lens depends on many things,
among which are the size of the camera, the make of plate, the
quality of the light, etc.   A lens has to do work under all sorts of
conditions, and therefore it is not so easy to say exactly which is
the most suitable.   There are a large number of makers of repute,
each of whom has his own peculiar method of manufacture.

The first point to be settled is whether a telephotographic lens
is to be employed, or whether a simple lens with long focal
length is sufficient.   The following explanations must be given
to clear up the matter.

Working with a simple lens the image of distant objects is at
a distance behind the lens equal to the focal length.   Therefore
the ratio of the size of the image to that of the object is the
same as that of the focal length to the distance of the object.   If
B is the size of the object, b that of the image, E the distance
of the object, and f is the focal length, then $b = \dfrac{Bf}{E}$.   Therefore if the distance is 100 times the focal length, the size of the
object will be 100 times that of the image.   In order to get
large images of distant objects, it is therefore necessary to use a
lens of great focal length.   It is often suggested that it would be
sufficient to take a small negative, and enlarge it in the usual
way.   But this is only possible within certain limits.   Probably
an enlargement which is five times the size of the negative is

the most that can be done. The grain of the plate becomes enlarged in the process, and obscures all the detail, if it is carried beyond a certain limit; and it is impossible in this way to conjure up any detail that does not exist in the original.

There is another method by which a magnified image can be obtained. A lens is used which produces a small image, and this is enlarged by allowing the rays to pass through a second lens, and then to fall on the sensitive surface. This is called a telephotographic method, the whole being actually a sort of photographic telescope. The first lenses of this kind were made by Dallmeyer of London, and independently by Stein-

heil of Munich and Professor Miethe of Berlin. They allow a considerable amount of latitude by using different focal lengths; the only necessary matter is that the distance between the lenses should not differ

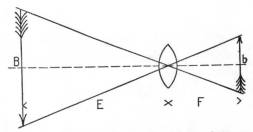

FIG. 197.—Diagram showing the relation between the focal length of the lens, the size of the image, and the distance of the object.

from the sum of their focal lengths by an amount equal to the focal length of the back lens.

The advantage of this arrangement is evident. The length of the camera can be considerably shortened, whereas with simple lenses of great focal length the camera must be of a corresponding size. It has been already stated that a focal length of 24 in. is the most that is possible for an amateur.

It may now be well to consider why telephotographic lenses are not employed under all circumstances. The reason is that the image is not so sharp, and the intensity of the light which falls on the plate is reduced. If two lenses, each of a focal length of 8 in., are placed one behind the other, and the second lens magnifies the image five times, then the image is as large as if it were given by a lens of 40 inches focal length, but its brightness is twenty-five times less. Therefore these combinations can only be used in moderately clear weather; in dull weather they become useless, because under such conditions and with such lenses instantaneous photography would be impossible.

Major Houdaille has stated that in his opinion telephotographic lenses are of no use in a balloon, but Baron von Bassus is not altogether of this opinion, thinking that they may do much useful work for military purposes. There is a good deal to be said for this latter view, but, as things at present stand, the

FIG. 200.—Pyramids of Cheops, Chephren, and Mencheres.
(Photograph by Spelterini.

amateur will probably save himself some disappointment if he uses the simple lens.

We must now consider the conditions attaching to the selection of a suitable single lens. The French Minister of War drew up a specification for lenses in 1900, when a competition was organised for the purpose of selecting the best. The conditions which were laid down still hold good, though for other than military purposes the requirements need not be so high. The specification called for a lens which was to be able at a distance of 5 miles in any light (always excepting fog) to give a picture of a battery, in which all the details, including horses, men, wagons, guns, etc., should be distinguishable with the naked eye without the use of a magnifying glass. The lens therefore must have a focal length between 24 and 40 in. At a distance of 5 miles a man of average height appears on the image thrown by a lens of focal length 24 in. to be about 0·005 in. high and 0·0016 in. broad, and consequently he could just be distinguished with the naked eye. The maximum length of the camera was to be 40 in. The sharpness of the negative was to be such that one man could be distinguished from his neighbour when standing at a distance of a couple of feet from him.[1] The lens was further to be capable of being used with an aperture of F/10; with a focal length of 24 in. this stop would have a diameter of 2·4 in., so that with a dull winter light it would be possible to distinguish objects which were at a distance from one another of F/10,000. This would require an aplanatic correction. Miethe considers that an aperture of F/20 ought to be possible in a balloon, seeing that the intensity of the light in a balloon is much greater than on the earth, but this would naturally not be the case in a very unfavourable light. At a distance of 1¼ miles the lens was to be able to include the whole of a battery, 325 yards long, drawn up across the field of view. Assuming that there was an error of 2 per cent. in estimating the distance, an angle of 10° would be required, and half-plates would have to be used. With a lens of this character work of the highest class can be done on plates of all the ordinary sizes. It would be better not to choose anything smaller than quarter-plate, and the most useful would probably be half-plate size.

The prize in this competition was won by a French firm; the second prize was adjudged to Voigtländer of Brunswick for a lens of 24 in. focal length with an aperture F/9; and the third to Zeiss of Jena for a lens of the same focal length, having an aperture F/8. Miethe considers that a number of other lenses would probably satisfy the conditions. Thus Goerz's anastigmatic lenses, Steinheil's antiplanat or aplanat, Zeiss's protar,

---

[1] For the results of the competition of long focus lenses for purposes of military ballooning, see the *Rerue du Génie Militaire*, April, 1902, and the *Illustrierte Aeronautische Mitteilungen*, 1902, vol. IV.

Voigtländer's collinars, etc., are all good and can be recommended as being of equal quality, while of English makers the names of Ross, Taylor, Beck, Dallmeyer and many others might be mentioned. The weight of the lens is probably a matter of minor importance as compared with its optical properties. Major Houdaille fixes the maximum weight at 6½ lbs.; some of the competing lenses weighed 16½ lbs. But it is doubtful whether anything is gained if the reduced weight sacrifices any of the optical properties of the lens.

FIG. 201.—Captain Spelterini, of Zurich.

It is certainly a little difficult to manipulate a camera with a very heavy lens at the front, and the best plan is to fasten a strap to the case, passing it round the body so as to take off some of the dead-weight.

The lens must be very carefully handled, and experience seems to show that a few words on this subject will not be out of place. A very important point is to clean the lens by means of a soft camel's hair brush from any dust that may have settled on it; the need for this is fairly obvious, and the reasons have been already mentioned. It is necessary to pay special attention to any alterations in the level of the balloon. As soon as it passes from a cold atmosphere into a warm, damp one, the surface of the lens will be covered with a thin film of moisture, and a blurred exposure would result. It is doubtful whether this matter always receives sufficient attention. Often enough the sky is perfectly clear, and yet failures are the only result. The cause is quite likely to be found in the fact that the lens has not been properly cleaned. In a balloon, moisture is very frequently deposited on the lens. The camera has perhaps been put away in a corner of the basket, where it is well protected from the rays of the sun, and it has about the same temperature as the surrounding atmosphere, which is generally far lower than that of the earth. A film of moisture has therefore probably coated the lens. It is possible to use a sliding tube of highly-polished metal to protect the lens from the sun's rays; and if the sun is low down it might prevent its direct light from shining on the lens. The inner surface of such a tube must of course be coated with a matt black paint, in order to prevent any irregular reflection.

The Development of the Plates.

Every photographer knows that he can do much to save a plate which has not been properly exposed by suitably carrying out the developing process. The developer can be strengthened or diluted; potassium bromide or caustic soda can be added, or a developer can be used which has already served for another plate. It would seem that balloon photography would derive much assistance from such methods, but this is unfortunately not the case. Development is a peculiar art. Everybody has his own special ideas and his well-tried mixtures, and he will hear of no others. In 1904 Miethe recommended the plan by which the plates were left to soak in a dilute solution for some time, as, for instance, in a solution of rodinal, containing one part in 250 parts of water. After an hour they may be taken out and carefully examined, when all the details will be seen very faintly. If the contrasts do not appear to be sufficiently vigorous they can be placed in another solution, containing one part in twenty, which has been prepared beforehand for the purpose. The whole operation takes two or three hours, if they have been properly exposed, whereas if the exposure has been too short, there may only be a sufficiency of detail at the end of five hours. The plates can be intensified or reduced as occasion requires.

In the light of experience, a totally different procedure must be recommended for balloon exposures, offering a better prospect of success. Professor Miethe has also changed his views as the

Y

result of some ascents he has made. In so far as the choice of a developer is concerned, rodinal can be recommended as being the simplest and the best. On the whole the best results seem to be obtained with it. Other developers have been tried, partly on general grounds and partly because rodinal causes with some people a soreness of the skin, which is unpleasant. But the change of developer has brought no improvement in the results. With rodinal it is quite easy to use rubber stalls, which protect the fingers from any unpleasant consequences. The whole manipulation is so simple that it requires little experience, and can be easily done even by the veriest tyro.

A solution of rodinal is prepared, containing one part in five parts of water. The plate is soaked till it is nearly opaque to transmitted light, and black when looked at by reflected light. This usually takes place in five minutes at the outside. It all sounds rather primitive, but it is undoubtedly the most successful plan. Everyone who has made a number of balloon exposures, knows that if a solution of moderate strength is used, a plate often looks quite unaffected for some time, and then suddenly the whole thing seems to become fogged, and nothing further can be done with it. This is due to the bluishness of the atmosphere, which has more or less fogged the whole plate. It is not easy to tell with great exactness what is the state of the atmosphere, and on developing there is little opportunity to counteract it. The best plan is, therefore, to put the plate in a strong solution and to get out as much detail as possible in the shortest possible time. Many who have tried this plan have found it successful, and none appear to fail, so that the correctness of the procedure, simple as it is, may be said to be proved. Other developers also give good results occasionally, but rodinal is much the most certain in its action. Its simplicity gives it an added charm.

CHAPTER XXII.

THE INTERPRETATION OF PHOTOGRAPHS.

Photographs which are taken from a fixed position are generally intelligible without explanation, especially seeing that they are not usually concerned with some very distant object. Balloon exposures produce a different impression on the mind, and one

Fig. 202.—Village in Posen, as seen from a balloon in winter.

has to accustom one's self to the bird's-eye point of view. The interpretation of an ordnance map requires some experience, and in exactly the same way with overhead photography it is necessary to learn to recognise the lie of the land. It is very difficult, and, indeed, almost impossible, for a balloon photograph to show the unevenness of the landscape; particularly is this the case when the balloon is at a great height, and the camera is pointed directly downwards. It is therefore well to say a few words about the means that exist for interpreting balloon photographs.

It may be pointed out in the first place that a balloon photograph often gives the impression that there are hills in the background, or at any rate that the level rises in passing from

FIG. 203.—Herrenberg in Württemburg.

the bottom to the top. This may be due to an effect of perspective, or to the peculiarities of lighting. The appearance of villages is curious; the houses look as though they had dropped out of a child's toy-box. The difference between light and shade is not very marked at great heights. The photograph of a place called Herrenberg, which is here reproduced, shows this very clearly. It was taken from a very moderate height, and it will be noticed that the shadows in the foreground are well marked, disappearing somewhat towards the middle and in the background. The effect is still more marked at great distances. The slope which appears on this photograph is well marked, and is emphasised to some extent by the low position of the balloon. It looks doubtful at first glance whether the whole town is on the side of a hill or whether the rise only begins near the church in the background. But a very simple sketch shows that the rise on the side of a hill would be much more marked, and the fact that one house appears to project above its neighbour is not enough to prove the ground to be hilly. The roads are very clearly visible, with their white dust and rows of trees. Country paths are often very indistinct, and could easily be overlooked altogether. There is always something characteristic about a railway, which catches the eye. But a light railway along the side of a road or a tram-line is not easily

Fig. 204.

found at once, even if its existence is already shown on the map.

Roads are often a good indication of a change of level. When a road disappears, as in the photograph of Blankenburg, between the points k-k, it is easy to see that it is hidden from sight by a slight hill. It is not so easy to see that the part marked e is a considerable rocky eminence, called the Regenstein, so little does it attract attention on the photograph. But the fact that it hides the road between k and k shows that it is a hill, though it is impossible to say how high it is. The low level of the balloon is also shown by the way in which the peaks in the background stand out against the horizon. The irregularities in the direction of the roads, and in the appearance of the ploughed land, all tend to show that the country is hilly. In the parts round a and b there are many gentle curves which fall gradually into the valleys or more evel ground lying among the hills. Such

FIG. 205.—View of Blankenburg in the Harz Mountains, with the Regenstein in the foreground. Taken from a balloon at a low level.

uneven lines as are shown between *m* and *m* would scarcely be possible on perfectly level country.   An ordinary road is generally fairly straight and turns abruptly at a bend ; in hilly country they become more serpentine in extreme cases with many gentle curves.   These peculiarities can be traced on the photograph of Rüdersdorf, and in many of the others.   The view of the chalk-pits near Rüdersdorf is particularly interesting ; at a first glance the uneven nature of the ground is not very striking.   The heights of the various points are shown in metres, and the incline of 1 in 4 in the foreground looks almost

FIG. 206.—Rüdersdorf.

level.   The number of small irregular pathways is also an indication of the nature of the ground.   They appear in great numbers on both sides of the railway siding, and would be clearly impossible on flat ground.

The distribution of light and shade depends on the lie of the land, and conclusions can often be drawn in consequence as to whether the one part is higher or lower than the other.   But a certain amount of caution must be exercised, seeing that a difference in the colour of the soil or in the nature of the

FIG. 207.—Chalkpits near Rüdersdorf. The figures denote the heights above the datum level. (über N.N. = above the datum level. Steigung 205 m, 1 : 4·02 = ascent of 1 in 4·02 over a distance of 670 ft.)

vegetation may cause an appearance of shadow. Water is generally easily recognised ; rivers run their course along well-defined
curves, which are at once recognised on paper. They probably
appear to resemble roads in so far as their brightness is

concerned; but there is likely to be little chance of confusion owing to the different nature of their outlines.   In the photograph of Rüdersdorf, three bridges are to be seen, which of course clearly indicate a river; besides which there are the shadows of the trees, and, further along, a small boat.

In winter time things are rather different.   The fields may be white with snow, and the roads black with slush and mud, while in the forest the paths may be still covered with snow, and

FIG. 208.—Village in the Uckermark in winter.

glittering in the dark trees.   If the whole country is covered with snow, and yet shows a number of black patches, this is a clear indication of a forest, and if the trees are not too closely planted, they can often be distinguished from one another. Fields and country paths disappear in the snow, and it is only the rivers and roads that seem to be black.   The railway, which passes through the middle of the photograph of the village in the Uckermark stands out from the snow, and the telegraph poles can be seen at the side of the lines.   The small declivity at the side of the line is shown by the dark patches,

where the snow has been unable to lodge.   In the photographs
taken by Spelterini, the snow, rocks, and glaciers are always
clearly to be seen.

It will therefore be seen that a little practice is all that is
required to interpret the photographic results, and to find out
the principal features of the country.   But much depends on
the nature of the light, and this may tend to lead one astray.

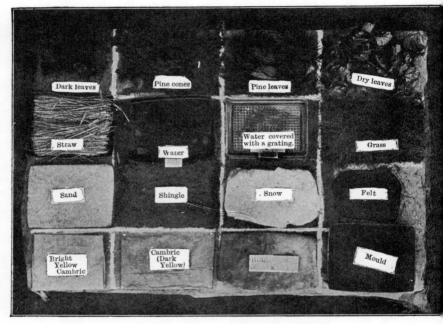

Fig. 209.—Objects of different colours, photographed from above.

Miethe's system of colour photography is a further useful guide,
which can hardly leave room for any doubt.

It has been already stated that the use of yellow filters or
isochromatic plates helps the photographic representation of
colour to correspond more nearly to the impression produced on
the eye.   In any case, marked differences of colour can generally
be understood, especially if the photograph is compared with others.
White, yellow, green, black, and the various shades of brown
and grey are the most usual colours in a landscape; in towns, a

red tinge is added by the roofs. Photographs can be taken of different substances, such as leaves, sand, straw, water, earthy soil, etc., and if they are grouped together close to one another, the contrast of colour becomes useful for reference. But the angle from which the objects are photographed makes a difference, and this has to be taken into account. Specially is this the case with water, which appears white in reflected light, but may appear absolutely black if looked at directly from above. Dry, brown leaves will also appear whitish if placed in such a position that they can reflect light into the lens.

Colonel Klussmann mentions the following points. The gradation of tone over a print may be either due to the different

FIG. 210.—This photograph shows the same objects as in the preceding, but it is taken from the side instead of being taken from above.

colours of the objects or to the varying illumination. Supposing the illumination to be uniform, the brightness of the various colours is in the following order, viz., white, yellow, grey and brown, red, green. Bright, polished surfaces often reflect so much light as to appear white, quite independently of what their actual colour may happen to be. The greater the distance of the object the less is the effect produced by its colour, and the greater the impression produced by light and shade. This effect is also produced on the eye when it looks at a distant object. The atmosphere produces so strong an impression on the plate that the distant landscape may be entirely blotted out, but colour photography is likely to make such a marked change that in the future we may expect to get plates with much greater detail than at present.   The first attempts in this direction have lately been made by Professor Miethe and Dr. Lehmann, who have made some balloon ascents, and taken some photographs with a special form of camera.

The methods of colour photography may be briefly explained as follows.   The colours that appear in nature can be analysed into red, green and blue.   With these three colours every possible tint can be produced by proper mixture.   By the use of filters, it is also possible to separate the three colours out of any mixture.

It used to be the plan to employ each filter in connection with a special plate, which had been so prepared as to be specially sensitive to the colour separated out by the filter; three different kinds of plates were needed, the one being for red, another for green, and the third for violet. With the three plates, exposures are made, the one after the other, as quickly as possible.   The camera has one lens and only one plate is used, a third of it being exposed behind the three filters in succession.   The whole thing is done automatically by pressing a rubber ball, and this changes the filters and the portion of the plate which is exposed.   Colour

FIG. 211. — Camera for three-colour photography.

photography is made very simple in a balloon by the fact that the three exposures can be made simultaneously, by using three lenses, one beside the other, the distance of the object being so great that no trouble arises from parallax.   If the three lenses are mounted so that their axes are at distances of about 3 in., and their focal lengths are from $6\frac{1}{4}$ to 7 in., no displacement of the image due to parallax can be noticed if the balloon is 800 ft. above the ground level.

Professor Miethe's camera therefore consists of a solidly constructed box, containing the whole of the apparatus, the front of which contains the three lenses, side by side, and has slight projections fitted to it in order to protect the lenses from any accidental injury that might be caused by jolts or knocks. The inside of the box is divided into three compartments, corresponding to the three lenses. The plate is $3\frac{1}{2}$ by $9\frac{1}{2}$ in., and is similarly divided into three parts. The focal length of the lens is about $6\frac{1}{4}$ in., and works with an aperture of F/4·5. Three carriers are provided for the filters, which are placed immediately in front of the plate. The camera has no focussing screen, seeing that it is adjusted once for all. A shutter of the slit type is used, and at the back there are the usual double-backs. The whole of the manipulation is done from the outside, and the double-backs are fitted with rolling blinds. Isochromatic plates must be used, and they must be sufficiently sensitive to red light to take an exposure in a tenth of a second. The plates are prepared with ethyl red in the following manner. One ounce of

FIG. 212.—Sliding screen carrier for three-colour photography.

Miethe's ethyl red (chinoline, chinaline, ethyl nitrate) is dissolved in 500 fluid ounces of alcohol, and forms a stock solution which must be kept in the dark. One fluid ounce of the stock solution is taken and mixed with 100 ounces of water. The plate is immersed in this mixture for two minutes and then washed in flowing water for another 10 minutes in the dark room. It is then dried in a draught in the hot oven for about twenty minutes, but not more than twenty-five minutes. The solution can be used for a large number of plates; probably it is better to take half the above amounts, which ought to be sufficient for six or eight plates. The plates should be packed front to back, in which case they can be kept for months.

The proper relative exposures for the red, green, and blue must be adjusted by means of suitable stops. The filters used by Miethe allow of stops of F/4·5, F/6·3, and F/15 for the red,

green, and blue respectively. The speed of the shutter is arranged
to suit the prevailing light, and the camera is either held by
means of a hand-strap, or is rested on the edge of the basket.
The length of exposure may amount to one-tenth of a second,
and it is therefore necessary to wait for a moment when there is
no oscillation in order to make the exposure. In Northern lati-

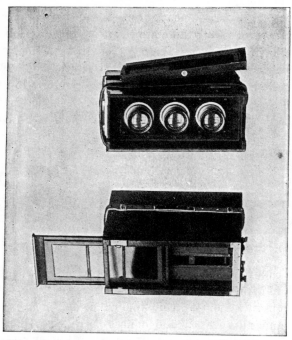

FIG. 213.—Miethe's camera for three-colour photography in a balloon.
At the top is shown the front part with the three lenses, and below is seen the sliding screen
carrier and the shutter.

tudes, colour photography is only possible in a balloon when the
weather is reasonably clear.

The development of the negative is done in the usual way in
the dark room by means of a moderately concentrated solution
of rodinal, containing one part in nine of water. Towards the
end of the development, the plate is examined on the back, and
the process is generally complete when the image begins to be
visible through the plate. A transparency is then prepared, and

this is treated in the usual way by Miethe's three-colour projecttion apparatus, or the negative may be enlarged and printed on one of the three-colour photographic papers. The projection apparatus gives far finer results than any print.

It may be well to mention a special photographic method which emphasises differences of level. It is known that the plastic effect is produced by looking at an object with both eyes at once. If one of the eyes is closed, it will be seen at once that the sense of solidity is lost, as well as of size and distance. At a considerable distance, the plastic effect ceases, even if two eyes are used, and one only judges by experience as to the actual distance. Colour and the nature of the ground give some assistance; but with large uniform surfaces one is often liable to make mistakes. This is caused by the fact that the effects of parallax are too small. This has been artificially increased by using prisms, and to a larger extent by the use of the stereoscopic camera, with lenses arranged several yards from one another. This undoubtedly adds to the plastic effect. The ordinary stereoscopic camera has two lenses, and gives excellent results if the distances are not too great. But for balloon work the parallax is still too small. This can be obviated in ordinary photography by taking two pictures, one after the other, from different points at some little distance apart. Experience shows that good results are obtained in this way if the distance between the two points from which the photographs are taken is from 1 to 3 per cent. of the distance from the object. In photographing from a balloon the method must be slightly modified. It is first necessary to determine at what speed the balloon is moving. The camera is then directed at an object, the distance of which is approximately known from measurements on the map. The second exposure is made a few seconds later, the exact interval depending on the speed of motion. Strictly speaking, the proper effect will only be obtained if the balloon is moving at right angles to the line drawn towards the object. But even if this is not the case it is still possible to get fairly good stereoscopic results, seeing that the distance of the object is generally very considerable. It is only necessary that the distance travelled by the balloon between the exposures, reckoned in a direction at right angles to the line of vision, should be approximately 2 per cent. of the distance from the object. But even this is not so important as might be thought.

If the balloon is moving very fast it is often impossible to make the second exposure at the right distance from the first. The best plan is therefore to have two cameras, fastened to the same baseboard. The plates in each are prepared and the speed of the shutters adjusted. The whole of the balloonist's attention can be directed on the object to be photographed, and he has not to bother about changing his plates. If the object is at a

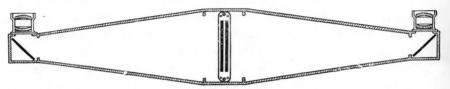

FIG. 214.—Boulade's stereoscopic camera.

distance of 1,000 yards, and the balloon is moving at the rate of 10 yards per second, the second exposure must be made between one and three seconds after the first.

If no great plastic effect is required, and the objects are not in the far distance, an apparatus described by Boulade can be used This camera is of the nature of a prismatic telescope with increased parallax, and is very convenient. The lenses are at a distance of about 3 ft. from one another, their focal lengths being $21\frac{1}{2}$ in. Mirrors are arranged at the sides to receive the images from the lenses and to reflect the rays to two plates, which are placed with their backs towards one another. The length of the path of the rays is exactly $22\frac{1}{2}$ in., and the apparatus is easily worked after a little practice.

CHAPTER XXIII.

APPARATUS has already been described, due to the designs of Triboulet, Cailletet and others, which necessitated a rather elaborate outfit, and might therefore cause difficulties in remote spots. But it is just in such places, *e.g.*, among the mountains, or in the polar regions, or in marshy land, that balloon photographs might be extremely valuable. A Frenchman, named Batut, therefore proposed in 1880 to send up lightly constructed cameras by means of kites. The size of the kite would obviously depend on the weight to be lifted, and also to some extent on the altitude to be reached. Batut used an ordinary kite of the Eddy pattern, 8 ft. 3 in. long, 5 ft. 9 in. broad, and weighing 4 lbs. The camera, together with all the other appurtenances in the shape of barometer, cord, etc., also weighed about 4 lbs. It was fixed to a block of wood at such an angle as to allow for an inclination of the kite to the horizontal of 33°. A time-fuse was arranged to release the shutter and to record the reading of the barometer. At the same time it rolled up a long strip of paper by means of a spring, and in this way the working of the apparatus was clearly seen from below. A German, named Wenz, had a similar method of working.

Gradually a kind of sport was evolved for the purpose of taking photographs in this way, principally by scientific men. The American meteorologist Eddy took some excellent photographs of Boston in 1896. Thiele in Russia and Scheimpflug in Austria have also lately done good work. The former was commissioned by the Russian Government to make photographs in Transbaikalia, Transcaucasia, and other places, and kites seemed to him likely to be suitable for the work, seeing that a wind was always blowing in these mountainous parts. In 1899 he constructed an apparatus consisting of seven cameras. The largest of these took plates 9½ by 9½ in., and was placed in the middle, pointing vertically downwards. The other six were arranged at the corners of a regular hexagon, pointing downwards at an angle of 10° to the horizontal. His first attempts were not very successful. At last he completed his arrangements, but it was then found that the plan was not altogether suitable. He afterwards built a lighter apparatus, and worked successfully along the coast and rivers. His first combination weighed 44 lbs., but this was reduced to 13 lbs. in the later designs. The lens, which

FIG. 215.—Batut's kite for photographic apparatus.

FIG. 216.—Panoramic apparatus for a balloon without observers.

was an astigmatic one by Zeiss, had a focal length of 2½ in., and the plates were 4¾ by 4¾, subtending at the lens an angle of 88°; the photographs therefore overlapped one another by 14°. At a height of 200 or 300 yards, he was able with one exposure to cover an area of 40 square miles. The photographs were subsequently enlarged, which naturally magnified any errors. For military purposes he devised a so-called perspectometer, by means of which all dimensions and distances were to be legibly marked on the photograph, after being magnified ten times.

Captain Scheimpflug constructed a panoramic apparatus for similar purposes, having lenses with converging axes. His apparatus, together with an electric device for releasing the shutter, and, including levels and plates, weighed 10 lbs. He originally proposed to suspend the camera loosely from a box-kite; but it was found that by placing it inside the kite it remained far steadier and was also protected from injury on coming to the ground. A Frenchman, named Denisse, has an original method by which he shoots rockets into the air, and in this way makes photographic exposures. The shutter is released when the rocket reaches the highest point, and the camera is protected from injury by means of a parachute. The main difficulty is to focus the lens on any desired object.

CHAPTER XXIV.

THE interpretation of these bird's-eye views for topographical purposes is a special science. It may be called photogrammetry, and the main principles have been expounded by Professor Finsterwalder, of Munich, and others. But it would take us too far to go into all the details.

A photograph is here reproduced, which gives an idea of the perspective effect produced by a balloon photograph. A place called Rudow is here shown, and a net-work, such as that drawn on this photograph, is easily constructed, if the altitude and the direction of the balloon are known. The general case cannot well be described, but a few particulars about this individual photograph may be of interest.

FIG. 217.—The village of Rudow, as shown on the ordnance map.

The exposure was made at an angle of 67° 30′ with a lens of 14 inches focal length at an altitude of 2,600 ft. The vertical and horizontal lines, X and Y, are drawn through the middle of the picture. The distance between two outstanding points is then measured and compared with that on the ordnance map. In this case it is found that the scale is 1 to 5,769. It may be stated that the

Fig. 218.—Photograph of Rudow, taken from a balloon.

original was taken on a whole plate, but in order to save space, it has here been somewhat reduced. From the middle of the network a line is drawn to P, making an angle of 67° 30′ with XX, and on this in the foreground a distance from the middle point equal to 6,300 ft. is measured off. The point P is thus obtained, and a perpendicular is drawn through P, cutting the line YY at H. If the central point is called O, the triangle OPH corresponds to that formed by the lens, the point vertically below the balloon, and the object. The angle PHO is 67° 30′, and HP is 2,600 ft.

A line through H is drawn parallel to OP, and this cuts the line XX in the vanishing point, V. On the line YY arbitrary lengths are laid off, each measuring, say, 500 yards. If the points on YY are then joined to V, the horizontal distances between these lines will be everywhere equal. It will be noticed that these distances appear to become less, and at the vanishing point they absolutely disappear. Similarly lengths equal to 500 yards are laid off along OP, and these points are joined to H. Through the points where the lines, drawn to H, meet XX, horizontal lines are drawn, and the distances between these parallels will be 500 yards. The effect of perspective in shortening some of these lines and lengthening others is again very evident. By means of a simple construction of this nature it is possible to make allowance for perspective in any balloon photograph.

CHAPTER XXV.

THE use of carrier pigeons was known to the ancients. It is reported that in the times of the Pharaohs, sailors used pigeons to send news to their families that they were on the point of returning home. Pliny relates that Brutus used them in 43 B.C. for military purposes at the siege of Modena. He was there besieged by Mark Antony, and sent the pigeons in order to invoke the assistance of his friends. The gladiators of Rome announced their successful feats to the provinces in the same way, and the orientals are said to have organised a regular postal system by means of the birds. The Sultan Nurr Eddin in 1167 communicated regularly with all the large towns of Syria from Bagdad, and similar means of correspondence were used between Syria and Egypt. For this purpose, blockhouses were arranged at intervals, where the birds were in the charge of the soldiers. The messages were fastened under the wings, and the Sultan received the letters with his own hands.

Dutch sailors are said to have first introduced carrier pigeons into Europe, where they were called *Bagdettes*, after their place of origin; according to other accounts, the Crusaders are said to have done this service. In any case, the birds were soon in common use in Italy and North Europe ; they were used at the siege of Haarlem in 1572, and at Leyden in 1574, and Venice in 1849, at all of which places the besieged kept up communication with the outer world with the help of these birds. The well-known house of Rothschild in London organised communication in this way in 1815 so that they might receive the earliest possible news of the outcome of the Battle of Waterloo. They consequently heard the result three days before it reached the Government, and it is reported that great gains were made on the Exchange in consequence. Before the introduction of the electric telegraph in 1850, banks, merchants, and newspapers used pigeons for conveying the latest intelligence; their importance was recognised in all countries, and in many places they were kept at the cost of the State. Their breeding has now become a kind of sport, and is encouraged by associations founded for that purpose.

Carrier pigeons played a very important part during the siege of Paris, which was completely shut off from the rest of the world in so far as other means of communication were concerned. Altogether 363 pigeons left the town in balloons, and of these only 57 succeeded in returning. Probably the reason for this poor result is to be found in the terrible weather of December, 1870, the whole month being cold and foggy with many heavy snowstorms. A large number of the birds were in Paris at the time, but they were not all employed. The siege of Paris was an entirely unforeseen event for the French Government, and although 800 pigeons were available, they had not been properly accustomed to their surroundings. The idea of taking them out of Paris in balloons was the suggestion of a Belgian, named Van Rosebek. The first attempt was made on September 25th in the balloon " La Ville de Florence," which carried three birds; and in consequence of its success, it was resolved to send birds by every balloon. Those of the Antwerp breed were the most successful, and several of them made the return journey on six occasions. A curious journey was that made by a pigeon which was set free from the balloon " Washington " on October 12th under very heavy rifle fire, and was only able to reach its home in Paris on December 5th. Many experiments have been made to find whether the flight of the birds is in any way affected by firing. It is certainly so in some cases, but, as a general rule, it seems that the birds are not deterred by the heaviest firing.

During the siege it became necessary to harbour their resources, and consequently a great number of messages were sent by one bird. This was largely due to a photographer named Dagron, who reproduced the letters by microphotography in the following way. A number of messages, together with printed matter, are fastened to a board, and then photographed by a camera provided with a very fine lens. The distance of the apparatus from the board determines the extent to which the image is reduced in size. Dagron succeeded in photographing about 1,110,000 words on a square inch of plate surface. If dry plates were used for such work, the image would not be sharp enough to be read with a microscope, so that wet plates had to be used, and these give an image which is sharp down to the minutest detail. As is well known, the plates must be prepared immediately before being used by dipping them in the sensitive silver solution after they have received a coating of collodion. By this process the upper surface is completely covered with a layer of the silver salt, whereas with dry plates the gelatine has a kind of grain which interferes with the sharpness of the image. After it has been developed and fixed, the thin film of collodion is stripped from its support. Its lightness is extraordinary. Assuming that the messages are reduced by photography in such a way that more than a million letters can be printed on a square inch, then one ounce of collodion film is

Fig. 219. — Photographic reproduction of messages on a reduced scale.

sufficient to take nearly 250 million letters. The films were rolled up and secured beneath the wings of the bird, as many as 20 such films being carried on one journey. When the bird arrived, the films were removed, pressed between glass plates and enlarged by means of a magic lantern. The words were thrown in this magnified form on a sheet, which was divided into sixteen squares, and clerks were employed to copy the words, each one having a square allotted to him. The messages were then delivered to their addresses. The microscopic reductions were made by Dagron at Tours, where he arrived on November 21st, after having left Paris in a balloon. Altogether 57 pigeons carried 100,000 messages for the Government into the besieged city together with a million private letters.

The instinct which leads the carrier pigeon to return to its home has been the subject of much dispute. Some have ascribed it to a kind of magnetism, but this is obviously impossible, seeing that if the birds are blindfolded, they are unable to find their way home, even if they should only be a few yards away. On a dark night they are able to do nothing. A test of this kind showed that the bird alighted on a tree and waited for the daylight, when it at once returned home, though on a moonlight night it was able to find its way without difficulty. Pigeons always rest by night for this reason, and there can therefore scarcely be any question of ascribing the instinct to some magical property of which we have no conception. It is quite possible that the nightly rest is to some extent due to a desire to escape from the attention of birds of prey. The losses are apt to be great if the ground is covered with snow, even if the distance to be travelled is very short, and this seems to show that the eye is unable to recognise its well-known landmarks. Added to this, the undoubted fact that they always wait till the sun rises before starting points to the idea that their movements are guided by the eye. It has been suggested that hearing plays its part, and that sounds help to tell the direction in which they are going. But this is very improbable, and gives no explanation of the way in which the return journey is made in a railway train. If the bird is sent up in some unknown neighbourhood it never starts off at once, but flies round in ever-growing circles till at last it finds its way. It then starts off at full speed, whereas the circles were described in a leisurely fashion. Possibly the sexual impulse plays its part in driving the bird home, added to which it knows well that it gets its food without exposure to any serious dangers. But its capacity for finding its way is due in the first instance to its keen sight; secondly, to the part which memory plays; and thirdly, to the speed of its flight.

These things are best understood in connection with the breeding of the birds. There are two different kinds, namely, those from Antwerp and those from Liège. The former are strong, with long necks and legs. They have long beaks but the head is flat, and marked with wattles. They are broad in the breast; the eye is surrounded by a circle of flesh, and the wings are long. The Liège bird is smaller, lower in the body, with short legs and toes. The beak is covered with small wattles, and is very strong and short, the head being convex in shape. Its eyes are surrounded with white or grey rings. The breast is full and muscular, and the wings are turned inwards and short. The Antwerp pigeon is said to be descended from the Persian bird and from the high-flier ; the Liège bird is said to be a cross between the rock pigeon, the high-flier, and the turbit. There have been many crossings between the Antwerp and the Liège types, and the carrier pigeon of to-day is the outcome ; in this way it has been thought to combine the homing instincts of the one with the swiftness of the other. In breeding the birds great stress is laid upon the appearance, the handsomest birds being also the best carriers. A really fine bird has a proud and somewhat elegant bearing, with a slightly arched head, the forehead being in a line with the beak, which must be strong and without very thick wattles. The eyes must be surrounded by a narrow ring of a white or grey colour, and the breast must be strong and muscular. Regularity in the marking of the birds is the result of suitable mating. Breeding begins in the spring, about March 15th or April 1st. It may even be later, and depends on the state of the weather. It lasts till the birds begin to moult at the beginning of September. The bird lays two eggs, and the period of incubation lasts about eighteen days ; but the young are likely to be stronger if there is only one to the family. On the sixth or seventh day a thin aluminium ring is put round the leg of the young bird ; on this is engraved such information as would lead to identification. After twenty days, they are fit to take their own food and drink, though a watchful eye must be kept over them. They soon learn to fly, and before long they reach the roof and describe circles round the house. They get good practice if they are sent up in all sorts of directions at a distance of two miles or so from their home.

The real training begins when they are three or four months old. At intervals of three days they are sent up at distances varying from three miles upwards, but always in the same direction. The distance is gradually increased till they are able to do fifty miles or so ; and the next year this is increased up to 120 miles. If the bird is very clever it may in its third or fourth year reach 500 miles ; but this is not the case with all. Before the training is begun the birds must be accustomed to their baskets; too many must not be packed together, and they should have something to eat and drink before starting on the return journey. If the balloon is likely to come to the ground with a bump it is well to release the birds before reaching the ground. If the pigeons have to be used for military purposes during the moulting season a great number will probably be lost. The distances should therefore be as short as possible, and unless there is great urgency it is well to suspend their work during this time. Only males or females should be taken on the same expedition ; but if this is not possible the males should be kept apart from the females. The male will return to the nest in the hope of finding his mate, and it is well that he should not be disappointed; both should not be sent out at the same time. In the breeding season, the female is best left at home.

Good results can be obtained with young male pigeons shortly before their first mating season, or with females who have been brooding for about ten days. In the intervals of training care must be taken that the birds have plenty of exercise in flying about. It is as well not to hunt them out of their cot, otherwise they are apt to become shy and to delay their return. A better method is for them to be obliged to go some miles to get their food. The common dove flies every day to the fields to get food and the carrier pigeon can be accustomed to do the same. The best plan is to give them a moderate allowance of food at home, and then to take them out into a field, and scatter the ground in and around the basket with grain. This is repeated for two or three days, and after they have eaten their fill they are allowed to return home. They will soon accustom themselves to undertaking the journey on their own account. But they often remain away too long, and it is as well to confine this plan to drinking. In the evening they are given a very small supply of water, and in the morning they are brought a distance of some miles to a quiet stream, and put in a basket without a bottom, which is allowed to project somewhat into the stream. They soon drink their fill and return home. This experiment is repeated for a few days, and they will soon be accustomed to seeking the spot for themselves in order to satisfy their thirst. If the water is near a wood, this has the additional advantage of accustoming the pigeons to the sight of the birds of prey, and they thus become more likely to recognise and escape them.

Birds that are intended to be used in balloons must receive a special training; and this can either be done by taking birds that have already been trained in the usual way, or by taking birds that have had no previous training. It is possible to train a bird to return from a balloon in any direction; or, on the other hand, birds can be trained to fly in certain directions from home. Herr Bernhard Flöring of Barmen has for several years provided pigeons for the balloons of the Lower Rhine Balloon Club; and he believes that the results did not depend on the direction taken by the balloon, though the birds had been trained to do their work mainly in certain directions. The performance of the pigeons is much affected by the fact that they are always obliged to return against the wind, if they are carried in a balloon. Ordinarily the birds are not sent out except in fairly clear weather, otherwise they are very liable to be lost. But in a balloon, little count is taken of such considerations, and consequently the birds often have to battle against a fairly strong wind, and this has the effect of greatly reducing the speed of their flight.

Professor Ziegler of Jena has studied the speed of carrier pigeons, particularly with a view to discovering the favourable conditions which react on the bird. By comparing the results of a large number of experiments, made at the various competitions, he found that for the longer distances up to, say, 300 miles, the average speed is about 20 yards per second. Some birds will reach a speed of 36 yards per second, while on other occasions, flying against the wind, they will only go at the rate of 5 or 6 yards per second; the best pigeons have a mean speed of 12 yards per second against a moderate wind. The

distance from Hanover to Hildesheim has been used for observation purposes; and it has been found that the journey is done
in 15 minutes with the wind, and 1½ hours against the wind,
the total distance being 18½ miles. On another occasion a
pigeon flew from a place near Bordeaux to Liège in Belgium,
and covered 508 miles in 8 hours, but this is a very exceptional
performance. Observations on the flight of migratory birds show
that they nearly always fly with the wind, and wait till the breeze
is in their favour before making a
start.

Attempts have also been made
to use swallows for this purpose.
An Antwerp trainer sent up some
swallows and pigeons at the same
time at Compiègne in France.
The pigeons covered the distance
of 145 miles in 3¾ hours, while
the swallows arrived in 1 hour 7
minutes ; the speed of the latter
was therefore three times that of
the former. Two swallows, which
had been trained at Roulaix, were
started from the Invalides in
Paris, and reached their home,
which was at a distance of 93
miles, in 75 minutes. It was

FIG. 220.—Dark slate-coloured carrier pigeon belonging to Herr
Flöring.

The bird, which is shown carrying a message
on its left leg, is 4 years old, has made
fifteen ascents in a balloon, and covered
2,400 miles on the return journeys.

proposed in consequence of this feat to start a training-station
for swallows in the fort of Mont Valérien.

Interesting experiments with swallows have been reported in
the papers from time to time, and the following deserves notice.
Two swallows had built their nest near the chateau of Nielles-
les-Ardres in the department of Pas de Calais. A gardener
caught one of the birds, and took it in a bag to the exhibition in
Paris. On the next morning it was let loose at 9.30 a.m. at the
foot of the Eiffel Tower. It rose up to the first gallery on the
tower, crossed the Seine, and disappeared in a northerly direction without a moment's hesitation. At 11.46 a.m. it reached

Nielles, and was recognised at once by the red ribbon which was tied round its leg. It had covered the distance of 150 miles in 2 hours 16 minutes. The country must have been strange to the bird, because it is hardly likely it would pass over Paris as it migrates from Calais to Africa, even supposing it did not go by the shortest course.

As a result of his experiments with balloons, Flöring gives the following as the mean speeds of the carrier pigeon; in good weather, 26 miles an hour, *i.e.*, 38 ft. per second ; in less favourable weather, 20 miles an hour, *i.e.*, 30 ft. per second ; and in bad weather, including rainy, foggy, or snowy days, the speed is only 15 miles an hour, *i.e.*, 20 ft. per second. Dr. Schultheiss, of Carlsruhe, gives rather lower figures. He made eleven experiments from a balloon in 1895 and found an average speed of 21 ft. per second. The velocity of the wind on these occasions was between 11 and 22 ft. per second. The distances were, of course, reckoned in a straight line from start to finish, but naturally nothing was known about the actual course.

The performances of two of Herr Flöring's pigeons were remarkable. The wind was blowing strongly from the west at the rate of 80 ft. per second, and the balloon soon disappeared at a height of 650 ft. into the clouds, whence it passed into the rain and snow. The first pigeon was released at a height of 3,150 ft., twenty minutes after the start ; five minutes later, at an altitude of 4,100 ft., the second bird was let go. They reached Barmen in little more than half an hour, and if allowance is made for the speed of the wind, their rates of travelling were about 118 ft. per second. On February 1st, 1903, the balloon started from Barmen with three birds in a heavy wind ; rain and snow were falling at the time. The first bird was let loose about the middle of the day, and reached home two days later, having travelled in a direct line a distance of about 60 miles. The second bird started about 1 p.m., and covered 100 miles in a very heavy snowstorm in three days, reaching home completely worn out. The third was released at Magdeburg at 3 p.m., and took seven weeks to cover the 185 miles, and reached home after having lost three or four of the pinions in each wing, owing to an accident of some sort. Flöring's pigeons also performed a feat on the occasion of a journey which took them to a distance of 25 miles from Barmen. On landing, they were released and reached home in 40 minutes, whereas a telegram, announcing their despatch, did not arrive till 2½ hours after they were safely in their cots.

The results of Flöring's experiments with balloons and carrier

Fig. 221.—Haynau in Silesia.   Taken from a height of 8,000 feet.

pigeons between 1903 and 1906 may be summarised as follows. Out of 109 pigeons that were released, 103 returned safely ; of the remaining six, two were killed by accidents, and the remaining four succumbed to the severe cold of winter. The author has taken pigeons with him on about 200 ascents, and has released about 1,500 birds in all. He has found that Flöring's estimates of speed are fairly correct, and that in foggy and cloudy weather it often takes more than a day to make the return journey.

In judging of performances in general, it is necessary to take into account the method of training which the birds have under-gone.   There is a great difference between birds which have been well trained in the usual way and are then taken on balloon ascents, and others which serve their apprenticeship on a balloon. In the latter case a certain number are sure to be lost, and the percentage of such losses will probably be rather serious.   It is also a matter of importance to consider the direction in which the balloon has been flying.   Often enough birds would fail entirely if released on the south side of Berlin at a very moderate distance, the wind and weather being favourable. They had probably flown often in other directions, but when released on the south side their memory seemed to play them false.   It is therefore necessary to adopt one of two principles ; either all the birds must be exercised and trained to fly from any direction round the given centre, or the birds can be divided into groups, some of which are worked on the north side, others on the south, and others again on the east and west.   It is generally possible to tell the course a balloon will take from observing the movements of the clouds ; but at higher levels the breezes may blow in other directions, and pigeons intended to work towards the south must therefore also be practised somewhat to the east and west.

The time of day at which they are released is a matter of importance.   If the birds are sent up in the early morning they learn a good deal from the position of the sun.   Several bal-loonists have noticed that a number of birds were lost without any very obvious cause, and it was discovered that the result was due to the fact that the balloon started at a different time in the day. Originally a start was made early in the morning, and the birds were released about midday ; but later, the start was deferred, so that the birds were only sent on their journey late in the after-noon.   As it was supposed that they directed their course by the position of the sun, they naturally lost their way altogether.

Better results are obtained if the birds are trained from the balloon.   It is very essential that they should be accustomed to fly at once downwards out of the clouds.   For this purpose it is well to take them up in a captive balloon, close to their homes,

A.   A A and to release them as soon as the clouds are reached, and while the earth is still in sight. On another occasion, it may be well to penetrate into the clouds, and later on, if the first experiments have resulted satisfactorily, to mount above them. The pigeons are very much afraid of plunging into a bank of cloud from above. Looked at in this way, it strikes them as being something new, and altogether outside their experience, and they become confused in consequence. They circle around for a long time and seem unable to make up their minds; at last when they have worn themselves out, they are compelled to descend. On a second attempt they appear to understand the situation a little better, and they soon learn to find their ways home. The intelligence of the pigeons helps them to make use of the sun as a guide, in the same way as migratory birds ; but their most important organ is the eye. The curvature of the earth is such that at a height of 300 ft., a bird can see about 22 miles ; actually the distance is a little greater owing to the effects of atmospheric refraction.

The wind affects them in many ways, partly by reducing the speed of their flight, and partly by interfering with their survey of the country. A bird soon finds out that the wind generally blows more strongly at great altitudes, and therefore flies higher if the weather is reasonably calm. Consequently it has a better outlook than it would have in rough wind, when it would tend to fly closer to the ground. If good results are to be obtained it is necessary to pay very careful attention to the pigeons in their cots. They consequently enjoy the pleasures of life, and are all the more strongly impelled to return. They must also learn to regard man with confidence, and it is possible to tell the sort of attention they receive from their behaviour to the keeper. Their cots must be clean and airy, and they will therefore delight to return home.

There are various artifices by which the performances of the birds can be improved, and it is well to know thoroughly the habits and peculiarities of all kinds of pigeons. A male pigeon returns to the nest as quickly as possible, and the same is true of the female bird. The weight of the messages carried by the bird is not without its effect on its strength, and the mode of attaching them to the body is a matter to be studied.   The usual plan is to write the message on thin paper, and roll it up in a rubber covering, fastening it to the feet of the bird.   Aluminium holders or spring cases are also used, which are fastened under the wing, and a great number of similar devices may usually be

FIG. 222.—In this photograph the shadow of the balloon is seen on the old fortifications.

(Taken by Count de la Vaulx.)

seen at the various shows.   Photographs can also be transmitted by their means, and this is useful in time of war for the purpose of sending plans, etc., from a beleaguered town.   Experiments of this kind were made in St. Petersburg in September, 1889.   The chief of the Balloon Corps, named Kowanko, made an ascent in company with an officer and two others.   They then prepared photographs on films of collodion according to the wet process. The negatives were developed in a primitive dark room, which was arranged in the basket of the balloon ; the collodion films

A A 2

were stripped from the glass, and secured to the birds. The results were considered successful. But the preparation of the negative in the car of the balloon is a tedious and awkward arrangement; and lately newer methods have been proposed by which the undeveloped film is entrusted to the bird and then developed at home in more convenient surroundings.

The carrying power of the birds is considerable, and they have been found to be able to carry weights of $2\frac{1}{2}$ ounces to a distance of 90 miles. Cages have been built in Warsaw, so that 150 or 200 birds could be released simultaneously in a besieged fortress by means of a balloon. The wicker baskets are put together in several sections and supported on the ring of the balloon; the ropes holding the car are longer than usual so that the birds do not interfere with the passengers, and the car itself is made somewhat broader. The birds are protected from the heat of the sun by a covering of oilcloth, which does not shut out the light, or bright metallic paper may be used. They have always stood the journey well, and the gas, streaming out of the neck, does not seem to cause them any inconvenience. They are, however, rather liable to be jolted about on landing, and before releasing them they must be well fed and have something to drink.

Various attempts have been made to train the birds to fly to a given spot and to return. Captain Malagoli succeeded in doing this in Italy, and Hoerter in Germany has trained birds by supplying them with water in Hildesheim and with food in Hanover. The results were to some extent satisfactory, but this method of training has been eventually abandoned. In spite of the developments of telegraphy, the use of carrier pigeons for collecting information for newspapers still continues. In time of war the pigeons form a means of communication which could hardly fall into the hands of the enemy, whereas the telegraph and telephone might be liable to all sorts of interruption. Duke Alexander of Oldenburg, who commanded the Russian Guards, trained falcons to hunt the pigeons; and at distances of two miles they did actually succeed in catching them and occasionally brought their prey back with them. But of course this kind of thing is only worthy of mention as a curious development of human activity; as a means of offence the falcon would be bound to be a failure.   On the other hand, attempts have been made to protect the pigeons from birds of prey by fastening small whistles to their bodies, but so far from serving its purpose it merely attracted attention to the pigeon, and this crude device has met with the fate it deserved.

It is a more difficult matter to prevent the pigeon from being snared.   On January 23rd, 1871, Gambetta announced special punishments for the offence of catching the birds in the following terms[1]:—

" In consideration of the importance of the carrier pigeon for postal purposes and the defence of the nation, it is hereby decreed that anyone killing a dove of any kind during the continuation of the war, either by shooting or snaring it or by hunting it in any way whatever, will be liable to six weeks' imprisonment. If it can be proved that the bird was killed notwithstanding the fact that it was known to be carrying dispatches or to be intended for that purpose, the punishment shall be a period of penal servitude, not exceeding five years.   Anyone giving information leading to a conviction will receive a reward between the sums of £2 and £4, according to the discretion of the court.   " CREMIEUX,

" *Minister of the Interior.*

" BORDEAUX, *January 23rd*, 1871."

Even nowadays, the pigeons are under the protection of the authorities, and it is a punishable offence to kill carrier pigeons and to keep stray birds that have flown from their cot.   Unfortunately there are many people who snare them on the roofs of their houses, and it is quite certain that a large number of carrier pigeons are lost by theft every year.

1 See Gross, " Die Ballonbrieftaubenpost während der Belagerung von Paris."

CHAPTER XXVI.

Traffic by land and sea is controlled by numberless statutes; but the balloonist has so far escaped legal limitation. It would almost appear as though he would be allowed to go on his way without let or hindrance; but many accidents have happened, imperilling the lives both of passengers and innocent bystanders, and the intervention of the law is bound to come sooner or later.

In 1902, an international legal congress was held at Brussels, when the position of ballooning was discussed. Some of the points may be here mentioned, especially seeing that they have since been debated at the congress of the Federation Aéronautique Internationale.

The first point is as to the distinction to be drawn between balloons belonging to the Government of a country and those belonging to private individuals. Balloons belonging to the State can either be used for military or civil purposes. A military balloon is defined as being under the command of an officer of the army or navy, who has been entrusted with the use of it by the military authorities, the whole of the equipment belonging to them. A balloon, belonging to the Government and used for civil purposes, must be in charge of an official, whose duty it is to make ascents on behalf of the civil authorities. All others fall into the category of private balloons, irrespective of the standing of the man in charge.

A balloon ought to be able to be identified in the same way as a ship. Colonel von Kowanko has stated that certain unfortunate occurrences have taken place owing to the want of an easily recognisable signal, such as a flag, denoting the nationality. Some Cossacks, stationed on the frontiers, have before now fired on German and Austrian balloons. All Russian balloons carrying passengers have a flag. Any balloon without a flag is

regarded as being of the nature of a recording balloon, carrying
meteorological instruments, for the capture of which a reward
is generally offered, and soldiers are therefore apt to fire on it
in order to bring it to earth. An accident of this kind is therefore likely enough to happen to any balloon in Russia not
carrying a flag.

It was therefore proposed that all balloons, whether belonging
to private persons or to the government, should carry a flag,
fastened to the net, half way down the balloon, and that this
should be easily recognisable both by its shape and colouring. All
balloons belonging to the Government should fly a pennant,
which, in the case of military balloons, should be attached to the
basket, and in the case of civilian balloons, should be attached to
the envelope immediately beneath the national flag. The shape of
the flags ought to be distinguishable with the naked eye at a
distance of $2\frac{1}{2}$ miles. Each balloon ought to carry the colours of its
own country and of no other, and the man in charge ought to have
an official certificate, which in the case of private balloons should
be produced on demand. The qualification of the man in charge
is a matter of importance. In connection with the army or one
of the larger clubs, a very thorough training can be had, and
examinations are held from time to time, as a result of which
certificates are issued to those whose knowledge appears to be up
to the mark. The Aero Club of Vienna divides its certificates
into those of the first and second classes, the higher distinction
being awarded to the man who is able to manage the balloon
single-handed.

At the present moment, any professional aeronaut, and indeed
any amateur, can make an ascent without any restraint, and
it must be said that in some cases the lack of experience is only
too evident. Some sort of legislation seems almost necessary to
prevent accident. A good instance of the preventable accident
took place last year in Germany. An engineer, named Vollmer,
made a few ascents, and then announced that he had assumed the
rôle of a professional balloonist. He found a man in Essen who
wanted to make an ascent, and they therefore sailed away in
clear weather and a moderate breeze towards Ostend, where they

fell into the sea and were drowned. The accident was undoubtedly due to the lack of experience on the part of the so-called professional aeronaut, whose qualifications had been assumed to be satisfactory by his companion without any very thorough inquiry. This was clearly a case calling for the interference of the authorities. Such men are not only a danger to their companions, but to anybody else who comes in their way. Very serious accidents may arise owing to explosions if the inflation of the balloon is not properly carried out, and, on landing, injuries may easily result from unskilful management. It would therefore seem to be in the public interest to demand that some sort of qualification should be necessary before being allowed to take charge of a balloon.

At the conference at Brussels, the following arrangements were proposed. Every private balloon must be registered, and have a name and number, which should be printed in large letters on the body of the balloon. The place of residence of the owner should also be stated, and the number and place of origin should be painted in red. Every ascent by a private person should be under the control of a State official. Government balloons should not be obliged to carry papers, but private balloons must have a copy of the official particulars, and a list of the passengers. The flags, etc., must be properly mounted in position, a journal must be kept, and the man in charge must produce his certificate on demand. Special flags should be arranged for signalling that a descent is about to take place or that help is needed, which latter would be likely to be specially useful if the balloon were to be in danger of being driven over the sea. At the congress, a series of regulations were drawn up with a view to preventing balloons from passing above fortresses. It was proposed that Government balloons should be allowed to pass the frontier in case of actual necessity, but that a flag should be hung out, showing that help was needed. An exception was proposed in the case of Government balloons, making ascents for meteorological purposes; but it seems only reasonable that military balloons should not be allowed to cross the frontier at will.

Several other proposals were made with the intention of obviating difficulties at the customs, and dealing with other cases which might arise. The use of balloons in time of war was also discussed, and it seems probable that they will require to be regulated in exactly the same way as traffic by sea. The question as to the treatment to be meted out to a captured balloon is important, considering the important *rôle* they may play in the future and have, indeed, already played in the past. Soldiers are often not available to man the balloon, and it has therefore happened that threats have been made to treat captured balloonists as spies. All regulations which prevent the balloonist from acting on the offensive or defensive seem absurd. At the Hague Conference it was proposed to forbid the throwing of explosives from balloons; but this regulation is no longer in force, as it was only valid for a period of five years. Moedebeck has pointed out that if the right of attack or defence is taken from the balloonist, it is only reasonable to expect that the enemy should be prevented from firing on it.

The proposals of the Brussels Conference may appear to go too far from some points of view, but it seems likely that some sort of international regulation will be necessary in the future, seeing that balloons are now much more common than they were, and that the dirigible airship is a practicable possibility.

INDEX.

BRADBURY, AGNEW, & CO. LD., PRINTERS, LONDON AND TONBRIDGE.